The
MOBOLOGIST'S STORY

A MEMOIR BY
Elaine Bonavita Jaquith

The Mobologist's Story

© Elaine Bonavita Jaquith 2017

ISBN 978-1-5213-3356-3

This book is dedicated to the memory of
MARIO ANTHONY FACIONE
For the courage to leave "the family"
for his Church family
August 14, 1939 - July 26, 2015

Mario (center), an associate of the mob before his conversion, is pictured here with missionaries from the Church of Jesus Christ of Latter-day Saints who knocked on his door in 1981, the same year missionaries knocked on Elaine Bonavita's door.

Mafia to Mormon: My Conversion Story
By Mario Facione

FAMILIES ARE FOREVER – EVEN IF "THE FAMILY" ISN'T

"When two clean-cut young men in dark suits showed up on his doorstep, Facione's main concern was to figure out the scam they were selling. Instead, he became surprisingly relaxed as these two answered every question he had unsuccessfully asked other clergymen. He learned real truth and began a journey towards knowledge. Yes, there is a reason why we are here on earth; yes, you can re-remember who we are and yes, it's true, Heavenly Father still speaks through a modern-day prophet." -- **Mario Facione's Book**

TABLE OF CONTENTS

INTRODUCTION

This mob memoir is not just another true story of someone growing up inside the Mafia like its author, Elaine Bonavita. It goes far beyond anything a mob fan could ever imagine. It is a real time mob whodunit that takes the reader into the author's own dark world of organized crime inside the Genovese family.

From the very first chapter to the last, you will be given clues from as far back as the year 1921 and they won't stop until you end up in Agawam, Massachusetts today.

What's the reason for the whodunit? Someone in her own crime family was determined to silence anyone who tried to help the author identify the mobsters behind the mob problem in Agawam that began more than 44 years ago.

Mob fans who enjoy a good whodunit will find themselves drawn into the author's own quest to know who was behind it all in this thrilling real time whodunit.

Follow the clues the author presents in each chapter and take notes so you can answer the 'Who do you think... questions when you get to Chapter 17.

It was not always desirable that the identity of some of the individuals whom I have addressed in this whodunit should be made known to the world and so I have withheld their names. These individuals are not suspect and as such will not affect the whodunit.

Good luck solving this non-fiction mystery and if you enjoyed this mob whodunit, tell your friends!

CHAPTER ONE:
INSIDE THE FAMILY OF A MOB

"But why do you want to know?" my grandmother asked me as we sat in her living room where my father, her son, had just left moments earlier.

"I just need to know," I innocently replied, as I watched my grandmother walk off into the kitchen hoping to avoid the subject. But I followed right behind her even though I knew she didn't want to talk about it.

Standing in the kitchen together, I waited. Again she asked, "What good will it do for you to know?"

"Come on, Gram," I pleaded. "You know the story of our family ties to the Mafia, why else did Dad come here today insisting how no one was gonna kill me and bragging how he was gonna stop it?"

My sudden interest in our own family's beginnings, in organized crime, stemmed from a recent run-in of my own with the Mafia. When I'd found myself in trouble, big time, with a notorious mobster in the Genovese crime family named Francesco "Skyball" Scibelli in the summer of 1972, I felt I deserved to know the truth if I was going to be running from them for the rest of my life.

Skyball Scibelli, the face of the Genovese syndicate's racket in Western Massachusetts for decades, was the father-in-law of my boss Victor C. DeCaro at the time he ordered the assassination of his own daughter's husband. Unfortunately for me, I was the only living person who had the dumb luck of witnessing what went down the night Victor disappeared. Victor was dead, but I hadn't said a word about it to anyone, not even my grandmother or father.

As for me, I didn't have a clue anyone in the mob wanted me dead, at least not until my father showed up so unexpectedly for a family sit-down right after Victor disappeared. And that was the day I discovered a dark family secret that went all the way back to the 1920's.

2

It is here in Chapter 1 that I introduce my readers to my birth family and its beginnings in the Mafia. I guess you could say if not for my grandfather Tony Bonavita's involvement in the Mafia, I might not be alive today to even tell my story, much less have one to tell.

Either way, I'll let my readers judge where the blame lays for the shattered life of a Mafia child forced into a life on the run from the most powerful crime family in America. And this is my story and how it unexpectedly evolved into a real time mob whodunit for my readers to solve.

I share another untold story of my life when I lived with Elvis Presley and the Memphis Mafia just before I witnessed a mob murder and had to go on the run. You can read all about it in Chapters 2 and 3. My own personal story of being wanted by the mob begins in Chapter 4 and from then on I take my readers on the most thrilling mob whodunit mystery ever told.

Should you decide to try to figure out this mob whodunit, be sure to take careful notes because I give ample clues beginning in this chapter on my own Bonavita family that will help you when you get to **Solving the Whodunit Mystery**.

But readers beware, what you are about to experience in this whodunit is nothing like any other book or movie, fiction or true, that you have ever imagined possible in the dark world of organized crime. In this whodunit, the Mafia finally meets its match in another powerful family whose boss is the Almighty God Himself!

Introducing the Bonavita family and the mob whodunit

My grandparents were both legal immigrants from Sicily, Italy. I really didn't know very much about my family's background, because growing up as child, no one ever talked about my grandfather or how he had died, not until now. While I had lots of Italian relatives who had settled in the Springfield Massachusetts area, I'd only heard unsubstantiated rumors claiming how he was a big shot in the Mafia, whatever that meant. But that's all I knew until I managed to convince my grandmother to tell me the real story about him and our family.

My Grandfather, Anthony "Tony" Bonavita, married my grandmother, Annunziata (Nancy) Maratea, in 1916. Both my grandparents came to America with their parents when they were children. As a young man, Tony was a smart wise-guy who rose up fast in the world of organized crime. He was what some might call a high profile Springfield mobster at the time he was slain in a drive-by mob shooting at the ripe old age of 27.

Depending on who you talked to in my family, it was unclear whether Tony was a boss, or a capo [crew chief] who oversaw soldiers in their family. One thing is certain: whatever position my grandfather held, it required that he must have killed a person in order to be considered "made." Given my grandmother's limited description of Tony during their short marriage, I'll never know anything more about him than what I was told after our family sit-down.

Undoubtedly, Tony was a boss of some kind and he was important enough to get himself killed. Doing research for this memoir, I learned that my grandfather's territory within the American Mafia in the 1920's included Springfield, Massachusetts. Online organized crime bloggers tell how his territory would later be controlled by the "Luciano" crime family until 1957 when, in keeping with tradition, they would eventually be named as the Genovese family in recognition of Vito "Don Vito" Genovese as one of its greatest leaders.

According to Wikipedia, the Genovese crime family is one of five families that dominate organized crime activities in New York City as part of the Mafia (*Cosa Nostra*).

Standing in the kitchen while my grandmother tried to evade my question about the Mafia, I wondered why I had waited until I was twenty-three years old to start asking questions about my grandfather Tony. Didn't most families like to keep pictures, and other mementos, to pass onto their descendants? Not ours. I never saw any pictures of Tony. It's as if my grandmother wanted to wipe out all memories of the past and in looking back I can understand why.

Even asking questions about Tony was taboo in my family. I still remember, like it was yesterday, a conversation I had with my father when I asked him about his father Tony. It was in the

'80's and I was working on our family genealogy for my own church records after my baptism into the Church of Jesus Christ of Latter-day Saints. My father's reaction was not like anything I had expected.

"Don't ask anyone about your grandfather," Dad angrily shouted. "Never mention his name again do you hear?"

"But why not Dad?" I innocently asked. "It's just for our family history records."

"Leave it alone!" he insisted, and with that he gave me such a look that it put the fear of God in me and I never brought it up again.

But going back to 1972, I did bring up the subject of our grandfather because now someone wanted me dead, the same mobsters who had just murdered my boss Victor and I wanted some answers. So I pressed Gram for anything she could tell me after the most chilling unexpected sit-down I'd ever had with my Dad who'd just left both me and Gram stunned by the bombshell he'd just dropped on us.

Dad had just left Gram's house where the three of us had been huddled in a family council called by my Dad after my boss had disappeared a few nights earlier. After Dad left I stayed behind so I could talk to my grandmother alone.

Minutes that seemed like hours passed before my grandmother, who died in 1991, reluctantly decided to open up and talk to me. I guess she figured she had to, seeing how I was worth more to my grandfather's crime family dead than alive. As the widow of a 1920's gangster, my grandmother's own story is chilling, but once she got started talking, I soon realized why she wanted to forget the past.

A Mobster's proposal

I followed my grandmother into the dining room where she liked to sit and relax, leaning comfortably on her huge antique carved oak dining room table, visiting with friends like we were doing now. Watching Gram pulling up a chair meant she was ready to talk, and I was ready to listen. I pulled up a chair right beside hers as I watched Gram take out a tin box from a cupboard

5

before taking her seat. Quietly, and carefully, she pulled out some old pictures from the tin box.

Although, there weren't any pictures of Tony or even herself, I mentioned to her how her sister Jenny once told me "what a pretty girl Nancy was when she was young."

Gram smiled when I told her what Aunt Jenny said. "Yes," Gram admitted rather shyly. "I was a cutie back then, but I was only fifteen when Tony asked for my hand in marriage."

Gram explained how her family being faithful Catholics, knowing Tony's reputation as a mobster, repeatedly refused his request to marry their daughter. Finally, the smitten young handsome gangster, used to getting his way, did what he knew best. Gram, not one to mince words, gritting her teeth and shaking her head, began her story. A conversation that went something like this…

"He threatened my family and forced me to marry him," she bitterly recalled.

I listened quietly as she shared some not so pleasant memories of her personal life with my grandfather Tony. They had two sons, Peter and Frankie, but from all accounts, it was not a happy marriage. I was sorry to hear how Tony had cheated on my grandmother and had brought so much pain and suffering into her young life and the family. Details I won't share out of respect for her privacy.

"I prayed for a way to get away from him," Gram confessed without any remorse. "I don't know if I was really praying for his death but that's what happened after we'd been married only five years."

I soon realized my grandmother was a survivor of more than an abusive relationship with a gangster. From the look on my face, Gram must have decided it was time to tell me our family's story of the day they were both wounded, in a spray of bullets, during a frightening home invasion that took place in broad daylight in their South End home in Springfield, Mass.

"Tony was home and we were in the kitchen having dinner when a car pulled up in front of our house," Gram recalled.

"Were you living in this house right here on Massachusetts Avenue at the time, Gram?" I asked.

6

"No. We were living in our home in the South End, where we had moved right after we married," she explained.

Now, I knew from my own experience, having lived in the South End myself until just recently that the Little Italy neighborhood was home to some mobsters, most of whom had originally migrated here from Italy.

"But Gram," I reminded her, "didn't you know you were living among gangsters involved in the Mafia when Tony moved you into that neighborhood?"

"Of course I did. Where do you think I was living when Tony fell in love with me at first sight?" Gram asked.

"Okay," I said, spurred on by this new information, "and if you knew about the reputation of the South End, then why didn't you warn me not to rent an apartment there like you know I did when I graduated high school?"

"I thought if I said anything, you would start asking me all kinds of questions just like you are doing now," she angrily replied. "And besides, would you have listened to me and just took my word to stay out of the South End?"

"Nope," I thought to myself. "I was a rebellious teenager by the time I was thrown out of my grandparents' home where I'd been living for a few months back then and I most likely wouldn't have heeded her warning to stay away from the South End."

But now, listening to Gram tell me about our family and the Mafia, I would have believed her and might've never rented an apartment in a neighborhood with the South End's reputation. Thinking it best not to get her all riled up, I shut my mouth. She had a story and I needed to let her talk.

"Fair enough," I said, trying to keep her focused on her story. "So, what happened after the gangsters got out of their car?"

Leaning on the dining room table, convinced I would shut up and let her finish her story, placing her head in her hands, this sweet little ole lady struggled to find the right words to describe what she'd been through. I reached over and gently laid my hand on hers.

"I'm so sorry, Gram, but I just need to know," I said.

Looking out the window, as if watching it play out all over again on a movie screen, she went on with her story. "As soon as

7

Tony saw the car pull up, he dragged me away from the table and told me to run and hide in the basement."

Haunted by my own dark memories of the South End, I thought Gram was going to leave it there and not finish her story when all of a sudden she gets up from the dining room table, where we were talking, and walks back into the kitchen and opens the back door. She points to the stairs leading down to the basement.

"We had only gotten about that far," she said, pointing to the bottom of the first set of stairs. "And that's when the armed men started shooting at us."

She just kept staring at those stairs until I asked, "What happened after that Gram?"

"We were both wounded in the gunfire while running down the stairs," she explained. "Tony managed to get off some shots, but I'd been shot and didn't see what happened after that."

As if by some miracle, both my grandparents survived that violent home invasion by mobsters sent to assassinate Tony. Thinking that was the end of the story, I followed Gram back to the dining room, at which point, she sat back down in her favorite chair with me sitting next to her. I waited.

Like grandfather like granddaughter

After the bungled mob home invasion, that left both my grandparents seriously wounded in their Williams Street home, life went on as usual for both of them after a slow recovery from their wounds.

Unlike other mob figures, some of whom have turned on their crime families after surviving failed assassination attempts on their life, Gram didn't say whether or not my grandfather Tony, sought vengeance. Instead, after surviving a gangland bid to kill him, Gram said he didn't even retire from the rackets as others might have done.

"Tony was crazy," is all Gram would say.

I didn't say it, but I sure wanted to know about Tony's dealings with the Mafia that made them want to kill him in his own home with a wife and family around."

8

"So what happened after they botched his assassination, Gram?" I asked.

"They waited and tried again," Gram said without so much as blinking an eye.

Gram explained how Tony was eventually slain in broad daylight, in a drive-by shooting, on Main Street in downtown Springfield. She said he was gunned down while getting out of his car. I didn't think to ask her so I don't know what happened to his bodyguard, or if he had one, because Gram never said.

Providing for mob widows

As for my grandmother, she managed to do pretty well for herself financially after Tony's death. One thing about the Mafia, according to mob wives like Barbara Fuca, who broke silence in 1962, "Usually the family will continue to provide for a wife while her husband is in jail. But when he gets bumped off, the women often end up on the welfare rolls, unless their husbands are high up in the organization."

Thinking about Fuca's knowledge of mob widows, I began to wonder just how "high up" was my grandfather Tony, given how my grandmother didn't end up on the welfare rolls after he was "bumped off" as other mob wives often did back then.

After Tony's assassination left my grandmother alone with two young sons, she moved out of the South End, bought a beautiful two-story home in Springfield where she opened up a corner store, a small neighborhood grocery store until she sold it years later. Gram never said how she got the money to open up a corner store, or about her second husband or either. I wish I knew, but I was only left with more questions listening to Gram tell her story.

"What does a mob widow do in those days," I thought to myself, "unless Tony's crime family provided for her after his death. Either that, or she inherited his "business" like another famous mob wife reportedly did in 1919." But I couldn't see my grandmother doing that and I would rather think she had some money stashed from Tony's "business" instead.

According to my grandmother, Tony's murder remained unsolved. Like so many others, my grandfather's assassination was just one of many "cold cases" in Springfield's history of mob murders. Just before sitting down with my grandmother to have this talk in 1972, I had already lost two friends murdered by the Genovese family, and both of those were filed as cold cases, too. For all I knew, I might be next.

At the time I was listening to my grandmother's story, I was only twenty-three years old and the mob had just ordered a hit on me, just like my own grandfather, who was only 27 when he was assassinated. What are the odds?

The Springfield Mafia in the 1900's

By all reports, the Genovese crime family is still active today in Massachusetts, as reported online by Joselin Estevez, titled Where Are New York's 5 Mob Families? As with most mobologists online these days, there is ample information out there involving the Genovese family that dates back to my own family. The best local updated source I found is put out on *masslive.com,* the online home of *The Republican* newspaper that operates out of Springfield, Massachusetts.

Incredibly, I could even trace my own grandfather's OC timeline, dating as far back as his 1921 assassination on *masslive.com* under Organized crime in Springfield evolved through death and money by Stephanie Barry.

As a mobologist, Barry's vignette was one of a two-part series addressing the evolution of the Mafia in Greater Springfield since the early 1900s dating back to Prohibition in Western Massachusetts. I appreciate Barry's research dating back to the 1900's that runs right smack dab into my own family line, who like so many gangsters I associated with, lived in Springfield's South End, also known as Little Italy.

I pulled up an interesting story on one of Barry's updates on Carlo Sinischalchi that reads like a chapter from my own gangster grandfather's life "When booze became illegal in 1919, Springfield's Carlo Sinischalchi was labeled "King of the Bootleggers" and moved from a cold-water flat in the city's South End to a bigger house and a lifestyle in which he was shuttled to work and outings in a chauffeur-driven limousine, historians say."

Barry drew an interesting parallel to my own grandfather's untimely death wherein she wrote, "However, his kingdom was less than a year old when he was shot and killed in that very Lincoln limousine, while waiting for his driver to bring him a cigar. His widow, Pasquelina Sinischalchi, inherited the business and married Antonio Miranda, a close ally of New York crime bosses Frank Costello and Vito Genovese."

Fast-forwarding to the 1960s and '70s, Barry informed her readers how "Organized crime figures in Springfield had a foothold in more contemporary, traditional rackets: street lotteries, truck heists, illegal sports-betting and casino junkets, among others."

No escape from the past

My grandmother's story didn't end with Tony's assassination. My grandmother blamed Tony's legacy for breaking up my own parents' marriage and even putting my life in danger several times. This was new information to me which I did not expect when I pressed Gram to tell me about Tony. But what she told me sure did explain a lot about why my parents never wanted me when they first learned my mother was pregnant with me.

Indeed, I am reminded of Shannon L. Alder who once said, "A legacy is etched into the minds of others and the stories they share about you."

Perhaps, Ray Bradbury's popular legacy quote says it all, "Everyone must leave something behind when he dies, my grandfather said. A child or a book or a painting or a house or a wall built or a pair of shoes made."

But it's Frank Herbert of Dune, whose legacy quote best sums up the real story behind my grandfather's legacy when he said, "There is no escape—we pay for the violence of our ancestors." As my grandmother began her story about my parent's married life, it wasn't until that day that I understood how much we had all paid for the violence left behind by Dad's father Tony. This is her story.

Mom's life in Italy

My mother, a war bride who came to America with my American born Italian father, grew up in a 1940's Nazi occupied Italy during World War II, in Naples, Italy. No stranger to violence, my own maternal grandmother died in my mother's arms from injuries sustained by shards of broken glass propelled by the explosion of a bomb, when the blast blew out all the windows in their home during the war.

I remember my mother telling me how she faced death many times when German soldiers were ordered to shoot looters. My mom, like so many others who'd been starving in her war torn neighborhood, was forced to search for food in stores that had been reduced to rubble from the bombs. Mom said she never knew why her life was spared so many times, like when a German soldier was killing looters in the very store where Mom was looting food supplies. The German had been lying in wait outside the back of the store for anyone trying to escape the German soldiers who were guarding the store front entrance.

As my mother stepped over each of her neighbor's dead bodies, she never knew why she wasn't shot in the back when, for some unexplained reason, the German soldier showed her mercy and let her walk away unharmed.

As for my father Peter, he was a veteran of WWII and had been deployed to Italy where he met my mother who had joined up with the Italian Resistance before the arrival of the first Allied forces in Naples in 1943. When Naples was liberated and the war ended, my parents were married in her hometown of Naples Italy in 1945 and Dad brought my mother home to America as his war bride. The newlyweds moved in with his mother, my grandmother Nancy, who had remarried for the third time by now and was still living in her Springfield, Massachusetts home.

When my sister was born in 1947, my parents happily welcomed her. A year later, when my mother discovered she was pregnant with me, it was evident to my grandparents that she didn't want me. According to my grandmother, my mother secretly made plans to end her pregnancy.

I'll never forget what Gram said to me when she decided to tell me about it. "For some reason though, you managed to survive the abortion. And we never knew why."

I didn't know about this part of Gram's story. It was all news to me. Up until now, sitting in Gram's dining room listening to her tell her story, I hadn't heard anything about my parents before I was born and I naturally had more questions. Our conversation went something like this...

"But Gram, why did Mom want to keep me from being born if she was married to Dad?" I asked.

"You survived that abortion she attempted, Elaine," she said. "That's all you need to know."

"But if she didn't want me, what happened after I was born alive?" I asked.

"After you were born," she explained, "your parents refused to name you."

According to Gram, my mother not only tried to get rid of me by an abortion, but also refused to name me and actually left me unnamed for days. Like the story behind her attempted abortion, Gram never said why my mother didn't want to name me.

"After so many days went by, and your parents still refused to name you, something had to be done," Gram said.

The way Gram tells the story, she didn't dare interfere and try to name me herself. She said Dad wouldn't have it.

"But everyone knew you had to be named sooner or later," Gram explained. "And that's how a bunch of college students came up with a plan to name you."

Whatever name comes out of the hat

At the time I was born, Gram ran a room and board for ten college students from Springfield College when she rented out rooms in her three-story Springfield home located just down the street from it. After learning about the unnamed baby in our family, the college boys suggested that each of them put a name in a hat, and whatever name my mother pulled out of it she would agree to name me.

13

"Your poor mother had no choice but to agree if you were ever going to be named," Gram said. "And that's how you came to be called Elaine."

Now I ask you, what kind of name was that to give an Italian girl? While I never said anything growing up, it had, nonetheless, always annoyed me that no one in our Italian lineage had the name of Elaine, as I did. In a weird kind of way, if not for my situation with Skyball's crew putting out a contract on me, I might never have learned about my naming story.

To this day everyone asks me why I go by a nickname instead of my birth name of Elaine. The bizarre naming story has everything to do with it I guess. But that's another story for Chapter 6 of how I got involved in fighting the mob while holding elected office. I just wanted to forget all about my naming story which seeing my name "Elaine" in the news would have been such a constant reminder!

A botched murder-suicide

According to *Wikipedia*, a "murder–suicide is an act in which an individual kills one or more other persons immediately before or at the same time as killing oneself." I was surprised to learn there was more to my mother's determination to end my life after the botched abortion attempt.

"There's more if you want to hear it," Gram offered.

"Sure," I said. "How bad could it be after everything Mom had already done to me?"

"Well, I kept something, and I guess you have a right to see it now."

Still sitting at the dining room table while Gram continued her story, I watched as she pulled out a small box with some yellowed aged papers inside it from a drawer in her china cabinet. Incredibly, my grandmother had kept an old newspaper clipping, all these years, of a police report filed on my mother and me.

It seems that, when I was born, my parent's marriage was already on the rocks. Dad was running around on my mother, and he beat her. Mom, in her defense, who died in 2002, had no family of her own in America and it had to have been even harder on her having only a third grade education and not being able to speak a bit of English when she came to America with my father.

It's hard to imagine myself in her shoes, but it must have been a hopeless situation for my mother, especially since, according to my grandmother, divorce was out of the question. I can still see that yellowed news clipping that haunts me even now. If memory serves me right, our conversation went something like this.

"Your mother never said a word to anyone about how desperate she had become," Gram explained. "Maybe if she had felt she could talk to someone, she wouldn't have tried to take your life again."

"What do you mean, take my life, again?" I asked.

"Your parents divorced when you were only three years old. But I always thought it's what your mother did that made your father finally divorce her."

Holding the faded yellowed newspaper clipping in her hand, I listened as Gram read the police report to me. Since moving out of Gram's place, my parents had been living on Pendleton Avenue in Springfield where they rented a house not far from the South End of Springfield.

"You and your mother were both unconscious when the police arrived and you were both taken by ambulance to the hospital," Gram explained.

Gram filled in the blanks. She sure was a good story-teller and I listened as she explained how my mother had put my sister, who was only a year older than me, outside in the back yard. Gram said the neighbors had called the police and that's how she learned what happened that day.

"Your sister was crying so loud that the neighbors came running to see what the problem was. And that," my grandmother explained, "is when they smelled gas and called the police."

"What happened to my sister, while me and Mom were locked inside the house?" I asked.

Staring out the window, seeming so far away, my grandmother continued her story. "It was because of your sister, the police got there in time, even though you were both unconscious and they had to break down the door," Gram explained. "Your sister was too young, she didn't know what was going on."

Gram explained how my sister was crying because she'd been left alone so long outside. It was her crying that got the attention of the neighbors and it's what saved our lives.

According to Gram, my mother had reached a point in her marriage and was determined to die and take me with her. Gram said Mom locked the doors, stuffed towels under them, turned on the gas to the stove, and kept me with her inside the house as the gas fumes filled the air.

"Dear Lord," I thought to myself. "Did my mother want to go to heaven and take me with her?"

I wasn't sure what place in Heaven there was for parents who kill their children, but because we both survived a murder-suicide, I guess no one wanted us to come back to Heaven just yet. Having time to think about what my grandmother had said, I still remember my next question like it was yesterday.

"But Gram," I finally asked, fully expecting her to know the answer, "why didn't my mother keep my sister inside the house with us?"

Gram just looked at me, closing her eyes, shaking her head and for a brief moment I actually thought she was going to tell me why my mother didn't want to kill my sister too. But she didn't say. And both Gram and my mother took the rest of the story to their graves.

Filicide is the deliberate brutal act of a parent murdering their own child. It's hard even today to understand why some mothers kill their children by abortion, but even harder to understand killing them outside of the womb too. As I listened to the sad story of my parents' dysfunctional marriage, I couldn't help but think maybe, like so many other women who kill their own children, my mother just wanted to end her pain here on earth too. But why take me with her?

My mother may not have ended my life that day, but she did end any chances I might've had for a normal happy childhood. Who knows, she might've saved me and my sister from something far worse if she and Dad had stayed married. Either way, my parents divorced shortly after my mother's failed

16

murder-suicide attempt and my sister and I were placed in the custody of my father and the three of us moved in with my grandmother Nancy and her third husband Teddy. Although Gram had remarried after Tony's assassination, and didn't want to talk about her own second husband, she seemed anxious about something else. So she continued her story as she filled me in on Mom's second husband.

Gram said my mother surprised everyone when she up and married her second husband right after her divorce from my father in 1951. According to the story, they'd only dated two weeks and just up and married to everyone's surprise.

I had known my step-father growing up but I didn't know the details of their marriage until talking with Gram. Being more familiar with monikers, nicknames given to mobsters, I find it funny that my mother married a guy nicknamed "Boots." No. He wasn't in any organized crime family that I ever knew about. But he was in an organized family in a way. Boots was an enlisted soldier in the Air Force when he met my mother.

According to Gram, they dated only a few weeks before marrying. "Your mother had a choice to make," she said. "Boots had just received his orders transferring him to Alaska."

I just had to ask. "So, if she chose to marry Boots, why didn't we go with her?" I asked.

"Your mother didn't have custody of you girls," Gram explained. "The court wouldn't let her take you out of Massachusetts."

And that's how it was that my mother found a way out of her dreadful situation. She remarried and left us girls behind. It would be several years before my sister and I ever saw our mother again.

Start packing

We lived with our grandparents until Dad remarried and we moved to the small rural town of Agawam just outside of the big city of Springfield. This time, it was Dad's second wife who cheated on him and I was only eight years old when he divorced her and asked his mother Nancy to keep us girls.

When my sister and I moved in with our grandparents we were both suffering from severe malnutrition. Dad's second wife wasn't the best step-mother I guess. The best thing about living with our grandparents was we got to eat good meals again and Gram surprised us when she enrolled us in a parochial school with Dad's help. I loved having nuns for teachers and for the next three years my sister and I were happier than we'd ever been.

But happy days in our family never lasted very long and looking back I recall the day our lives would forever change. If memory serves me right, the conversation went something like this.

"Why are we being sent away Gram?" I asked while trying to hold back the tears. "Did I do something wrong?"

Walking into the bedroom where Gram was helping us pack, Dad said, "What are you worried about? Your foster parents will let your grandparents visit you whenever they can."

"It wasn't Dad I'd be missing," I thought to myself, as I recalled how he had once left me hanging by the scruff of my shirt on a door hook for punishment when we were living in Agawam with his second wife. He took his belt to me too many times and I sure wouldn't be missing that, I thought, as I cried while packing to leave Gram's house.

"You've got to understand," Gram was saying as she pulled me aside, "we didn't want it this way, but your father has turned you and your sister over to the state."

"Say goodbye to your grandparents," Dad said as he led us out the door.

The worst of it was when my sister and I were separated when we were put into foster care. The next year passed slowly for me without her around. I was miserable and acted out a lot after being turned over to the State. I even ran away a few times, but the police always found me and brought me back to whatever foster home I was living in at the time.

Somehow, by the grace of God, both my sister and I got out of foster care in 1963 when the State made my parents take custody of us. All I know is that I was suddenly being sent off to Germany to live with my mother where Boots had been stationed.

According to Gram, both my parents wanted my sister, but not me.

It was finally decided that my Dad would take my sister, leaving our mother with no choice but to take me. Thanks to growing up with the nuns while living with my grandparents, I had gotten in the habit of daily prayers on my knees and I kept up with my prayers while in foster care. That was good, because unknown to me at the time, I was being shipped off to live with a woman who had already tried to kill me twice.

I was, understandably, nervous about leaving America and moving in with my mother's new family, who thanks to Dad's resistance to keeping me, I knew didn't want me either. Seeing as how I only had three years left to graduation, I figured I could survive Germany if I survived foster care.

I was too young to trust in God enough to believe I could ever happy again. And so it was, I never imagined how living in Germany would bring me into the glamorous world of Elvis Presley and the Memphis Mafia.

CHAPTER TWO:
ELVIS, THE MEMPHIS MAFIA, AND ME

"You going out with that Elvis guy again?" My mother asked me as I was getting dressed for my date.

"Yep. And stop calling him that Elvis guy. He has a name," I replied.

"He looks just like Elvis and you know it," Mom insisted.

"Okay. But that's not why I like him," I explained.

Growing up a teenager in the rock-n-roll era of the 60's, I didn't follow Elvis Presley. I barely knew who Elvis was and didn't care. In fact, I didn't even listen to his music while I was living with my mother in Germany on the Bitburg Air Force Base where my stepfather was stationed from 1963-1966. While most of Elvis' adoring fans dreamt of meeting him one day, I never did.

The story of my brief visit in Germany is only worth mentioning in its own chapter because I did get to meet the real Elvis in 1969 when I returned to the states. And so, this is my story of how I came to hang out with Elvis Presley and his guys, better known as the Memphis Mafia.

Before I ever met Elvis and his Memphis Mafia during the filming of his movie, *Change of Habit,* I spent some time dating his look-alike in Germany where I lived with my mother. Looking back, I can say that dating his Elvis look-alike kind of prepared me for the day I would meet the real Elvis.

Elvis, Nuns, and Guns

After I was moved out of foster care and placed in the custody of my mother I soon found myself on a plane heading for Germany to join both her and her second husband Boots. I got settled in and faced the grueling task of making new friends in the middle of my sophomore year on the Bitburg Air Force Base where I attended high school until I graduated in 1966.

It was in my senior year on Valentine's Day that I met and began dating an American soldier who bore an uncanny resemblance to Elvis Presley. Heck, he even sang like Elvis too.

My step-father Boots was a Master Sergeant in the Air Force. As a Non-Commissioned Officer's kid with more baggage from my past that I left behind in the states than most teens my age could ever imagine, I never fit in with the popular crowd in high school. Thus I ended up dating mostly servicemen, stationed on our base, in my senior year of high school.

While I can't recall his name after all these years, I've never forgotten my Elvis look-alike crush. He was an enlisted Airman and we met while taking square dance lessons at the recreation center on the base.

Everywhere my look-alike crush went, people mentioned how much he closely he resembled the real Elvis. Yep. Except for his blonde hair, he could've passed for the real thing.

Like the real Elvis, he liked to sing and serenade me with Elvis songs. If anyone had said I'd meet the real Elvis Presley, in less than three years, who would do the same thing, I would never have believed them.

My Elvis look-alike and I had fun while it lasted and when I graduated, we said our goodbyes as I packed up to go back to the states. I didn't have time to miss him what with my step-father's rush to get rid of me. I was sent back unescorted to America, but I will never forget Boot's parting message as I walked out the door for the last time.

"Don't let the door hit you on the way out," Boots said, kind of sarcastically.

"Thanks," I snapped at him. "You never wanted me to come here and live with you and Mom did you?"

Picking up my bags walking out the door, he merely replied, "You'll be happier in Massachusetts around your grandparents."

"More like he and Mom would be happier," I thought to myself.

Well, to be fair, I was forced on my mother when the state made my father take me and my sister off foster care. All I was ever told, before I left for Germany, was that neither of my parents wanted me and since Dad had refused to take both of us; that left my mother who was forced to take custody of me against her will.

As for me, a teenager whose entire childhood was spent thrown around from home to home, I was just glad to head back to the states despite being scared not knowing where I was going to be living once I got there. My grandparents weren't real excited about my homecoming while my sister was pretty settled in living with Gram's sister who took her in when I went to Germany.

It's all still a blur on how I left Germany and got relocated in the states but I had a plane ticket to Springfield and Mom assured me she would call my grandparents to let them know I was on my way back. The shock of realizing I was on my own finally hit me when my plane landed at Bradley Field Airport.

As soon as I stepped onto American soil, I made plans to explore my options, which included entering the convent, that I'd put on hold when I was shipped off to Germany.

Nun of that for me

Growing up in the Catholic Church and then hanging around the nuns as I did when living with my grandparents, I really wanted to be a nun too. I never did get to meet any nuns while I was in Germany, so I was excited to be reunited with some of my favorite nuns in Springfield like Sister Mary Gervase.

Even though I wasn't the same good little girl that I was before I started dating servicemen in Germany, I had never stopped praying or attending church. Although I was pretty mixed up by the time I showed up at my grandmother's doorstep in the spring of 1966, and probably needed a psychiatrist more, I sought out the nuns instead.

The first thing I did was make a visit to the convent where I had gone to school during my childhood. Seeking solace, I decided to visit the Sisters of St. Joseph who lived near my grandmother.

The nuns had always been like family to me. I spent more time visiting the convent then I did hanging out with school friends. Visiting the nuns, like Sister Gervase, always felt more like a spiritual retreat from the world. I envied their life living as a bride of Jesus and having the church for a family as they did. Convent visits always made me want to stay and never leave.

Hoping for good news when I was reunited with Sister Gervase, I was disappointed to find myself preparing to enter the real world instead. After talking with Sister Gervase, a former teacher of mine who took the name of a second century Christian martyr St. Gervase, I was heartbroken as she gently broke the news to me.

"You can't just enter the convent straight out of high school my dear," she explained. "But we can help you prepare for that day."

As Sister Gervase explained to me what I would have to do, I was disheartened to learn that if I wanted to be a teaching nun, I would have to put myself through college first.

"But I'm only seventeen and I don't have any money for college, much less a place to live." I reminded her.

I guess I started crying because the next thing I knew, Sister Gervase was holding me in her arms like a small child who had lost its way. "Are nuns angels Lord?" I asked myself as I rested my head on her dear shoulders. She was my earthly angel and I loved her.

"Now, now, child," she said. "I think we can figure something out to help you."

True to her word, Sister Gervase came up with a plan to help me prepare so I could plan to enter the convent one day. Within a few days I found myself starting a new job, at Massachusetts Mutual Life Insurance Company, thanks to the nuns who arranged for me to get into a keypunch operator trainee program.

I decided to take Sister Gervase's advice and enroll in a secretarial course at Andover Institute of Business in Springfield. I needed a better paying job to fund my college plan. I also needed to get a car. Using the public bus system to get to school downtown late at night, wasn't very safe for a young girl alone, so I signed up for a driver's education course and got my driver's license.

It was a lot on my plate and I was overwhelmed for sure. If not for the nuns, I don't know how I could have overcome so many challenges on my own. But I did, and I must have had some angels watching over me as I got settled into my new life.

The nuns got me into the YWCA in Springfield, so I could have a safe place to live temporarily, and that's how I found a roommate, Jill, and my ticket out of there.

At seventeen, I couldn't rent an apartment on my own, but it didn't matter since I couldn't afford one on my meager

Keypunch trainee job paycheck anyway. To my delight, Jill was eighteen and could sign for an apartment but like me, she couldn't afford one on her own either. We were a match!

"You're going to just love the apartment I found for us in the South End," Jill exclaimed as I got in from work one day while staying at the YWCA.

"I can't believe you did it," I said. "We're really going to get out of this place?"

Unaware yet of my own grandparents' close brush with death so long ago in the South End, I was clueless about the South End's reputation in the '60's. I was just thrilled to be moving out of the YWCA with my new roommate.

According to Jill, we could manage the rent on both our salaries and it was a comfortable apartment too. When we moved in, we acted more like two excited college girls moving off campus. Unaware of the pending danger in my new surroundings, I felt inspired to get on my knees and pray for guidance and safety as I settled into my new home. I should've done that before moving out of the YWCA and I don't know why I didn't.

The next year passed rather quickly. Although I was never a party girl before meeting Jill, I soon was, thanks to her bad influence and willingness to show me the ropes. Jill, I soon learned, was an alcoholic and I began spending more time with her and her friends in bars than with the nuns.

"It's only 10 o'clock in the morning and you're drinking already?" I asked in disbelief as Jill started on her second beer.

"You gotta lighten up and have some fun girl," Jill said while tempting me to join her for a drink.

"You know my plan Jill," I reminded her. "I want to join the convent one day."

"Yes. And you can too," Jill replied. "What's the harm in a little drink once in a while and going out with the girls?"

And that's how I got introduced to the wild night-life in Springfield at the ripe old age of seventeen. I was led like a lamb to the slaughter as I followed Jill on her nightly rounds of favorite night spots. Like Jill had done, I too had to get a fake ID so I could get in the clubs. Looking back, I walked right into Satan's trap as I made one bad choice after another.

What was I thinking? Looking back I can see how those choices brought me right smack dab into the very "family" that my grandmother never bothered to warn me about even when I told her I was getting my own apartment in the South End.

But Gram never had the "talk" with me until it was too late for me. In 1966, I didn't know to watch for the typical signs warning me to stay away from the Genovese family. I had a new mentor now—Jill. In no time at all, I realized I could never be a candidate for the convent. I liked the life I'd been introduced to and I soon began partying with some real tough guys who packed guns.

Seventeen was way too young for me to messing around with mobsters. But I was. I remember the time I was held at gunpoint when I changed my mind about partying with some of Jill's friends that got too rough for my taste. It got real ugly when I said I wanted to go home. They let me know in no uncertain terms I wasn't going anywhere. I was scared alright.

"I need help. Send the police!" I cried ever so quietly into the phone.

"Hang up the phone," a husky male voice demanded.

I squeezed my eyes shut and waited as I felt the cold metal of a gun pressed up against the back of my head. I dropped the phone. You didn't have to ask *me* a second time! With one hand grabbing me by my hair, and a gun in his other hand, he dragged me away from the phone.

It's never too late to pray

"Our Father who art in Heaven…" I prayed ever so loudly and more fervently than I ever remembered doing before.

I was being held captive against my will and when I found myself alone with two men in a bedroom I knew there was only one way I was going to get out of it unharmed.

"Shut up!" ordered the thug with the gun. Leaning over me, he demanded, "What are you doing?"

"…Hallowed be thy name. Thy kingdom come…" I continued reciting The Lord's Prayer just as I'd done every night all my life.

Pressing the gun up against my forehead now, he threatened, "I'll give you something to pray about if you don't shut up."

"..Thy will be done on earth as it is in Heaven…" I began crying out to the heavens as loud as I could.

The next thing I knew I was being thrown into a cab and I was on my way home. Who says praying doesn't help? Who says God doesn't hear and answer prayers of sinners like me? The thugs never laid a hand on me and I knew then, as I know today, it was the power of God that compelled them to let me go unharmed that day. Else why was I released unharmed?

I'd had a few other close calls, thanks to Jill's friends, and each time, I prayed as I did before. At some point, I knew I had to get away from Jill but I didn't have a way to do it alone. Praying for the strength to get out of my situation living with her in the South End, I got a temporary reprieve when my grandparents agreed to let me move back in with them just until I got myself together.

"You sure you won't change your mind and stay here?" Jill was pleading.

"I can't do this anymore, Jill," I said. "It's not the life I want to stay in anymore."

Yes. I know. I should've spent more time hanging out with Sister Gervase than Jill. If I had, I might have turned out differently maybe even became a nun. Instead, thanks to some bad choices, I found myself visiting the parish priest every Saturday before Sunday Mass confessing my sins.

Confession didn't seem to make much of a difference I'm sorry to say. Nevertheless, I did keep to my plan. I kept busy working a day job. I was no longer going to night school as I had completed an Office Secretarial course. Living with my grandparents, I found that I had more time on my hands than when I lived with Jill.

I made new friends and tried to stay away from the places where I'd been hanging out with Jill. Despite my attempts to straighten out my life, I managed to find enough time in the spring of '68 to get into trouble when I met "Big Al" at a local night club with some friends.

My first true love

"Hi. Can I buy you a drink?" the drop dead gorgeous guy was asking as he leaned in ever so close to me.

"Sure. But I'm only drinking ginger ale," I answered, stupidly.

"We can change that," he said as he ordered me a nice red wine.

I was underage sitting at the bar with friends in a popular night club when the bouncer approached me. I wasn't drinking but at nineteen I sure didn't look twenty-one. I didn't like to drink alcohol in these places just in case I got ID'd and got in trouble. But I wasn't going to tell the club bouncer that.

Instead of checking my ID, he was hitting on me. Yep. He had actually left his station at the door to come flirt with me. Heck, if he wanted to buy me a drink, I wouldn't have to be worrying about getting thrown out for being under age.

Looking at the guy standing next to me, I thought to myself that this is what love at first sight must feel like. At 6'2 weighing in around 220, his rugged good looks reminded me more of a Don Juan than a bouncer.

Looking around, it didn't take me long to figure out he was definitely a chick magnet. I liked it and I liked him. I was totally caught up in the moment when a sudden noise erupted behind us, and I watched as he morphed from Don Juan to Iron Mike in a split second.

"I wouldn't want to be on the other end of his fist," I thought to myself, "if I was a guy that got on the wrong side of him." Looking around I noticed several beautiful women giving me the evil eye. "Any of them your girlfriend?" I asked, when he returned to take up where we left off.

"Friends," he whispered into my ear, "but I like to make new friends, too. What say we go find a more quiet corner to get to know each other better?"

"I see you met Big Al." A tough looking wise guy smiled at me as he slapped Al on the back.

27

"Hey. Not now. Can't you see I'm busy?" Al kind of jokingly shot back as the guy shrugged and wandered off smiling.

While Big Al was at the bar ordering my second red wine, one of his guy friends came over and sat down next to me in the booth where we'd been sitting. His friend was chattier than Al and I soon learned "Big Al" Brooks was a former heavyweight boxer in his late 20's.

"Was he a pretty good boxer?" I asked Big Al's friend.

"Good enough to get a match in Madison Square Garden," he replied. "We're real proud of our Big Al. He even held the "Home City Heavy" title."

Al's friend didn't stick around once he returned with our drinks. One thing led to another and after closing the bar, Al took me home.

Unlike his big-mouthed show-off friends, Al was your typical quiet type who never bragged on himself but never smiled much either. Instead, Al would just squint his eyes and look at you like he was about to eat you for lunch. If battle scars built character, then Al had a lot of character. Sporting a broken nose, like a badge of honor from his days in the ring, his reputation as a battle hardened warrior made me feel safe any time I was with him.

I never seemed to run into any scary characters that bothered me anymore after taking up with Big Al. His guy friends, I noticed, always managed to keep an eye on me when he wasn't around. I was flattered by his attention and never gave it another thought, although I should have. I never knew much about him until years later in our tumultuous on again, off again love affair.

Al, who died in 2008, was involved with the Springfield crew and had been hanging out with made members of the Genovese family when we met. I'm sure that had something to do with him ending up serving time in prison a few years later. I guess Al didn't talk or he would've ended up in the river like other wise guys he had hung around usually did.

While Al never talked about himself or what he did for a living around me, I had always suspected he had been drafted as a soldier in the Mafia like so many other former battle hardened warrior boxers. It was no secret that besides seizing control of the rackets and drugs, mobsters were partial to insider boxing.

I didn't care what he did. I only knew that I fell in love with my Big Al the moment I laid eyes on him. We started seeing each other regularly over the next few months and I should have suspected something when he didn't make real dates with me. Unless I was at the club where he worked, I would only see him when he came by my place after hours.

It wasn't until months later that I learned he was married to the woman who owned the club where I had always assumed he was just the bouncer—never thinking he might have been the owner.

Watch what you pray for, you may get it!

"I don't think it's a good idea for us to be seeing each other anymore," I told Al one night after keeping a doctor appointment. I was still reeling from the news I'd been given a few hours earlier his office.

"Miss Bonavita, your blood tests have come back, and we need to talk," the doctor politely explained.

"Is everything alright, Doc?" I asked.

"Yes. Everything came back normal except it seems that you are pregnant," he explained.

"What?" I cried. "I don't understand. You've had me on birth control pills. How can I be pregnant?"

The doctor, half joking, tried to explain how such a thing could've happened. But I wasn't laughing, and he was. What was wrong with that picture? I was devastated.

I was barely nineteen the day my doctor told me I was pregnant. In 1968, I was single and living with my grandmother. Sitting in the doctor's office that day, I knew one thing—I did not want a baby right now. I couldn't even take care of myself yet.

On the drive home from the doctor's office I had time to ponder my situation and how my praying might have played a part in all of this. I distinctly remember praying for a family of my own. I distinctly recalled how I had prayed for a child that no one could take away from me.

"Wait a minute," I thought to myself. "What was I thinking? But yes, I had unconsciously been praying for a baby all those years of my crying on my pillow every night unto God hoping to rescue me from my lonely existence."

Somehow, in all the praying, it never crossed my mind to pray for God to send me a good husband first. The realization that my unborn out-of-wedlock child's father was already married left me bereft and inconsolable. On the drive home from the doctor's office, I contemplated my options. Telling Al wasn't one of them.

Here I was, three months along and not showing a bit either. For obvious reasons, I never told Al I was pregnant. I didn't know how he'd react if he knew. Heck, I didn't know how I was supposed to react to the news, either. Neither did my family.

"You're pregnant?" my grandmother cried out. "Who's the father?"

"I don't know" is all I could say for the time being.

"Some nun you turned out to be," my father declared when he heard about it. "Sister non-existent." Dad always used to say that whenever I mentioned I wanted to be nun as a kid growing up.

"Yep. Dad had a way with words sometimes," I thought to myself, but I wasn't in any mood to hear it. I was a young girl who honestly had wanted to be a nun and here I was pregnant by a guy married to the mob whose wife had a story that no one ever talked about either.

For all I knew, Al could never claim an out-of-wedlock child. The Mafia had a code and I didn't know where Al and I stood with that situation. I was naïve of so many things inside the Mafia that I was clueless of the world I had wandered into with Big Al. I never knew about his wife or whether she had ties to the mob, but did it matter?

I knew enough back then to know that people got killed for violating any of their codes. I sure didn't want any harm coming to Al or me. Fearing for his safety and mine, my only option was to keep silent and go on the run after hearing what my family expected me to do.

Finding myself alone and pregnant, I contemplated keeping and raising my baby myself. My Catholic priest advised against it. My grandparents argued in favor of adoption. Others talked of abortion like my crazy cousin Gina.

Gina had recently married at the ripe old age of nineteen and growing up had been like a sister to me. One thing she never outgrew was her angry temper.

I'll never forget the day I was visiting her and we were standing at the top of the stairs outside her back door discussing my situation, when all of a sudden she started screaming "I'll kill that little b___ of yours!" Before I knew what was happening, she had punched me in the stomach and thrown me down two flights of stairs.

My poor unborn baby survived crazy Gina's attempt to get rid of him and I thanked the Lord. As unpopular as my decision was with everyone around me, my fight to keep my unborn baby must have bewildered my grandmother more than anyone else. Not yet knowing about my own mother's attempts to get rid of me by abortion, I find it all the more amazing I chose to keep my baby. But Gram knew my mother's story all along and yet she never said a word to me.

Looking back on it all, it would be another three years before I would be called in for that infamous sit-down with my father at Gram's house and learn of my family's darkest secrets.

"If angels watch over us," I thought, "surely the Lord must have wanted me not to follow in my own mother's footsteps." While I never understood at the time, I nonetheless felt the promptings of the Holy Spirit instructing me that I must not kill my unborn child.

I had always been stubborn, and so, when everyone including my parish priest advised me to give up my baby, I refused to do it. When others insisted I have an abortion, I cringed at the idea.

In those days, no one ever talked about the real facts of abortion. They didn't tell us unwed young girls the real horrors and dangers of abortion to both the unborn baby and its mother. Heck, they still don't today very much as I discovered when I volunteered to serve as a pro-life counselor to unwed mothers while living in Iowa years later.

Back then, in 1968, I didn't know that babies feel every bit of pain during an abortion. If I had, I never would have even listened to all that abortion talk when trying to make a decision to keep my baby or not.

It's about making choices

Knowing how most young girls finding themselves as I did, are not given the facts before getting abortions, I feel it is my duty to share my own experience even if it only saves one more unborn child an excruciating death in the womb of its mother.

While writing this chapter, I found an article online when I googled questions about the unborn child, titled <u>Did You Know That an Unborn Child Can Feel Excruciating Pain During an Abortion?</u>

No, I didn't know back then and I never even knew this until ten years after my own pregnancy.

The Silent Scream

In an article I found, titled <u>The neural pathways are present for pain to be experienced quite early by unborn babies</u> by Steven Calvin, Perinatologist, University of Minnesota says "unborn babies can't cry out when they feel pain, but all biological indicators suggest they are capable of feeling pain by at least 20 weeks after fertilization, if not earlier."

Calvin further explains how "Surgeons entering the womb to perform corrective procedures on tiny unborn children have seen those babies flinch, jerk and recoil from sharp objects and incisions. Given the unborn child's ability to feel pain, imagine how excruciating their pain must be during an abortion!"

Not wanting to get an abortion, I turned to my Father in Heaven more than ever over the next week. I prayed for the courage to make the right decision for me and for my unborn child. Realizing I would have no family support if I stayed in Springfield, I decided to run away to Hollywood, California.

It's while there, leaving my family and their crime family far behind in Springfield, that I end up running into another family—the "Memphis Mafia."

32

Hollywood and the Good Samaritans

"I don't understand why you're going to California," Gram questioned. "Who do you know there that's going to help you with a baby on the way?"

"I don't know anyone out there, Gram," I admitted half-heartedly. "But I heard from friends that it's a great place to start over, and besides, no one will judge me like I would be if I stayed here."

Yep. I was starting over and I was determined to do it in Hollywood. I didn't tell Gram I really just wanted to get as far away as I could from Al and his Mafiosa friends. She didn't know Al was the father of my baby or that he had anything to do with the infamous Springfield crew, and I was going to keep it that way, at least for a while, anyway.

Looking back, I don't really know what possessed me to run off to Hollywood. I didn't pray about my final decision, I just up and did it! So, that's how it came to be that I gave two weeks' notice to my job after learning I was pregnant, and, with only the cash from my last pay check, I was off to Hollywood.

Running into Elvis and away from Big Al

The long plane trip was uneventful until I disembarked the plane and looked around for a ride. Having no money to waste on a cab, I bought a shuttle-bus ticket to Hollywood.

"Yes, Miss," the bus driver answered. "Destination Hollywood."

I quickly took a seat satisfied I was on the right bus. But looking out the window, I kept asking myself, "Where am I going? Who would help me?" Once before, when on the plane ride home from Germany I had asked the same questions. And like before, I hadn't a clue.

Not getting any sleep on the plane from Massachusetts, I was tired but it had given me plenty of time to think about what I was doing. However, it didn't all sink in until I boarded the shuttle-bus. Suddenly, sitting on the bus, the flood of tears I'd been holding back finally threatened to break free like a floodgate to my heart.

I wanted to scream out, "Someone help me, please! God, let someone help me!" And that's when I heard a gentle voice call out to me. "What?" I asked, while turning away from the window and trying not to look as forlorn as I was feeling.

"Is this seat taken?" a fellow passenger asked.

I found myself staring up at a handsome stranger, whose striking appearance made me wonder who this saintly looking person was, as he took a seat beside me. He didn't look like your average travel-tired passenger. His warm smile, and gentle soothing voice, had an amazing calming effect on me.

"No. You can sit there," I replied while trying harder to hold back my tears.

When he spoke again, the bus had pulled out of the terminal and we were on our way to Hollywood. I was mesmerized by his warm penetrating eyes as he looked deep into my own eyes repeating his words just slightly above a whisper, more stating a fact, than asking, "You're here alone, aren't you?"

"Yes. Yes, I am," I replied, although much too quickly. All the while thinking, how I had been praying just moments ago, before he boarded the bus, for someone to help me. "Was he the one to help me Lord?" I asked in silent prayer. Knowing our next stop was Hollywood, the kind stranger startled me with his next question.

"Are you pregnant and needing a place to stay while you're in Hollywood?" He asked.

Normally, that would give cause for any young girl to run when approached by a stranger asking such personal questions as he was doing right now. But, instead of fear, I again felt a calming spirit impressing me to trust this kind stranger.

"Yes," I replied too quickly, no longer able to hold back the floodgate of heartbreaking tears.

We traveled on in silence after that understanding between us. As we pulled into the bus station, the kind stranger stood up and reached out his hand to help me up out of my seat. Without speaking another word to me, I watched him walk away and before I knew it, I was standing beside him as he hailed a cab.

He didn't ask me where I was going. If he had, I would have had to tell him I didn't have a clue. So, I said nothing when he helped me into the cab.

"Where to folks?" the cab driver asked.

My kind stranger gave him an address and I just went along for the ride in silence. I felt such a calming spirit that I became lost in my private thoughts.

"If this stranger was no threat to me," I wondered to myself, "then who was he? And...." My thoughts were suddenly interrupted by the cab driver announcing our arrival.

The cab stopped in front of a building that reminded me of my former residence at the YWCA back in Springfield. Shaking off memories of what was now my past, I followed my kind stranger into the building.

I stood at the door and watched, unsure of what was going on. He walked up to a neatly dressed matronly looking woman whose soft voice and twinkling eyes immediately made me feel welcome. I could tell they knew each other by the friendly way they greeted each other.

He asked the proprietor of what I soon learned was a boarding house for women to give me a room for which he paid a month's rent in advance on my behalf. To my surprise and relief, it included room and board, which meant I would eat for the next month while getting myself adjusted to my new surroundings.

"Who was this kind stranger," I thought to myself, "and why was he going out of his way to help me, a total stranger?"

Looking back at that experience, I am reminded of the *Good Samaritan* in the bible who did the same thing for another stranger stranded and alone as I was which begs the eternal question, "and who is my neighbor Lord?"

To this day, I regret not keeping in touch with him. I don't even remember his name. I lost his business card that he gave me and I never did see him again. But I do know the Lord sent him to me.

I know, because He answered my prayer that day on the bus when I cried to God for help. I know God hears and answers our prayers because He sent me a *Good Samaritan* who reached out and helped me, just like I prayed someone would do.

The nuns prepared me

I only stayed in the boarding house until the month that my kind benefactor had paid for was up. The room and board was wonderful but much too expensive for me to stay there long term.

In no time at all, I found a one-room efficiency apartment in a run-down neighborhood off of Hollywood Boulevard. It was affordable but it wasn't anything I was used to living in and it had roaches! I never saw roaches in any home of mine before moving to Hollywood and I didn't like it. They gave me the creeps. I mentioned it to the Lord and I fervently prayed my living there would be only temporary—only until something better came along.

In the meantime, thanks to Sister Gervase who got me my first job in Massachusetts, I found a job right away working as a keypunch operator. I felt a bit guilty about taking the job, because I had to lie on my application when asked if I was pregnant. At three months, I wasn't showing yet.

I recall the day I was sent out on my first job interview for a keypunch operator. The woman doing the interview just kind of looked at me and I thought for sure she was going to call me out on the lie on my application. "Who asks if you're pregnant?" I thought. I didn't check the box.

But she never said anything even if she suspected. For some reason unknown to me at the time, I was hired on the spot and told to show up the next day if I wanted the job. "Did I ever!" I nearly gasped out loud.

I showed up the next day, and every day after that during my Monday through Friday day-shift as a keypunch operator. Everything seemed to be going well at work and I was quickly promoted to a keypunch operator verifier that even came with a raise. As the months flew by, I was able to keep my condition hidden pretty well and as my due date got closer, I decided I shouldn't mention my condition until the subject came up by itself.

"The boss wants to see you in her office, right away Bonavita," one of my co-workers said with a worried look on her face.

I didn't know what I had done to get called in like that, but it couldn't have been anything good. I closed the door as I walked in and took a seat as instructed. My employer had always been more than fair to me and she was a good boss to work for, despite running a tight ship.

I took in my surroundings and watched her just sit there for what seemed like an eternity before saying what was on her mind. She never smiled much, so I didn't take it as a bad sign that she wasn't smiling now, either. She was a good looking middle aged woman who dressed for the job usually wearing a business suit as she was now.

Finally, leaning forward in her seat, hands folded on her desk, she came right out and asked the question I had been dreading. "Are you pregnant?"

Before I could answer, she got up from behind her desk and came and sat down right next to me. My boss, more understanding than I deserved, informed me that she sort of suspected I was in trouble the day she interviewed me. She even said how she didn't know why she hired me but never regretted it for a minute.

"I made an exception in your case, and I don't know why I did," she explained.

"And now she can fire me if she wanted to," I thought to myself. But she didn't.

Sitting there alone with my boss, I thought back to the kind saintly stranger on the bus. Given Hollywood's sinful reputation, pilloried from pulpits across the country for years before I ever arrived, I was humbled by the unexpected outpouring of charity and love shown to me since my arrival. Maybe that's why Los Angeles was originally named *City of Angels*.

"How many angels like this were there in Hollywood?" I wondered to myself. Phew! It didn't take long to find out. Instead of giving me my walking papers, which I rightly deserved, my boss instead gave me a referral to more angels who could help me so I could keep working and, more importantly, keep my baby.

City of angels

"I have some friends who might be able to help you Elaine, if you're interested," my boss said, as she handed me a brochure.

"It's a home for unwed mothers run by the nuns?" I asked in amazement as I stared at a picture of nuns.

"Yes. They're the Franciscan nuns who sponsor the Queen of Angels Maternity Home for girls like you who are alone and needing help," she explained.

"I never thought I'd be helped by any nuns way out here in Hollywood," I replied.

Smiling ever so kindly, she said, "You'd be surprised to know that the nuns actually have the financial support of some of the best stars in Hollywood. I'll tell you what, go ahead and take the afternoon off today, and go visit with the nuns so they can help you, my dear."

My wonderful boss didn't have to tell me twice. When I hesitated, only because I was thinking I couldn't afford to take the time off, she seemed to read my mind.

"And don't worry about the money," she said. "You can make up the hours you miss today."

Sitting in the waiting room of the Queen of Angels Hospital in Los Angeles, I couldn't help but feel like I was in the arms of God's own angels now. I calmly watched as the nuns busied themselves helping girls, some younger than me, who looked as frightened as I felt.

"Don't worry, my child," one of the Sisters said, comforting me when I couldn't hold back the tears any longer.

"Oh, Sister," I cried. "How I have prayed to find you. I prayed to Jesus so hard that I thought my heart would break at the thought of going through this alone without the nuns in my life out here."

It's true. I didn't know about this program for unwed mothers and I never imagined there was one around me, much less run by nuns—and not in Hollywood, of all places. "How the Lord works!" I thought. Looking back, I am still convinced

Heavenly Father led me here to Hollywood where His angels could watch over me.

I was accepted into the Franciscan Sisters' program for unwed mothers at St. Anne's Maternity Home at the Queen of Angels hospital. I was given the best care and, thanks to many more Good Samaritans who funded the program, I didn't have to pay anything, either.

Just like my boss had informed me, my benefactors were mostly from Hollywood's community of actors. In fact, the room I was assigned, on the day I delivered my baby, was donated by the actress Loretta Young. Back in those days, Ms. Young was quite popular and I was an avid fan of hers.

The nuns made me feel safer again and it helped to have a boss who was supportive of my situation too. But I was still alone and struggling to make ends meet, and I really wanted out of that efficiency apartment and away from those roaches! And so, I kept up my prayers, and the one blessing I asked Jesus to grant me was for something, or someone, to help me get out of my apartment.

In the midst of adversity often comes the blessing, or so I'd been taught growing up in parochial schools. And so it was for me, on the day of one of my pre-natal doctor appointments that I caught the attention of another Good Samaritan, and this one was just as amazing as my kind saintly stranger like the one the Apostle Luke described in the New Testament.

A Mistress and an attorney

"I gotta get out of this storm," the kind lady whose umbrella I was sharing explained as she ran off to take cover in a nearby restaurant. "You coming?"

"I can't," I shouted back over the thunder. "I have to wait for my bus. I can't miss it."

The day I first met Yvonne, I was standing at the bus stop of a busy intersection. I was drenched to the bone with the rain coming steadily down with the clash of thunder sending all other pedestrians running for cover—but not me. I was determined to wait for the bus.

I had an appointment to keep at the Queen of Angels hospital, and if I missed it, I might be dropped from the program. I had no umbrella with me because I hadn't bothered to listen to any weather report before leaving home that morning.

I must've been a sight to behold, looking like a wet mop, when one of the passing cars at the intersection where I was standing, suddenly pulled over.

"Quick. Get in," the driver called out, throwing open the passenger side door.

Water dripping off my wet clothes, leaving a puddle where I was sitting, I meekly looked over at the driver half apologizing to the beautiful young woman behind the wheel of a Mercedes Benz.

"Now, don't even think about it," she said, half laughing in a kind way. "Let's get you somewhere so you can dry off. Where you headed?"

"The hospital on North Occidental Boulevard," I replied.

"I know where that is," she said. "I can take you there."

It was a terribly cold blustery rainy day, and I'd been shivering and struggling to stay warm, waiting for the bus that was running late. I was sure glad to get out of the storm, and having a ride to my appointment was answered prayer indeed.

Sitting in the waiting room at the Queen of Angels clinic, I watched Yvonne calmly flipping through the pages of a magazine that had caught her interest. I figured her to be at least twenty-one or older.

"So how old are you Yvonne?" I asked, trying to take my mind off my surroundings.

"Seventeen," she responded without looking up from her magazine.

"Seventeen, and driving a Mercedes Benz?" I asked out loud, wishing I hadn't.

"We'll talk later," she whispered. "There'll be plenty of time for chatting when we get you home."

At seventeen, Yvonne was a sexy looking woman for her age, slim in all the right places with big brown eyes and the longest lashes that made you forget anything else when she batted them at you, as she always liked to do. Besides being a real looker, she had impressed me as a good, caring person. Hadn't she rescued me from the storm and brought me here?

"You okay?" Yvonne looked up from her magazine as if reading my thoughts.

"What made you stop and pick me up like you did?" I asked.

"I really don't know," she admitted. "I never do that sort of thing what with all the weirdo types in Hollywood. You just never know who you might be picking up."

"Well, I'm sure glad you stopped for me, Yvonne," I replied.

"Who was this angel," I thought to myself, "and should I tell her how I had been praying to Jesus for someone to stop and give me a ride just like she did?"

Actually, I had been praying for more than just a ride standing at the bus stop that day. And now here was Yvonne, who just appeared out of nowhere, exactly like the kind stranger on the bus.

"Bonavita. Elaine Bonavita?" The nurse, a Franciscan sister, called out my name letting me know they were ready for me.

A second chance

We hit it off right away, and Yvonne even drove me home from my doctor appointment. I was surprised when she gave me her phone number and promised to get together over the weekend.

"What a nice place you have here," I exclaimed as I made myself comfortable in Yvonne's apartment. I couldn't resist looking around for those unwanted guests called roaches. Nope. Didn't see a single roach the whole time there.

I was thinking of the dump where I was living and tried not to compare my life to hers but it was hard not to do. I was envious and it must have showed.

"You'll have a place like this of your own, one day," Yvonne tried to assure me.

"I don't know how," I thought, as I took in the magnificence of her surroundings. Yvonne lived in a gorgeous luxury apartment off of Hollywood Boulevard near Warner Brothers Studios in a nice safe neighborhood, unlike mine. She said she

41

didn't work or hold down a job, but from the looks of everything she seemed to have a lot of money, or so I thought.

I was surprised to learn that my new friend Yvonne, who was only two years younger than me, had been living in Hollywood for more than a year already. And, like me, she was on her own with no family either. We had a lot in common, or so I thought. Boy, was I in for a big surprise.

I soon learned that Yvonne was a kept woman. Her boyfriend, Luke, was a married man, and she had been his mistress long before we met. I liked Luke and despite their relationship, he was a kind soul. I was especially impressed with how generous Luke was with her.

Luke, I learned, paid her rent, bills, food, car, and clothing. He paid for everything. That "everything" I would soon discover would include me too. But with me it was more like an act of charity than his arrangement with Yvonne.

Shortly after I met Yvonne, I had been awakened one night to find a burglar in my room. I screamed and scared him off. He ran out of the building leaving behind all the stolen goods piled up in the hallway, from other apartments, he had just broken into that night. I was a hero, and everyone thanked me, but all I wanted was out of there after that frightening experience.

An offer I couldn't refuse

After I told Yvonne about finding a burglar in my room, her plan was to figure out how I could get out of there. But we both knew I didn't make enough money for an apartment in a better section of town. I prayed after I left Yvonne's apartment that night, and over the next week, she and Luke came up with a plan.

At the time I met Luke, he was busy taking on high profile cases like Sirhan B. Sirhan who on trial for the 1968 assassination of Senator Robert Kennedy. Luke had been assigned on the criminal defense team for Sirhan and was also a TV legal analyst during the O.J. Simpson criminal trial.

Luke, who died in 2010, was a prominent Los Angeles criminal defense and civil rights attorney, with a heavy case load, leaving Yvonne with a lot of spare time on her hands since she didn't work. That worked out good for me in a strange sort of way.

"You mean I would be your companion whenever you wanted to travel to places without Luke?" I asked when she gave me the wonderful news. "I don't know what to say," I told Yvonne, half crying and half laughing.

"Well, we'd be more like travel buddies whenever Luke couldn't get out of town to go with me to places like Vegas," she excitedly explained.

She was a clever girl, alright. "You've been wanting to make weekend road trips to Las Vegas, and now I guess you can, if I go with you, right?"

"Yes," she replied with a twinkle in her eye. "When I asked Luke if he would pay your rent, so you could come live in my apartment building, he agreed to do it on the condition you would be my travel companion."

She had a big heart, my new friend Yvonne. She didn't cry so easily, but I noticed she was holding back the tears as she helped me up from the big chair I was sitting in and gave me a big hug, whispering in my ear, "It's gonna be okay. Luke and I will take care of you."

"How great is God," I thought to myself. Once again, He sent me the help I had been praying for so desperately. Just like the Good Samaritan in the Book of Luke, Yvonne stopped to help me when everyone else just kept on driving right past me in the storm. And, like the Apostle Luke's Good Samaritan, Yvonne not only stopped to help me, but to my amazement my new benefactor, also named Luke, was now offering to give me shelter, too.

There were no vacancies in her building for another month. So, I stayed in my rundown apartment until one came available. I remember the night I was invited to stay over at Yvonne's because she was worried I was so close to my due date.

"Luke and I have been talking," Yvonne said as she started up a conversation after dinner. "We're worried about you being all alone over there in your apartment. What will happen if you go into labor and you're all alone with no telephone in your apartment?"

"I know Yvonne." I replied. "I've been worried about that too. I have a hall pay phone in my building but it's on the first floor and in that neighborhood I don't want to go outside my apartment late at night—God forbid."

"It's late," she said, looking at the clock. "Spend the night here tonight, and then we'll get your things tomorrow so you can stay here until you deliver your baby."

Babies come when they want to come, and my son was no exception to the rule. My due date wasn't for another two weeks according to my doctor back east. So it was that, while I was getting ready for bed that night at Yvonne's, my water broke and we were off to the Queen of Angels hospital where the nuns were waiting for me, thanks to Yvonne's phone call.

Yvonne stayed with me while I was in labor, which continued until the next morning, and finally, on January 14, 1969, I gave birth to a healthy 6 lb., 10 oz. baby boy with a head full of hair that made all the nuns joke about how he needed a haircut before going home.

The naming that wasn't

"We need a name for your son's father," the Sister was patiently instructing me.

I was staring at the birth certificate form the nuns wanted me to fill out before leaving the hospital. Looking back, I can't explain why I held back from naming my son's father other than the fact that Al and I hadn't ever married.

Maybe it was because he was already married. For some reason I felt prompted not to give his name. To this day, his birth certificate shows the word "unknown" in the space for his father's name.

Although I hadn't been told about my own naming story before the birth of my own son, looking back, I appeared to be carrying on some kind of surreal tradition by not naming my son's father.

By leaving that section blank on his birth certificate, I had done just as my own mother had once done with me when I was born. Unlike my mother who did not want me, I did want my son, and so I named him. But like others including my siblings

44

who are still alive during the writing of this memoir, I personally will not name him publicly.

Unlike most young married mothers with husbands or family to help support them, I had to work full-time, which left me little time or money to raise a child alone. As the Franciscan sisters had done so many times with other girls in their care, they offered me a plan that would allow me to keep working my day job and, more importantly, keep my baby.

"You'll be meeting your son's new foster family as soon as they get here," the Sister in charge of foster care placements assured me while I was waiting in her office at St. Anne's Maternity Home.

The Franciscan sisters had made arrangements for my son to stay in a foster home for the next three months, giving me time to get back on my feet.

The sisters figured I would get to bring him home on weekends once I moved out of my one room run-down apartment in Hollywood. No place to raise a child. So, I was thankful for the blessing of knowing he would be safe until the Lord provided a safer home for us in Yvonne's apartment building, as she and Luke had promised me they would do.

One good promise deserves another and Luke made me promise I would never talk to any reporters about his private life. I just assumed it was because he was married and probably because he was in the public eye all the time as one of Sirhan's attorneys.

"That was fine with me," I thought. "I could keep a secret." I promised Luke I wouldn't talk to any reporters. And I never did, right up until his passing at the age of 72.

Even though Luke is gone now, it is his story that I find so interestingly connected to my own. I had no way of knowing, at the time I met him, that I was destined to be involved in notorious assassinations of my own throughout my life. In Chapter 8, I recount a similar experience I had with the mob in Agawam. They had made a deal with my father in exchange for my life when they helped to get me elected to the Town Council in 1979.

It's common knowledge that President John F. Kennedy was assassinated for going back on a similar deal as my father had

45

made with the mob for me. Robert Kennedy was appointed Attorney General after his brother won the presidential election. It seems Robert had invited what is referred to as "violent retribution" by the mob when he, like his president brother, went back on their deal to set up a complaisant Justice Department ignoring the mob activity in the country.

CALIFORNIA | LOCAL OBITUARY
Luke ... dies at 72; L.A. criminal and civil rights lawyer
Los Angeles Times

Luke ..., a prominent Los Angeles criminal defense and civil rights attorney whose clients included Sirhan B. Sirhan after his conviction for the assassination of Sen. Robert Kennedy and an Army private charged with the hand-grenade killing of two officers in Vietnam, has died. He was 72. ..., who also was a TV legal analyst during the O.J. Simpson criminal trial, died Sunday of complications from brain cancer at his home in Los Angeles.

As soon as an apartment became available, I moved into Yvonne's building. Luke, good to his word, made up the difference in the rent that I'd been paying. My son was doing fine in his foster home, an hour's drive from me, and I visited him every week.

Now that I was looking forward to moving into Yvonne's apartment building, I was anticipating the day I could get my son out of foster care. I actually started believing my life was finally coming together, thanks to the Lord, who sent Yvonne to rescue me on that cold rainy day at the bus stop. I couldn't imagine it getting any better.

There was a familiar knock at my door and I watched as Yvonne let herself in.

"Hey girl, what are you doing up so early on a Saturday, it's only 10 in the morning?" I asked. It must be important, I thought, for her to come visiting me in this neighborhood.

CHAPTER THREE:
TORN BETWEEN TWO KINGS

"Get dressed Elaine. We're going shopping. You can't be going to Vegas in those clothes." Yvonne called out to me, sounding more like the high school girl she really was instead of a mistress in waiting to Luke.

"It's true? Luke really is gonna let us go Vegas without him?" I asked in amazement.

"Yes. And we're going this weekend." She confirmed. "So get dressed. Let's go shopping!"

I couldn't believe it. It was official. I really was going to be Yvonne's travel companion, which meant one or two weekend monthly road trips to Vegas.

With Luke's blessing, Yvonne and I made plans to mix with the rich and famous in Las Vegas even before I had the chance to move into her apartment building. In the meantime, my new benefactor spent all of his weekends with Sirhan Sirhan's criminal defense team while his mistress spent hers with another high-profile newsmaker.

A change of habit for me, Yvonne, and Elvis

When I met Elvis, in 1969, he was filming the movie *Change of Habit*, a story about nuns. It wasn't lost on me how my own desire to enter the convent had been sidetracked only to find myself one day in the company of Elvis and his co-star nuns. If it hadn't been for a series of missteps in my life that resulted in an unexpected pregnancy I might've actually become a nun and would've never had this chapter to write.

"You think you feel up to making a road trip this weekend?" Yvonne was asking because she knew I usually planned my visits to my son's foster home around the weekend. "You okay with not seeing your son this weekend?"

"I made plans with his foster parents to visit him before we take off for Vegas." I replied. "So, I'm good. Thanks."

On our first road trip, Yvonne and I learned very quickly why Vegas was nicknamed *Sin City*. Gambling, show girls and movie stars were everywhere you looked. And that's how Yvonne and

I met Elvis Presley our first night in town. We were celebrating my birthday. I had just turned twenty and still looked like a freshman in high school compared to my glamorous companion Yvonne.

Looking for a less expensive place to stay for the weekend, the cab driver directed us to the Aladdin Hotel. It was just by chance, that Yvonne and I ended up staying in the same hotel where Elvis, in May 1967, had married his child bride Priscilla Beaulieu whom he'd met while stationed in Germany. We found out later that Elvis preferred the Aladdin Hotel, with its location off the main Vegas strip, where he had a better chance of escaping the flashing paparazzi bulbs and throngs of fans. In 2007, the Aladdin became the Planct Hollywood Casino.

I remember it like yesterday. Yvonne and I had signed in and freshened up in our room after our long drive from Hollywood. It was way too early to take in any of the shows yet, so we opted to kill some time by grabbing a bite to eat in the Hotel. We'd just been seated at our table, and were looking over the menu, when Yvonne caught the eye of a cute guy sitting at another table. I looked up to see a confident, good looking, dark haired young man in his mid-twenties, walking towards our table, keeping direct eye contact with Yvonne until he was standing right beside her.

As he leaned towards Yvonne, ever so sexy, he quietly asked, "May I join you ladies?"

As I checked him out, I thought to myself, "He's a lady killer, alright. But we hadn't discussed what she'd do if Luke's mistress met someone in Vegas."

I didn't have long to ponder that thought when Yvonne turned to me and said, ever so coyly, "What do you think? Shall we invite him to join us?"

"Uh oh," I thought to myself, "she used the word *us*. Yvonne definitely wanted to make it look like I was the one who wanted him to sit with us. Poor Luke."

After the usual small talk and introductions had been made between everyone, it was obvious that Yvonne's new friend whom I will call Nick was smitten with her. Thinking I had a duty to Luke, who was paying my rent for me to chaperone his mistress while in Vegas, I had to come up with a plan to lose this guy.

"Excuse us Nick, but we should get going and check out the lobby," I said.

"Oh, I forgot," Yvonne told her new friend. "We saw Elvis Presley at one of the Craps tables when we came down for lunch."

"Yes. And we want to see if he's still out there," I said, nodding my head towards the lobby discouraging any further flirtation between the two of them.

Smiling and winking, he surprised us by asking, "Say, would you lil ladies like to meet Elvis?"

A wide-eyed Yvonne turned to me not knowing what to say. But I did. "Who wouldn't want to meet Elvis?" I asked my new best friend Nick.

Leave it to Yvonne to say, "But we don't know him, so there's no chance of that happening."

Before I could say another word to feel out this guy and see if he was for real, or what, Nick got up from the table holding out his hand to Yvonne.

To our amazement, Nick said, "Come on. Let's go, and I'll introduce you to him."

At first, we both thought it was just a cheap pick up line, with Yvonne winking at me and saying to Nick, "You don't really know Elvis," at which we both laughed and got up to leave the table.

Without another word, holding onto Yvonne's hand, Nick gently pulled her up out of her seat. Sure enough, there was Elvis still playing at a Craps tables. Thinking how it might be fun to humor our new friend, we followed right behind him and watched as Nick walked right up to Elvis and, bold as day, he tapped him on the shoulder.

"E, I'd like you to meet my new friends." Nick even used Elvis' nickname, "E," as he threw us both a sideways glance.

Elvis, in the middle of a play, with dice in his hands didn't act annoyed with Nick for interrupting his game. Instead of scowling for being interrupted, we soon found ourselves face to face with a smiling Elvis as he turned away from the Craps table to check us out. And then, Nick, with the biggest grin on his face, actually introduced us, just as he said he would.

I thought Yvonne was going to faint when Elvis spoke to her. I didn't expect him to give me a second look in the presence of Yvonne's beauty. So, I was surprised when Elvis turned to me, looking as if he knew me. It seemed like an eternity before he spoke to me. It was the way he kept looking at me that had me mesmerized. Heck, I figured he might've been more attracted to Yvonne who had the figure and looks of a more mature Vegas showgirl—not me.

At nineteen, I looked years younger for my age. It was a curse growing up. I had inherited young looking genes from my mother's side of the family. Mom always looked fifteen years younger than she was, right up until the day she died. I was an Italian girl, brunette and cute as a button, or so I was told, growing up. But my girlish figure hadn't quite caught up with me yet.

If I had known Elvis was fascinated with the idea of young teenage girls, as confirmed by Lamar Fike, a former member of his entourage, in an interview with the Daily Mail, I might have had more confidence coming face to face with him. But I didn't know it at the time I met Elvis. As I held out my hand to take his, I thought to myself, "What do you say to the King of Rock-n-Roll?" But I didn't have to wait for something to say.

"Do you have any plans for tonight?" Elvis asked us when we mentioned we were in town for the weekend.

Still holding my hand in his, smiling like only Elvis does, I nearly gasped out loud when he invited Yvonne and I to join his party to take in the shows with them. Later, we would find out that the guys around Elvis often called him "E." Pulling Yvonne aside, I whispered into her ear, "Nick really must be Elvis' personal male secretary." At least, that's what Nick told us before walking up to Elvis the way he did.

Yvonne just stood there, frozen, while looking at me wide-eyed until I said what we were both thinking. Trying to act cool, I muttered something like, "Didn't have any plans. We just checked in and thought we'd get a bite to eat before heading out to the strip ourselves."

Turning to Nick, Elvis invited us to join them in the Hotel's restaurant where he told us to wait for him while he finished up at the Craps table. Looking around, I noticed the hotel lobby was nearly empty. It was way too early to catch any shows on the strip. Everyone knew to wait until darkness falls—it's when Vegas comes to life.

"Come on ladies," Nick invited as he walked us over to a comfortable booth where we could wait on his boss.

It was relatively quiet while we were in the lobby, with hardly anyone standing around the Craps table with Elvis which normally would be the scene of people cheering loudly every time a number hits. Later, Nick would tell us that's how Elvis liked it.

"And how lucky can a gal get," I thought to myself, "to just happen to walk into the same Casino where Elvis was staying?"

About a half hour later, Elvis, true to his word, sauntered over to our booth and sat down right next to me. Nick, who had sat himself in the middle, was preoccupied with Yvonne by now, so I got to chat with Elvis. Suddenly, I felt like I was back in Germany, chatting comfortably, just like I used to do with my Elvis look-alike crush. Only I must admit, it was much more thrilling with the real Elvis.

Elvis had a date he was planning on taking with us when we went out on the town. "I never met her until today," Elvis admitted. "She was in Vegas for the weekend and wanted to meet me. So I invited her to take in the shows with us tonight."

I knew Elvis' was married and wondered how his child bride Priscilla of only two years, whom he'd met while a soldier stationed in Germany, felt about his public escapades with other women. No sooner had Elvis mentioned his date to me when a tall thin blonde woman walked up to our booth.

"Let's head out," someone, in another booth, called out to Elvis as I followed everyone out the door of the hotel lobby.

I was the odd girl out when Elvis' date showed up and Yvonne paired off with Nick. Elvis' entourage stuck close to him and I just went along for the ride. Only after everyone had piled into the two waiting limousines that had been pulled up at the curb, Elvis had his date get in the first limousine. Yvonne had left me behind when Nick ushered her into the second waiting limo.

I was afraid of being left out of the party, so I made a beeline to get into the limo with Nick and Yvonne. That's when I felt someone grab my arm and pull me towards him.

"You're coming with us in this one." Elvis said to my surprise as he climbed into his limo with his date while extending his hand to help me in after him.

As the limousine pulled out, it was just the three of us, with Elvis in the middle sitting on the back seat of the limo. A couple of Elvis' entourage were seated across from us and I wondered what I was doing there when Yvonne was with Nick in the limo behind us. As I turned around to gaze out the back window, trying to see if Yvonne was following behind us, Elvis must've read my mind.

"They're okay," he assured me. "The guys know where we're going. You'll see them in a few minutes."

I had just leaned back ready to enjoy my first ride in a limousine and my first ride with Elvis Presley, when he gently laid his hand upon mine. I was glad now that I had chosen my new yellow low-cut mini dress, compliments of Luke, to wear out on the town that night.

"Someone pinch me, I must be dreaming," I thought to myself, as I wondered what his date must be thinking. "Who does that when on a date with someone?"

Partying with the King

We spent the rest of the night taking in the shows on the Vegas strip with Elvis and his entourage, and he was every bit of a gentleman to me and his date. The paparazzi must've wondered what Elvis was doing with two mystery women on his arm all night. Heck, I was just along for the ride. And what a ride it turned out to be!

Christmas had already past, but it felt like Christmas all over again the night Elvis took in a show to see Diana Ross and the Supremes. When Diana was told about Elvis being in the audience, the spotlight was put on our table where we were all sitting. When Elvis stood up, the room went wild!

Later, after the show, Diana came up to us out in the lobby and Elvis introduced her to me and Yvonne. We got to meet more celebrities, like comedian Dick Shawn as we took in another show later that night. "Boy, would my friends, even my crazy cousin Gina, back East ever be surprised," I thought to myself. "Eat your heart out Gina!"

The next day, as Yvonne and I were packing up getting ready to drive back to Hollywood, Nick invited us to dinner. Seeing Elvis with his entourage in the lobby, I wanted to say goodbye to him and thank him for one of the best nights of my life.

As for Yvonne, I got worried when I overheard Nick making plans for them to see each other again after Vegas.

"Oh no," I thought to myself, "she hadn't bothered to tell him about poor Luke back in Hollywood." And here I was sworn to secrecy as her trusted traveling companion."

The Memphis Mafia

Well, Nick must have told Elvis he wanted to see Yvonne again, because before we left, Elvis made us an offer we couldn't refuse. In his deepest sexiest voice, Elvis looking right at me said, "How would you girls like to meet up with us next week in Palm Springs?"

All I kept thinking was "Poor Luke, but happy me!"

Nick happily filled us in on the details on where to meet up Elvis' entourage the next weekend. We learned that while Elvis was filming the movie *Change of Habit,* on location in Hollywood, he was leasing a villa from Warner Brothers in Palm Springs for their weekend getaways. You'll be safe out there ladies, Nick assured us. I believed him. Heck, I didn't know about Elvis' entourage that had been nicknamed by the media as the "Memphis Mafia."

"So what are you going to tell Luke where you're going next weekend?" I asked on the drive back to Hollywood.

"What Luke doesn't know won't hurt him," Yvonne tried to convince herself. "Besides he has his wife and I have no one when he's not around."

The following weekend Yvonne and I drove out to Palm Springs. To our delight, when our arrival was buzzed in at the

53

security gate at Warner Brothers Villa, we really were expected. The gate swung open and we were in! And so was the "Memphis Mafia."

The villa was gorgeous. Nick explained how Elvis didn't like staying around in Hollywood when not on the set and we were glad he didn't. Thanks to Elvis, over the next few months, Yvonne and I enjoyed some very special weekend road trips to Palm Springs.

Nick and Yvonne ended up sharing his bedroom while we visited at the villa. As for me, I was assigned the only bedroom with twin beds. That was fine with me, I had no plans to share my bed with anyone while in Palm Springs. There were plenty of girls hanging around to keep the guys entertained and Elvis always had his weekend girlfriend.

I didn't think anything about it at the time, but looking back I can see how Elvis' guys came to be called the "Memphis Mafia." Their behavior did mimic a Mafia family in the way his guys protected Elvis and seemed stuck to him like glue all the time. I thought of my own Big Al, as I watched Elvis who had his own bodyguards just like the mobsters I'd known back east.

Having been around the real Mafia, I felt safer around the Memphis Mafia than I'd been in a long time actually. Heck, these guys weren't going to kill me if I said no. And that was fine with me.

According to *Wikipedia*, "The "Memphis Mafia" was the nickname given by rock 'n' roll icon Elvis Presley for a group of friends, associates, employees and "yes-men", whose main functions were to accompany, protect, and serve Elvis from the beginning of his career in 1954 until his death in 1977. Several members filled practical roles in the singer's life. For instance, they were employed to work for him as bodyguards or on tour logistics and scheduling. In these cases Elvis paid salaries, but most lived off fringe benefits such as gifts, cars, houses and bonuses. Over the years, the number of members grew and changed, but for the most part there was a core group who spent a lot of time with the singer."

As for all the wild partying going on lately, I wasn't ready for it as much I thought I would be. I figured my giving birth to

54

my son only a few weeks before meeting Elvis had a lot to do with it. I was just along for the ride. That's what I kept telling myself.

One thing that did remind me of the real Mafia, however, was Elvis' rule of no cameras allowed on the premises. Another request he made of us, reminded me of Luke when like him, Elvis also asked me not to speak to any reporters if anyone came around asking questions if we were seen in public together.

Not a problem Yvonne and I assured Elvis. "If no one spoke to the paparazzi," I thought, "then how did all the stories of Elvis' mystery women make the news all the time?"

"What does that mean?" I asked Yvonne when we were alone.

She said, "Guess they don't want us selling our story like some of the women who knew Elvis have done."

"Okay," I muttered under my breath, "but it would be nice to have some pictures for a keepsake."

We never sold our story about Elvis in Vegas or Palm Springs. I don't know what Yvonne did after I moved back east the following year. But I never did. And if Yvonne did, I'd never know because we lost contact with one another before I had even left California. But that's another story that I'll get to later in this chapter.

As for selling my Elvis story, this memoir is the first time I have ever spoken publicly about my adventures with the Memphis Mafia. Writing my story about Elvis, titled **Torn Between Two Kings**, is just an idea I got to promote this memoir.

My only regret is that I have no pictures. Memories fade through the years, but pictures are forever. I only vaguely remember two of Elvis' associates who made the most impression on me back in 1969—Nick and Red.

Besides Nick who was Yvonne's weekend date, there was the unforgettable character of Red West who was Elvis' longtime friend from High School. I never forgot Red's name, like I did with Yvonne's lover, because I liked watching the Wild Wild West television show. I was surprised to learn that Red was a stunt man on the show.

As for using Red's real name, I figured he wouldn't mind seeing as how he wrote a tell-all book about Elvis himself shortly before his former boss died.

It didn't take long for me to find out why Elvis had a no camera rule. On our weekends in Palm Springs, Elvis usually partied all night, did drugs, slept in the day and had an underage sleepover nearly every weekend too. He also had a mystery visitor who came by every day while we were in Palm Springs.

"Say Red," I asked, "why does a doctor come out to see Elvis every time we're here in Palm Springs?"

"Elvis gets his daily shot of vitamin B to keep him going," was the only answer I got back.

I soon learned why Elvis needed those daily shots. Getting more familiar with him, I had a chance to observe his eating and sleeping habits which were not good. I worried watching Elvis party the way he did. Watching anyone use social drugs, the way Elvis freely did, was new to me. When he offered me something one time, I said "no thanks."

Maybe it was his look with that sexy smile of his, or the twinkle in his eyes that said more than words that gave me the courage to broach the subject one day with Elvis. I did, but afterwards he made me feel like I should just mind my own business. If memory serves me right, he took it with a grain of salt when I commented on his unhealthy life style.

"I'm okay. Don't worry about me," Elvis insisted, as he cleaned up every last bite of the egg omelet I had made for him.

Watching him finish off his meal, I said something stupid like, "I wish you would eat better," but quickly changed the subject when he gave me that look.

Despite the drugs during the nightly parties, staying in Palm Springs with Elvis was exciting. When he wasn't partying, stoned or sleeping, I remember how he liked to practice his Karate moves during the day and play records while singing along to his own songs.

The King of Cool comes to town

"Dean Martin owns the villa next door to you?" I asked Elvis one day when I overheard him and some of the guys talking.

"Would you like to meet him Elaine?" One of the guys called out to me.

"Are you kidding?" I shot right back. "I love Dean Martin."

"I think we can make that happen," Elvis said while reminding one of the guys to invite me the next time my idol was in town.

"I can't believe I'm going to meet Dean Martin." I reported back to Yvonne as fast as my legs would carry me. As usual she was preoccupied with Nick.

"You're here with Elvis and you are going crazy about meeting Dean Martin?" she asked in feigned surprise.

And so it was that I found myself anxiously awaiting the day that Elvis would announce "He's here." "He" being the King of Cool. I was thrilled I was going to meet Dean Martin and sure enough, true to his word, the next time my idol came to Palm Springs, I was invited to go along.

"He's here." Elvis called out to me as he walked into the kitchen where I was making breakfast, but more like lunch on his crazy schedule.

"At last." I rejoiced. "Oh Elvis!" I nearly cried. "Am I really going to get to meet Dean Martin?"

In his sexy chuckle, Elvis nodded yes as he checked out the meal I'd prepared for him.

"Are you gonna be there too?" I asked.

"And miss the chance of seeing you meet your idol?" Elvis jokingly asked as he ruffled my hair which he often liked to do when we were kidding around.

But alas, it was not to be. As it would happen, Elvis had one of his famous all-nighter parties the night before we were to visit Dean Martin.

Although I didn't drink or do drugs around Elvis, and had no love interest like the others usually had during parties, I was their designated hostess. It was fine with me.

And so it was, that instead of turning in early as I should have done, I ended staying up all night with everyone and Elvis, at his pool party. Not used to staying up like that, I slept in the next morning missing out on meeting the King of Cool.

"Why didn't anyone wake me?" I asked when Elvis and the guys returned from their visit with Dean Martin.

"Thought you needed to sleep more than go visiting," one of the guys said.

Elvis must have seen the disappointment on my face, because he said "There'll be another time and you'll get to see your idol." But that time never came.

Years later, I was reading online the August 16, 2007 interview Priscilla Presley did with Larry King Live about her ex-husband Elvis which reads as follows:

> "Some stars want to meet other stars. Some stars have to hang out with other stars. Not Elvis. I can't remember him once telling the Colonel to arrange a meeting with anyone famous. He saw Hollywood as the home of phonies. He certainly felt out of place, which is why the minute the movie (*Change of Habit*) wrapped he was gone." –Priscilla Presley

As for missing out meeting the King of Cool, I never did know the reason for Elvis wanting to meet with Dean Martin.

Judge not, lest ye be judged

Besides my infatuation with Dean Martin, I had wanted to meet some other actors too, like Elvis' *Change of Habit* co-star Mary Tyler Moore who played the part of Sister Michelle. I was just getting over missing out on meeting Dean Martin when Elvis hinted one day on how he was going to invite some of the actresses, who were cast as nuns in his movie, to join us in Palm Springs for the weekend.

Much to my disappointment, Mary Tyler Moore did not come with the rest of the cast of nuns. I don't recall the names of the actresses who came out that weekend or if Jane Elliot, who played the part of Sister Barbara Bennett had been there.

Although it was rumored they'd had a romantic fling on the set, I only recall one special love interest of Elvis during his filming of *Change of Habit* while me and Yvonne were staying with him in Palm Springs.

I've since forgotten her name, but I remember the cute little sixteen year old blonde Elvis had brought in for most of the weekends I was there. If he was having a fling with Jane, as rumored, then she had to have been his weekday love interest in Hollywood during the filming of the movie.

Come to think of it, his underage love interest didn't show up the weekend Elvis invited Jane and the cast from *Change of Habit*. Hmmm.

Elvis sure loved his women but I never judged him. I knew he had a wife at home but I never brought it up, just like I never said anything to Luke about Yvonne's affair with Nick.

"Who was I to judge?" I thought, "Seeing as how I was in love with a married man myself. Heck, I even had Big Al's out-of-wedlock son."

As for Elvis' cheating, I can honestly say in all the time I was in his company, I got to see a different side of him from what the public saw. Despite cheating on his wife Priscilla, and his wild partying in Palm Springs, I was touched by how much he cared about those around him—even me.

I remember, one weekend in Palm Springs, when I'd gotten upset over some silly little thing and took off without telling anyone.

Ever since I was in foster care, I'd gotten in the habit of going off by myself until my head cleared. And that's all I intended to do when I took off that day too. I didn't think anyone would miss me, especially not Elvis. But he did and he even came looking for me because he was that kind of a guy.

The way the guys in the house told it, when Elvis noticed I was gone, he set out to find me. They said he was really worried about me.

"Why would Elvis even notice I was gone for Pete's sake?" I asked innocently when I'd returned.

"He keeps an eye on everything and he's very protective of you little ladies," one of the guys volunteered.

And that's how it came to be that Elvis called for his limousine and piled in with a few of his associates determined to come looking for me after he'd searched the property and couldn't find me.

"Elaine? Elaine where are you?" I recognized Elvis' voice calling out my name.

I was sitting under a palm tree down the road from the villa where Elvis was staying. At first, I couldn't believe it. "Elvis out here, and looking for me?"

I listened to make sure and yes, it really was Elvis calling out my name alright. There it was again. "Elaine, where are you?"

I didn't answer, and I felt bad about that. He just kept calling out for me until they finally gave up and I watched them turn around and drive back to the villa. When I decided to go back an hour later, I had to get buzzed in at the security gate. Elvis was waiting for me like a worried parent whose daughter had missed her curfew or something. He even made it clear that I wasn't to take off like that ever again without telling someone first.

"You had me worried Elaine," Elvis said.

I knew he really meant it. Thinking back I recall another incident like it was yesterday when Elvis handled a problem I'd had with one of his men.

Red West was a character indeed. I liked him as much as any of the others who worked for Elvis. It was fun just knowing he was in the cast of the TV show The Wild Wild West that I liked to watch. Born in 1936, Red was a lot older than me—by thirteen years.

Red had gone to high school with Elvis and they were close friends. Up until the incident with Red, none of the guys had ever made a move on me during my entire time at Palm Springs. I kidded around with the guys and told them I was holding out for Elvis.

As luck would have it, Red got drunk one night and tried to make a move on me. He got a bit rough and I managed to get out of it unharmed. Heeding Elvis' warning not to take off again without telling someone, I couldn't run away and find a quiet place like I had done before. So, I went crying to Elvis' underage girlfriend when I couldn't find Yvonne.

His weekend girlfriend and I got along good and I knew I could talk to her without mentioning any names. Worried about me, she passed it on to Elvis who didn't waste any time coming to my room demanding to know who it was. So I told him.

60

"It's okay Elaine," Elvis reassured me. "He won't be bothering you again. I promise."

I don't know what Elvis said or did, but all I know was that he took care of it. Red never bothered me again. To be fair to Red, I felt kind of bad knowing he would never have tried anything with me if he hadn't been drinking or whatever. Up until then, he'd always been every bit a gentleman around me.

Looking back, I know Elvis could have easily ignored the whole incident, even dismissed it as letting his guys have some fun. But he never did that around me. That day, I saw a kind soul who could've easily defended his best friend Red, but didn't.

I never forgot what Elvis did for me. Despite hearing all the stories I'd read years later about Elvis and his disrespecting women and wild parties with the Memphis Mafia, I never saw that side of Elvis in Palm Springs and it's the truth.

"In The Ghetto" was our song

One of the endearing traits that I loved about Elvis was how he liked to listen and sing along with his own songs. At the time I knew him, I didn't know it was something he liked doing. I'd only heard about it years later.

According to reports, it seems whenever making a movie, Elvis liked it better when he sang to someone rather than sing to a camera. And so it was that while staying with Elvis in Palm Springs, I too had my own rehearsal love scene with the King--or was it?

His hit song, *In the Ghetto*, hadn't yet been released the day he played it while we were at the villa. I remember it was one of the songs Elvis sang to me when he found me alone one day in the main room of the villa. With so many people around that day, finding myself alone was really rare indeed.

I was bored and reading through a magazine when I looked up to see Elvis walk into the room. Seeing me alone on the couch, he just smiled and instead of walking out of the room, he sauntered over to his record player and put on some vinyl records.

I was surprised when Elvis came over and sat next to me. I was more surprised when he placed his arm around me. When the song began to play, Elvis got right into character and started serenading me just like a scene from one of his movies. Heck, I thought he was rehearsing a scene with me. But what he did next was no rehearsed scene.

Elvis didn't know too much about my situation. When I first met up with him, I didn't want anyone to know my story. Yvonne must've told Nick, or else how would Elvis had known to sing me his song *In the Ghetto* the way he did that day in Palm Springs?

"He's singing my story," I thought, as Elvis began serenading me to his song about a poor little baby child that was born in the ghetto.

I wanted to cry, but didn't. As I listened to the words of the song that could've been my own story, I thought to myself, "Wouldn't he want to practice a love song on me instead of this one?" But I'd never know, because I didn't have time to ask him.

As the music faded out, like the first slow gentle kiss with a new partner, Elvis gently and slowly lifted my chin with his second finger until my face was uplifted towards his. His gaze was so intense I was mesmerized. It was only when he dipped his head to kiss me, that I closed my eyes.

One of the guys, who happened to walk in just when Elvis was kissing me, said out loud, "Looks like Elaine is gonna get her wish."

"Whatever that meant," I thought to myself. And I was out of there. The moment was ruined.

I couldn't figure out just what "the moment" was we had shared until years later when I read what a blogger wrote on the *Elvispresley.com* website, titled <u>For Elvis Fans Only</u>, "He (Elvis) even seemed to be trying to impress Priscilla with his songs he'd play her."

That made for a much better memory for me knowing why Elvis had done the same thing with Priscilla too. As for my own memory back in Palm Springs in 1969, it would stay with me for the rest of my life as would what happened next.

We had all just retired earlier than usual the night I woke up to find Elvis watching me as I lay sleeping in my bed. My room was the only one with twin beds in it because everyone knew I slept alone and had no love interest on these weekend getaways.

Going into town and picking up beautiful girls was one of the benefits of working for Elvis. The Memphis Mafia had a habit of going into town with the limo and picking up pretty girls to bring back for late night pool parties who'd join them in the many bedrooms of the villa. As for Elvis, his underage girlfriend was actually in his bed the night he visited my bedroom.

"What is it Elvis?" I asked when I awakened to find him standing over me in the middle of the night.

Gently touching my face with his hand, all he said was, "Nothing. Go back to sleep."

Maybe it was the twin bed…But I'll never know what was on the King's mind when he came into my bedroom that night so long ago. When morning came he never said a word and neither did I. His underage girlfriend was by his side most of the time anyway. What was there to say?

It wouldn't be until I was doing research for this chapter on Elvis that I would gain some insight as to why he never touched me. I don't want to taint the memory I have of Elvis, so suffice to say that it was commonly reported how Elvis was fascinated with "real young teenage girls."

When we first met, I never bothered to tell Elvis about my personal problems or that I'd just had an out-of-wedlock baby. I figured Nick must've told him else why would Elvis sing *In the Ghetto* to me like he did? Years after I'd met Elvis, I read reports claiming how he'd stopped visiting his wife Priscilla's bedroom after she gave birth to their daughter. Ironically, our own serenade scene and the no-touching in my bedroom hinted of similarities Priscilla and Elvis had also shared.

Of all the memories I have of him, Elvis treated me with respect and I felt safe around his Memphis Mafia because of it. I remember him for being a caring kind spirited person around me. And that's my memory of Elvis.

Farewell to the King

When Elvis wrapped up the filming of *Change of Habit*, he left California leaving me with only my memories of Palm Springs. I never saw Elvis again. Less than eight years later, when the world heard of his death on August 16, 1977, I was not surprised to know how he died, but I was saddened. I couldn't help but think of the drugs he'd been doing when I knew him.

"What a waste," I said to friends, "Elvis had everything and everyone to live for."

Now, 39 years later, never intending to coordinate my memoir around the anniversary of the King's death, it amazes me how I found myself writing this chapter about Elvis in the very same week of August 16th.

As for Red, who had reportedly tried to intervene to save Elvis several times, I'm sorry he didn't succeed and even more sorry to hear about his parting with Elvis. Red made the news.

According to *Wikipedia*, "On July 13,1976, Vernon Presley, Elvis' father, fired West, Sonny West and Hebler after criticizing what he believed to be their heavy-handed tactics. The three of them collaborated on a book about their lives as Elvis' bodyguards, which was published just two weeks before Elvis' death in 1977."

When Red was fired, just before Elvis' own death, some claim it was because he was trying to get his former boss to stop doing drugs. Red responded and claimed Elvis wouldn't listen. I could believe it. But then again, Elvis didn't listen when I knew him either. Regrets? Sure, doesn't everyone who ever had a chance to make something right but missed the opportunity?

Did you think to pray?

Looking back, I regret I never prayed with Elvis. His wild lifestyle and my unfortunate circumstances when we met might've played a major role in distracting me from listening to the Spirit of the Lord. Otherwise, I surely would have been praying wouldn't I? Come to think of it, I recall how I didn't pray anymore during those days in Vegas and Palm Springs. If I had been, I like to think I would've prayed with Elvis.

For me, praying was no longer a regular habit once Yvonne and I chummed up. As for Sunday Mass attendance, I didn't do that anymore either. I even stopped going to confession just before I signed on as her travel companion for our weekend getaways.

Two Kings and only one choice

Undoubtedly, I was distracted by the fast life and glamour that Yvonne introduced me to. I never even realized when I'd stopped praying on my knees. But I did stop praying and I know that's why I messed up with the King, Elvis himself, the way I did. I should've been praying with him not partying with him. Why was I his party hostess instead of his prayer partner? What was I thinking?

Sharing the King's own living quarters as I had done, was I so distracted that I failed to recognize the possibility that the Lord might have had another purpose for me meeting Elvis the way I did my first night in Vegas? Right up until I met Elvis I'd been praying for the Lord to help me. I needed so many things and had no way to do it myself.

From all reports, Elvis was generous with everyone he met. And yet, I never told him about my situation. I never asked for a handout.

Sure, I'd always asked my Father in Heaven every day in my prayers to get me through life's challenges, but I never thought how meeting up with Elvis might've been answered prayer.

To be honest, I never even thought about it until writing this chapter about Elvis. I never cried to Elvis about how I had no money to get my son out of foster care, much less tell him I didn't even own a car. If I had I know he would've given me a car. Wasn't he known for giving away cars? Heck, he even gave away a car while I was staying with him in Palm Springs. And still, I never said anything.

He must've seen Yvonne's Mercedes Benz parked in the driveway of his Palm Springs Villa each weekend and figured we were both loaded with dough. I wasn't thinking about the scripture "Ask and ye shall receive."

If I'd been talking with another King, my Lord and Savior Jesus Christ, who'd always been there for me every time I prayed, I might've shared my personal story with Elvis. But I didn't. Regrets? Sure, I regret that I walked away from my relationship with my Lord and King only to have one with another King instead—Elvis the King of Rock-n-Roll.

65

As all, who abandon the King of Kings, I too paid the price by not sharing my testimony of faith in prayer and by not praying with Elvis like I started doing with others in my life ten years after meeting Elvis.

What is it that the bible says about praying together? In the Book of Matthew Chapter 18 Verse 19 Jesus taught, "Again I say unto you, that if two of you shall agree on earth as touching anything that they shall ask, it shall be done for them of my Father which is in heaven."

After wrapping up his movie and leaving Hollywood, little did I know it would be Elvis Presley's final film before his death on August 16, 1977 at the age of 42.

According to *Wikipedia, "Change of Habit* was Presley's 31st and final film acting role; his remaining film appearances were in concert documentaries."

Yvonne and I never saw Elvis or Nick again after Palm Springs. As for me, I stayed around in Hollywood for another year before heading home myself in 1970 with my one year old son. Yvonne and I lost contact with one another before I had even left California--and it was all Gina's fault. Not one to judge, but it was her fault--really. Read on dear readers.

Crazy Gina does it again

"Who is this?" I asked a familiar voice on the other end of the phone. Praying it wasn't who I thought it was.

"It's me Gina," my crazy cousin confirmed.

I got the phone call right after Elvis wrapped up the filming of *Change of Habit* and moved back home to his wife and family. Yvonne and I had just settled down, but before we had a chance to make any more road trips to Vegas again, I heard from my cousin Gina saying she wanted to come visit me in Hollywood.

Barely married two years, Gina wanted to come out for a visit after her husband walked out on her. And that's how that crazy cousin of mine ended up in Hollywood.

No surprise to me, Gina did not approve of my friendship with Yvonne. Gina, for some weird reason, never took to any of my friends and Yvonne was no exception. I remember my crazy cousin even taking a knife to poor Yvonne during one of their heated arguments.

Gina didn't let it go and she took it to Luke.

"Why Gina?" Why would you do such a thing?" I asked her when Yvonne told me how Gina had told Luke everything we'd been doing behind his back.

Up until then, Luke didn't know anything about Yvonne's affair with Nick. But thanks to Gina, he did now. I was with Yvonne in her apartment when Luke dropped by the next day to tell us what he had decided to do. The conversation went something like this.

"I'm sorry Elaine," Luke said as he was walking out the door. "I can't do this. I hope you'll find another place to live. Your rent and Yvonne's is paid up for the next month."

Luke broke it off with Yvonne with the snap of a finger and cut her off from everything. Being cut off meant she had no place to live anymore and neither did I. Gina was happy though and planned on staying in Hollywood with me. And that's how my son and I ended up sharing an even fancier apartment, a block from the famous Grauman's Chinese Theater on Hollywood Boulevard, with my crazy cousin Gina.

I only saw Yvonne once after her breakup with Luke and then I lost track of her. She was driving a Mustang now instead of her beloved Mercedes Benz and had moved in with a nice guy in another less affluent neighborhood in Hollywood.

I sure felt sorry for Yvonne. She wasn't living the life of luxury she had with Luke, but at least she wasn't out on the streets either. And I missed her terribly. I still do. She was a friend who never judged me. She just accepted me for who I was.

Even today, I wonder if Yvonne is alive or dead. I recall Yvonne telling me how she had changed her name so no one could find her when she ran off to California. I wonder what name she goes by now. Everyone has a story and Yvonne had hers.

Like so many others in my life before I met her, she too will have taken her story to her grave-- if she lies in one today. If not, and she comes across this memoir of mine, I pray she will find me again, and forgive me for what my crazy cousin Gina did.

As I prepared to leave Hollywood, I took to my knees. Living with my crazy cousin for nearly a year was starting to make me crazy too and, luckily for me, I turned to prayer again. I prayed for help as I faced the challenge of going home back to my family in Massachusetts.

I remember praying that the Memphis Mafia would be the last time I'd be around any kind of Mafia again. I had some bad memories of the mob back east and wasn't anxious to take up where I'd left off any time soon. Still, Big Al was never far from my thoughts.

Like the adult salmon, each year that make the long journey back to the same natal streams they were born in to spawn, I felt drawn to return where Al had fathered my child. I didn't expect to face death, but then don't all Pacific salmon die after spawning?

And so it was I left with my memories of Elvis, and the Memphis Mafia, and said goodbye to Hollywood.

In the spring of 1970, I headed back to my natal streams not knowing, that like some Atlantic salmon that don't die after spawning, the Genovese crime family had spawned while I was gone and were swimming in my natal streams of Springfield.

CHAPTER FOUR:
WANTED BY THE MOB

"Your grandfather and I think it's time you find a place of your own," Gram said as I walked in the door.

"You've been talking to Gina again, haven't you?" I asked in feigned surprise.

In 1970, I returned to my birth home in Springfield, leaving Hollywood behind me. Elvis and the "Memphis Mafia" would soon be just another memory for me. Leaving behind the memory of so many Good Samaritans, I prayed things would be different once I returned home. While my grandparents didn't have the kind of money to help get me back on my feet, like Luke and Yvonne had done, they gave me something much more valuable than money--they accepted my out-of-wedlock son who was now a year old.

At first my homecoming was a happy reunion—but it didn't last long thanks to my crazy cousin Gina. I thought she was out of my life for a while since she had decided to stay in Hollywood after I left. But if not for her, I'd have no chapter to write about what happened next in my life.

Leaving footprints with my Arrest Record

"You want me to move out Gram? I asked in disbelief, trying to hold back the tears.

I had a pretty good idea, thanks to Gina, why my grandparents were anxious for me to move out after moving in with them since my return home. I'd messed up pretty good this time, and now, not even my step-grandfather, who favored me, dared interfere when Gram gave me my walking papers. I remember Grandpa Teddy as a kind hearted laid back kind of guy, but even he had his limits after I was arrested for something really stupid.

I didn't have an arrest record, before I took off for California in 1968, but I did manage to get one right after I moved back to Springfield in 1970. It was just minor stuff like selling an ounce bag of marijuana to an undercover cop while working as a topless dancer in an out of town night club.

I was taken in and fingerprinted, and luckily for me, the drug charges were dismissed. At the time of my actions that led to the arrest, it never dawned on me I'd have an Arrest Record that would follow me for the rest of my life. You don't think about mistakes of the past or protecting your future when you live in the present, at least not until you run for public office like I would eventually do one day. But looking back, I know this arrest incident would've never happened if it wasn't for my crazy cousin Gina.

In fairness to Gina, I gave my grandparents plenty of reason to kick me out before she messed up. Since hanging out with the Hollywood crowd and Elvis I had gone inactive as a Catholic and even lapsed in my prayers and that left the door wide open for Satan to lead down a path that I would never have taken had I stayed close to the Lord.

Like a child being chastised, I listened as my grandmother made it perfectly clear how she didn't like the crowd I was hanging around with.

"Ever since you came back from California, your grandfather and I have tried to make you welcome." She said. "But you wouldn't listen to us when we tried to help you."

I reminded her how I was attending Sunday Mass with her and Gramps every week since moving in with them. I even started going to confession again but who was I fooling? In the Catholic Church you can go week after week confessing the same sins and expect to be forgiven and you partake of the sacrament and go right back to sinning all over again during the week.

I couldn't get myself back on track no matter how hard I tried. With no spiritual instruction in the home and no family prayer to guide me toward the right path, I didn't find my way back to the young girl who wanted be a nun.

"I don't blame you." Gram half apologizing said. "I blame your mother for putting you on that airplane and shipping you off to the states all alone like she did."

"You knew I didn't want to go." I argued with her. "And still you all let me go to Germany with a mother who never wanted me."

"We had no choice. We couldn't keep you with us after you got out of foster care." Gram tried to explain. "It's your father's fault you ended up going off to your mother."

"Why is everything always my father's fault?" I argued. Knowing full well, Dad would only take custody of my older sister, refusing to take me.

"Well, you can't undo what's been done," she replied. "Just stay out of trouble and try to find better friends to hang around with from now on and keep going to Church. Can you do that?"

The "trouble" Gram was talking about, was my getting arrested for selling marijuana to an undercover cop where I'd been working as a topless dancer. I have often wondered what she would've said if she knew the bad company I'd been keeping, that got me in trouble and arrested in the first place, was her own grandniece my crazy cousin Gina. She thought Gina was the cat's meow who never did anything wrong.

I can still remember the look on Gram's face when I walked in from the police station that night.

"What were you thinking?" She demanded to know.

The Marijuana stash at Gram's

Up until then, I'd been staying under the radar pretty good while living with my grandparents. It never was my intention to get them upset or do anything to get me kicked out. I liked living at home with my grandparents. I could work nights and they were happy to watch their new great grandson for me. Heck, I was just beginning to think I could make a life for me and my son out here again.

"I don't see their car. Are you alone in the house?" Gina asked as she walked through the door one day while my grandparents were gone out.

"Yep. We're alone." I replied. "Why? What's up?"

When Gina came back to Springfield, a few months after I left Hollywood, she'd taken up with a drug dealer. Oh, he was a nice guy alright-- for a drug dealer. I even liked Duff. They were deeply in love and I was actually happy for her. Living with Duff, I figured she wouldn't have time to make trouble for me, so I was happy for her and for me.

My life would forever change the day Gina walked through that door wanting a favor that I should have had the sense to refuse. But I didn't and so I stupidly agreed to help her stash Duff's marijuana when she begged me to help her so he wouldn't go to jail. Unlike today in many states, marijuana was quite illegal in the '70's which meant Gina was worried Duff would get busted if the police raided his house. And that's how I ended up getting busted instead of her beloved drug dealer.

"This is the craziest thing you've ever done. And you want me to help you?" I asked dumbfounded. I was thinking about my grandparents. "What about them?"

"What are you worried about? They won't know if you don't say anything Elaine." Gina kept insisting, knowing I would do anything she wanted as I usually did.

"How many trash bags filled with marijuana are you gonna hide in Gram's basement?" I asked.

"Only the few we have left in our place." She promised. "And then when it's safe, I'll get them out of here. Okay?"

She was my crazy cousin, but I sure didn't want anything to happen to her, so I stupidly went along with the plan. Gina knew I was a sucker and I'd let her do it. I watched as she ran out to her car and started unloading large trash bags filled with Duff's stash.

I'd forgotten about the marijuana in the basement, until Gina dropped by for a visit a few weeks later.

I still remember sitting at Gram's kitchen table and making up one ounce bags of marijuana with her. And that's when, I, who had never dealt in drugs or marijuana before, stupidly accepted her gift of a few ounce bags in exchange for my help.

Truth be known, I had no idea what I was doing or I never would have ended up getting arrested. Not knowing what I was doing, I sold an ounce bag of marijuana to an undercover cop posing as a customer at one of the night clubs where I worked. Hey, it was my first time doing anything like that and I got caught. So much for Gina's generous gift.

And now here I was being kicked out of Gram's house because I'd gotten arrested thanks to my crazy cousin. "Where was I supposed to go?" I thought, as I contemplated my options.

I couldn't help but think I had been through this once before with Gina—hadn't she ruined my set up with Yvonne and Luke and gotten me kicked out of that living arrangement too? I was lost in my thoughts until Gram walked up to me with a wooden spoon in her hand shaking it in my face as she liked to so often do.

"Did you hear me?" Gram repeated. "What were you thinking to go and get yourself arrested like that?"

"I don't know." I wanted to say. "Why don't you ask Gina? Why ask me?" But I didn't say that. Instead, I tried to talk Gram out of throwing me out.

"I don't know. How you can do this to your only great grandchild?" I said, as I tried laying a guilt trip on her about my son.

I was hurting and I was sorry I had let her down. But I was alone with a child now and what did she expect me to do?

The dentist who changed my life

Gram loved me and she gave me time to find another place so I wasn't homeless right away. I took advantage of program for low income people like me and got a nice two bedroom apartment in a housing project outside of Springfield. I had no car yet so it was hard to move that far away from Gram.

I also took Gram's advice and made new friends in my neighborhood who like Duff used and sold marijuana. I continued working as a topless dancer saving up my money to get a car. In the meantime, I made a plan to have some dental work done but the closest dentist was nearly a mile from my apartment. I walked to the dentist every week for months until I had all the work done. What I didn't know, and what the dentist didn't bother to warn me, was the fact that he was putting mercury "amalgam" fillings in my mouth.

Up until I started seeing the dentist, I had great health and energy of mind of body. But within a short time I noticed symptoms that were interfering with my daily activities. I began struggling with depression, anger, even suicidal feelings but I just dismissed it as my missing my grandparents and stressing over living alone with my child for the first time since he was born.

To make a long story short, I didn't know to ask my dentist the golden question about his choice of material for fillings. How could I, if he never informed me of the dangers of mercury or that I had a choice to have a safer type of filling? And that's how it was that I never suspected it was the mercury fillings suddenly wreaking havoc in my life. Looking back, I paid a bigger price for those eleven fillings than I would ever know.

Since I didn't know about the mad hatter story and mercury, I didn't have a clue what was happening to me and wouldn't discover the source of my ongoing health issues until fifteen years later. Thanks to a mercury-free dentist I found in Iowa, while serving on the school board, I was finally diagnosed with mercury poisoning and was able to get the mercury fillings replaced with white plastic fillings and get the help to detox so I could get on the road to recovery again.

I found a good article at *dentalwellness4u.com*, titled <u>Basic Facts about Mercury</u>, wherein it suggested that "it will be impossible to fully understand the toxicity of mercury unless you first understand some basic facts such as how Mercury is the most poisonous, non-radioactive, naturally occurring substance on our planet. The report further warned, "There is no safe or harmless level of mercury."

What most people don't know is that the first exposure to mercury in newborn babies "from amalgam fillings occurs at the moment of conception." I recall a show I did on mercury poisoning when I had my own cable television talk show, *Telling it Like It Is* when I lived in Iowa. One of my guests had suffered several miscarriages and was only able to carry a child full term after she had all her amalgam fillings removed.

I finally got a car and was able to get around better and that's when I decided I wanted to move back to the Springfield area again. I'd also been working less hours since I didn't have the energy to keep up longer hours as I had been doing before my visit to the mercury dentist. I prayed for a roommate so I could find a decent place to live that I could afford.

Her name was Jodie and she was a topless dancer where I'd been working. Lucky for me, she had just lost her roommate and we soon found ourselves apartment searching together. I was

74

eager to move into the brand new apartments we'd found in West Springfield.

Jodie turned out to be a real lifesaver indeed, especially since we were both working rotating shifts in the clubs where we danced. Our work schedule meant Jodie could babysit for free while I worked. I'd been spending so much money on doctors, trying to figure out what was making me so sick all the time, I didn't have money for a sitter anymore.

Having Jodie for a roommate worked out for me much better than when I took up with Jill whom I'd met at the YWCA. Unlike Jill, Jodie didn't do drugs, drink or smoke. We got along good in that department. After Gina's escapade, I sure didn't want to get mixed up with any drug dealers again. And besides, I knew my crazy cousin didn't hang out in West Springfield. "No." I thought to myself, "I wouldn't be getting any unexpected visitors out here." Or so I thought.

The return of Big Al

The doorbell rang and when I opened the door there stood Big Al, himself, more handsome than ever.

Looking around, he asked, "Aren't you going to invite me in?" Coming from Al, it sounded more like an order than a question. I just stood there staring at this man whom I loved more than life itself. But there had been another man in my life and he had just been taken from me and now here was my son's father at my door.

For some unknown reason, I had always been the favorite of Gram's third husband, my step-grandfather Teddy. I loved him dearly, more like a father than anything else. But shortly after I moved in with Jodie, Gramps died rather suddenly and I took his death hard.

In May of 1970, I remember how I'd had a dream three days before Gramps died. In my dream, I saw three coffins. In the third coffin lay my grandfather Teddy. I remember waking up the next morning and calling my grandmother who confirmed he'd had been rushed to the hospital the night before—the very night that I saw him in my dream.

As a child, I often had dreams, more like visions that usually came true and continue even today. So when I had the dream about my grandfather laying in that third coffin, I knew it couldn't be good. Although I worked nights, I spent as much time at the hospital with Grandpa as I could. As in my dream of the three coffins, he died exactly three days from the night I dreamt of him.

Not understanding the purpose of our earth life, I hadn't yet gained a testimony of how death is merely a birth that brings us back into the presence of God. Losing my grandfather, I was understandably inconsolable at his funeral. Teddy was the only grandfather I had ever known and he loved me unconditionally, despite all my faults. He loved me and how I loved him for that.

I remember trying to throw myself on his coffin when it was being lowered into his grave. Years later, I came across a similar story about my beloved friend Elvis Presley who had done the very same thing when his mother Gladys died in 1958 just before he was shipped off to Germany.

Struggling with Gramps death, missing Al and wandering around like a lost lamb looking for its leader, I looked forward to making new friends at the club where I'd been working. That's one thing I did really good. I loved meeting new people and bonding to those I can trust.

I soon got to know the regulars at the club and I remember showing a picture of my son to one of the girls who worked there. I carried his picture around with me, but I didn't think it would get back to Al. It did and that's how Al came looking for the child I'd hoped to keep secret from him.

So when the doorbell rang, I picked up my son and put him in the playpen to keep him out of mischief while I was at the door. Jodie was gone and I had the apartment to myself.

"Now you be a good boy while mommy sees who's at the door." I said looking at my son and believing he understood every word too.

My heart skipped a beat to see the man, I loved more than life itself, standing in front of me after nearly two years. The passion was still there, but I didn't know if he still had feelings for me. Not knowing the reason for this unexpected visit I held the door partly closed until I could get my thoughts together. But

Al didn't wait. He pushed the door open and walked right in as if he owned the place.

"How'd you know where I lived Al?" I asked as I stepped aside.

It was the first question out of my mouth, which was stupid, because as long as I'd known Al he'd always had connections to anyone and everyone. If he wanted to find you, he did. And here he was. But acting more in character like Big Al, he ignored my question and without so much as a word, I watched as he marched right over to the playpen where our child was playing.

"So, what brings you around after all these years?" I tried asking again, but Al seemed to be more interested in what was in the playpen.

Still ignoring me, I watched as Al reached into the playpen and picked up the child he didn't know he had fathered.

I will never forget what happened next. Holding him high in the air above his head, keeping his eyes on our child, Al called out to me asking, "Is this my son?"

"You could never have such a beautiful child," I said without even thinking.

Yes. It was cruel. But what could come of his knowing that this was his kid? Besides, I was not prepared to discuss it with him either. I needed time to think, didn't I? Thinking my response would put an end to any further talk on the subject, I waited to see what he would do.

"I got some stuff to do and then I'll be back." And that's all Al said, just like he had never been gone.

I found out later, at work, that it was the girl I'd shown my baby's picture to who had run straight to Al to tell him. It seems she told him how much my son looked just like him. Yes. Once he got a good look at my baby, Al knew it was his kid alright and that's how it was that I had to let him have "visitation rights" because no one says no to Big Al.

Al wanted his son in his life, and that surprised me given how he was still married. I knew I wasn't part of the package deal, and I didn't expect I would be. Things had changed in Al's life since I came back from California. For one thing, he'd found another love interest on the side in my absence.

Despite my determination to not get involved with Al, old feelings got me turned around again, not to mention I was not making good decisions after my dental experience. I was still struggling from the effects of those doggone mercury fillings. I recognized the change in my behavior. How could I not?

If I hadn't been thinking clearly before Al's unexpected visit, I sure couldn't now. To make matters worse, Jodie met a guy and was making plans to move in with him. Naturally, I was happy for her but my mind was on other things the day Al showed up at my doorstep. I was trying to figure out how I was going to make it without a roommate. Al's sudden appearance in my life came right at a time that I was able to find and rent an affordable house back in Springfield.

As for Al, he liked the idea of my moving back to Springfield and being closer to him. While Springfield may have been good for him, it wasn't so much for me.

Another Arrest Record

I quickly got settled into my new home and happy to be in a safe neighborhood in Springfield, with a school-age babysitter only a few doors down from me. I was getting really good tips at work and things were looking up again. Maybe it was because I saw more of Al who embraced his newfound fatherhood much to my joy. But seeing him only made it harder on me since I still loved him.

"I got a friend who wants to meet you," one of the girls at the club offered.

"Is it that cute guy Jackson sitting over there at the bar?" I asked.

"That's him and he likes you Elaine," she replied.

I still wasn't making good decisions since all that dental work I'd had done, so that's all I can attribute to what happened next.

The big heist

Jackson was a cute guy that often came into the club and enjoyed watching me dance whenever I worked my shift. Unlike some guys, Jackson never gave me a hard time and I appreciated that. Right now, my mind was on Al these days. And I have to admit, I wanted his mind on me again too. And that's how I found myself conjuring up a crazy plan to win him back.

It all came about when I saw Al in the club on the same night one of the girls tried to hook me up with Jackson. I figured it was my one chance to make Al jealous.

"Hey, Jackson," I called out when I saw him walk back in the lounge where I'd been dancing. "Wanna go out for breakfast when my shift ends?"

Poor Jackson, he didn't know he was being set up or that Al had overheard us either. But I knew Al did and that's why I did what I did. I even made sure Al saw us leaving the club together at the end of my shift.

"You want me to do what?" I asked in surprise, while we were sitting in a booth having breakfast 3 a.m. in a popular after-hours diner.

It was only then for the first time, that I noticed he was packing. Normally, that wouldn't bother me. Most of Al's friends were armed with concealed handguns too. But this was different. I worried what he might do to me if I refused his offer. Suddenly, I was finding myself wishing I'd never gotten into this situation in the first place.

"My partner went missing on me and I've got a job to pull off," he tried to explain.

"And you want me to take his place?" I asked incredulously, as I wondered who was setting up who?

"Sure. I'll show you what to do and your share from the job will pay your rent," he promised.

Al had gotten into the habit of leaving cash on the table every time he dropped by to pick up our son for one of their weekly visits. But the extra money, Jackson offered me, was tempting. And that's how I ended up getting arrested for the second time in my life. Turns out Jackson's partner had the job set up but something went wrong and we both landed in jail.

Right back where I started

I was charged with breaking and entering and should have been sent to the big house for sure. Instead, I was surprised to

79

learn that the police wanted Jackson more than me and so I walked when I talked. I watched as Jackson was led off in handcuffs never to be seen again.

While I didn't end up going to jail, I was faced another problem when I got home. I was evicted by my landlord and told to vacate the premises immediately. It seems he was none too happy about the police raiding his property to recover all the "swag" Jackson had stashed at my place. Most likely a habit I picked up from my crazy cousin Gina.

Miserable to find myself out on the streets again, I was more relieved just to get rid of Jackson and his stolen weapons. I never figured why I let Jackson stash his swag in my home like I did. With Gina, I was just trying to help her when I agreed to stash Duff's marijuana at Gram's, but with Jackson it was not the same thing. "What was I thinking," I thought, "when I let Jackson do it to me too?"

Had I known about Mercury poisoning back then, I would've blamed it all on that dentist. But I didn't have anyone to blame but myself since I still didn't have a clue why I was doing such crazy things.

As it turned out, I wasn't going to be homeless for long. Thankfully Al stepped in and that's how I ended up right back in the South End of Springfield—Little Italy, the home of mobsters.

While packing up and making plans to move I had the sense enough to put two and two together since my second arrest. Some might say it was the hand of God that got the charges dismissed both times and let me go free despite getting caught red handed each time. And here's where I find my story evolving into a real time mob whodunit when I found myself being drawn deeper into the dark world of organized crime after my second arrest.

Welcome to the whodunit!

From this point on, my story will lead you the reader through an intriguing real time whodunit. I leave ample clues in each chapter "how to figure it out." Never doubting for a minute that this book will make a great a movie, I invite my readers to take notes if you want to solve this murder mystery mob whodunit.

The plot begins in this chapter starting with the cover-up of a murder in Agawam Massachusetts with me as its star witness!

The best way to manage this real time whodunit is to suspect everyone so that no one should be above suspicion--not even a police chief whom my readers will be meeting shortly.

Prior to 1972, I had no cause to suspect anyone in the Mafia had enough pull to get me a get-out-of-jail-free card, both times I was arrested. Sure, I suspected Al's connections with the Mob, but not my father yet. Heck, I was just happy to be free, so I wasn't thinking about how I'd been leaving some mighty fine footprints for anyone in the Mafia to use against me one day.

What about the Police?

What was it about the Mafia and the police that I'd heard Al and the guys talking about whenever they thought I wasn't listening? Growing up, I always liked to see police in our neighborhoods.

Thanks to the internet today, we gain greater insight to the Mafia and our local police. As OC bloggers like to remind us, "the Mafia held sway over every element of society, from police to the judges and politicians." Knowing the Mafia was active in places where they dominated organized crime activities, like they'd been doing in the Springfield area where I'd been living, I never had any reason to think I was immune to prosecution like local mobsters usually enjoyed.

Looking back, whether acting as enforcers or associates of the Mafia, no one usually makes that connection with its own police. Unfortunately, that's how our communities find themselves with a mob problem like the one I stumbled onto with the Agawam faction in 1979 as an elected town councilor.

As you will find out soon enough in Chapter 9, I actually had the chance to personally witness how the Mafia holds sway over our towns and its police. And if you're every unlucky enough to stumble onto them and stir up that bee's nest, watch out if you have an arrest record past like I did. But I get ahead of myself.

It's what I did after I got arrested that got me into even more trouble with the mob in Agawam.

Life in the South End

Having an Arrest Record, I fit right in with Al's crowd even though that didn't go over too well with him, given the nature of our relationship recently. Instead of a lover, I was his son's mother. For Al, that meant I had to stop doing stupid things like getting arrested. He didn't know about the dentist, so he just figured I was messing up on my own. I knew he cared when he called for a sit-down with me.

Up until then, I hadn't said anything to Al about my arrest. Turns out, I didn't need to say anything. He already knew every little detail leading right up to my arrest and he wasn't happy either! Not surprisingly, I got my walking papers when Al told me in no uncertain terms that I was retiring from the topless dancing business. Our conversation went something like this...

"You know I can't afford to give up dancing, Al." I said. "The tips are too good. I need the money to live in a decent place with our son."

"I know a guy who owns a nice apartment building in the South End," Al explained. "I can get you in there. Get packed."

"Uh oh, not the South End again," I thought to myself. And then, as if reading my thoughts, he just gave me that look of his, which made me wonder, "Did he know about my days with Jill in the South End too?"

"Don't worry about the money. I got a friend and he owes me a favor," Al said. "You can trust him and he'll keep an eye on you and the kid. You'll be safe there."

"Heck, that was fine with me," I thought to myself. "I'd been through so much I needed someone to watch out for us right about now." A new start sounded good. A new home and a new job. What could go wrong with that plan?

Al, a man of few words, signaled our talk was over and, as I walked him to the door, he turned and threw me a warning look saying, "And stay out of trouble, will ya?"

"Sure. No problem Al," I promised.

But Al didn't know who my crazy cousin Gina had just taken up with and what she about to do that would forever change our lives.

A murder in Agawam

Al kept his word, and I met my new landlord who, like many of his gangster friends, had a real fancy moniker for a nickname. I won't use it, because I don't know if he's still alive and I don't want to bring him into this mess. Suffice to say, thanks to Al's friend, I was soon set up in a nice two bedroom apartment in his apartment building.

I'd just gotten settled in to my new place in the South End and wondered what I was going to do with my free time while in-between jobs, when the phone rang.

"Hey. What are you doing tonight?" Gina was asking.

"How'd you get my new phone number so quick?" I asked, only because I knew she didn't get it from me.

"Your grandmother gave it to me," she replied.

"So much for staying out of trouble," I thought to myself. Unknown to me, my crazy cousin had moved on and was dating a gorgeous mobster named Victor C. DeCaro, whose wife's "family" just happened to own the Living Room Lounge in Agawam. Victor's father-in-law was none other than "Skyball" Scibelli, a notorious mobster in the Genovese family. At the time, Skyball's name meant absolutely nothing to me and I would never have run into them if not for Gina.

When Gina called me I thought she just wanted to talk about what had happened to a mutual friend of ours named Gary J. Dube. But she didn't mention him. She had someone else on her mind that day.

After moving into the South End, I began spending more time hanging around with the same rough crowd as Big Al and I met more of his friends like Gary J. Dube of Agawam.

I remember the last time I saw Gary alive.

If memory serves me right, it was a nice spring day and some of the guys decided to take our party outdoors. I was with Big Al, but not everyone had a date. Like Gary, there were a few of the guys without a date, so when I noticed the new girl sitting alone I introduced myself. "What was she doing here?" I thought to myself. She was a shy lovely tall slender girl with shoulder length blonde hair. I marveled at how she calmly

83

ignored each of the guys who tried to hit on her, until she took one look at Gary.

Gary, a known lady-killer with a ruggedly handsome look about him, liked a challenge and I wasn't surprised when she hooked up with him that day. Despite her being taller than him, they were a couple after that-- but not for long.

Soon after our outing, it was rumored that the 24 year old wise guy had taken a bullet to the head and his body had been dumped in the Connecticut River. No one ever said who did it, but I knew someone in our circle of friends had to know. How else could anyone know how Gary had been murdered if his body wasn't even discovered until six weeks later, as reported in the news on June 23, 1972?

According to an online file with *masslive.com*, organized crime articles updating Dube's murder were published in *The Republican*, by Jack Flynn and Stephanie Barry. It seems that in 1972, Francis Soffen shot Gary Dube twice in the head and dumped his body in the Connecticut River.

Since moving back to the South End, people around me started disappearing. Shortly after Gary was bumped off, my new boss met the same fate. Two friends killed within weeks of each other. It all seemed so unreal to me at the time. Why was the mob going around killing people I knew all of a sudden? In the wrong place at the wrong time people might say, but for me it was all about being in the wrong family at the wrong time.

Just a family tradition

This is where I bring my readers up to date on my father Pete who died in 2005, and who like his father, he too had ties to the Springfield mob. But unlike his gangster father Tony, no one in Dad's lifetime ever talked openly about it. Not even my grandmother mentioned it to me. Growing up as a Mafia child, I guess they thought it was for the best that I didn't know. Unlike today, there were no computers back then and no internet to google all the things I'd been getting mixed up in.

Today, thanks to the internet, we can read about the evolution of the Mafia in Greater Springfield since the early 1900s. As readers may recall from Chapter 1, my own family's involvement in the Mafia can be traced back to the 1920's as well. Little did I know that one day my own life would depend on my family's association with the most powerful crime family in the country.

Online organized crime news updates tell of how "the roots of the Mafia in Western Massachusetts date back to Prohibition, and its growth mirrors the history of organized crime across the United States." In the 1970's I can tell you the Springfield Mob was alive and well, even in the small rural town of Agawam. I know, because I witnessed first-hand how my family's association with the Springfield Mob interacted with the Agawam faction.

I may have lived and hung out in the South End neighborhood of Springfield but it was in Agawam when I stumbled into the dark world of organized crime. It's been said how "every town with a mob presence was called Little Chicago." But the South End of Springfield, where my grandparents had once lived and where I was now living, had always been known as the stomping grounds of the Mafia—Little Italy.

Even the boss of the powerful Genovese family faction in Springfield, Francesco "Skyball" Scibelli, born in 1912, grew up in the same South End neighborhood where my grandparents had miraculously survived a botched mob assassination attempt on Tony in 1921.

Despite my family's roots in the South End, that's not how I managed to get on the wrong side of Skyball. If I had stayed out of Agawam, maybe I might never have ended up being wanted by the mob. But thanks to my crazy cousin Gina, who introduced me to the Agawam night life, Skyball found me, and that's how I came to know about the dark secret of Agawam—another little Italy.

Gina's new boyfriend was a real killer

The phone rang and I heard an all too familiar voice on the other end.

"So you want to go out dancing tonight at The Living Room Lounge in Agawam?" Gina asked.

"Sure, I got nothing better to do tonight," I said without thinking.

I loved to go dancing and Gina knew it. She had her friends but I was her backup when she needed someone to hang out with at the last minute. She loved dancing and she knew I was always up for a fun night of dancing. What I didn't know was that Gina was not interested in dancing at the Agawam lounge. When we got there, I noticed she was spending most of her time cozying up to some handsome guy in a suit.

"So, who's the cute looking guy?" I asked when she walked back over to me leaving the suit to take care of some business in the back room.

"Victor DeCaro and he's my cute looking guy," she snapped, while giving me a look that said don't even think of moving in on him.

"Relax girl, he's not my type." Trying to change the subject, "I heard someone say he's the manager of this place." But all I could get out of her was, "Yep."

Over the next few months, I found myself spending a lot of time at The Living Room Lounge with Gina. It hadn't occurred to me why she kept asking me to go with her when she had so many of her own friends that would've gone with her. I didn't know much about Victor and I sure didn't know he was married. Gina, of course, never bothered to mention it.

Looking back, I guess she didn't want anyone knowing she was dating a married man. In those days young women didn't go to bars alone, unless they were going to meet up with someone, so I never suspected she needed me as her decoy.

I'd heard rumors in the lounge that Victor had served time in prison for manslaughter. I didn't know if it was true or not, and Gina didn't seem to care either. At twenty-four, and looking more like a model, she was happy and obviously in love with the 28 year old lounge manager. And that's all I thought he was, and if Gina knew, she never said anything to me about Victor being the son-in-law of a notorious crime boss in the Genovese family. If she had, I would've told her to go back to her drug dealer whom she'd long broken up with.

I was worried that Gina had graduated from dating a drug dealer to a big time mafiosa when she took up with Victor. I never asked Gina about Victor's father-in-law "Skyball" who was rumored to have owned the lounge. Heck, back then, I didn't have a clue myself.

As for the rumors about Victor's manslaughter charge, I wasn't bothered by it at all. Who was I to judge anyone? Me with an arrest record of my own, I just wanted to stay out of trouble and Victor made me feel real safe for some strange reason that I could never explain.

Much to my dismay, shortly after I started working for him at the Agawam Lounge, Victor broke it off with Gina. She was crushed, but I was happy. I still had a good paying job. She had fallen in love with the guy and I could understand how she didn't want to hang around the lounge anymore after that. I stayed on because it made no difference to me.

For some unknown reason, Victor had taken a shine to me, more like a kid sister might be, and he didn't mind that I had no experience serving alcohol before he hired me as a cocktail waitress. He even paid me under the table which I thought at the time was a good thing. As I considered my options whether to stay on or not after their break-up, I thought to myself, "Why would I ever want to leave? I liked working for Victor and the tips were really good."

Witness to a mob murder

Working for Victor, I never knew he was dating another mobster's wife after he had broken it off with Gina. In fact, it wasn't until I began doing research for my memoir in 2016 that I learned the real story behind Victor's assassination. Mobologist Scott Burnstein wrote up a report on my former boss under the title, Mafia Hit List-Top Springfield, Mass. Mob Murders reporting for the East Coast -- Featured Mafia Mob Hits and News: Genovese Family.

Victor C. DeCaro, Skyball's son-in-law disappeared and later turned up in the Connecticut River on July 3, 1972. It seems he'd been continually warned about cheating on Skyball's daughter with the wife of another gangster.

It seems that even the Mafia has a code they live by and Victor had broken one of its most sacred rules—don't mess with another Mafia member's wife. If you did, it was punishable by death and sadly, as the story goes, a reluctant "Skyball" Scibelli was ordered to have his own son-in-law killed. Since it was a cold case, like Gary Dube's murder, no one was charged in both murders.

Meanwhile, in real time 2016 while researching the story behind my former boss's murder, I decided to contact my crazy cousin Gina who'd been Victor's love interest before he went and got himself killed. Just part of my research I told myself.

Seeing how Victor's cheating ways got him killed, it was good that they broke it off when they did. I knew Gina was a good kid, albeit a bit crazy, but she didn't need to get mixed up in any of what I had walked into after they broke up. I never told her or anyone what I am about to tell now. Until the writing of this memoir I never brought it up with Gina. We kept in touch over the years, so I knew how to find her and I sent her a text.

"Do you remember Victor DeCaro?" I texted Gina.

"Yep." She replied back.

"Did you know Victor was married when you were seeing him?" I asked wondering what she would say.

"Yep!" Gina texted right back.

When I tried to get more information out of her, she refused to talk anymore. She just wanted to let the past stay in the past she said. Gina knew my story. Heck, if it wasn't for my crazy cousin's meddling in my life, I wouldn't even have a story to tell.

Today, Gina is no longer the same person I knew back then. My rehabilitated crazy cousin is just plain good old model citizen Gina today who went to college in her mid-40's and turned her life around in an amazing way. As for me, I have never spoken about what happened to my boss Victor since the night he disappeared in Agawam--the night I became a threat to the Genovese family when I alone had the dumb luck to witness what they did to him. That night still haunts me and it plays over and over in mind after all these years especially since the Feds, years later, have linked "Skyball" to its cover up.

Today I finally get to tell my story of what really happened and that up until now has never been told. I remember it like it was yesterday.

The Good Daughter

On May 22, 1972, I was closing up with Victor DeCaro on the night he disappeared from the lounge. Victor usually had a driver who would come by to take him home after closing up the place. As for me, I usually took off before he locked up, but that night I sensed something was amiss. It was a dark feeling that came over when I saw Victor's ride come through the back door of the lounge. It was what the guy said and what he did that was out of the norm and I didn't like it.

Instead of minding my own business, I said something about it to Victor. "I don't think you ought to get in a car with this guy Victor."

I'll never forget how he just looked at me and said, "Don't worry. I'll be okay."

Worried about him, I hung around for a couple more minutes while he closed up the place. When I walked out to my car it was then that I noticed someone else in the car besides the one who was his ride home. That was the last time I ever saw my boss Victor alive.

I had no idea what happened or if he ever got home or not. So, I showed up the next night for my scheduled shift. I looked around but didn't see Victor anywhere. Someone had to have opened up the place. There was that dark feeling again. Only it was so intense I could barely breathe.

I didn't know why Victor hadn't come into work yet, but I was starting to get a pretty good idea. One thing you learn when hanging around mobsters like I did, you knew enough not to ask any questions. I played it dumb and went about my business of setting up the place. That's when I noticed two familiar faces huddled together at a table, talking loud enough for me to hear them from where I was working. Skyball was here!

I busied myself and left them alone to their business. I'd been told it was Victor's father-in-law "Skyball" Scibelli who was supposed to have been the owner. Back then, mobsters like Skyball reportedly owned businesses like bars and lounges to wash their cash through. I knew nothing about that, but looking back, I guess that's why I always got paid in cash all the time.

The room was dark and Skyball seemed so intent on their conversation, I was hoping they didn't notice me as I set up nearby. I sure didn't want them thinking I could hear what they were saying. It sent chills up my spine—they were talking about Victor.

Blessed with excellent hearing, I was close enough to hear every word so I couldn't help but overhear them talking about what happened to Victor and how his ride home had been a set up to kill him. Of course, I pretended not to hear them. I just kept ignoring them. But I don't think it mattered at that point. They knew I'd been there last night and had closed with Victor and now they knew I had heard every word they had said too. Maybe that's why they didn't care if I did hear what they were saying. Looking back, they probably already had a plan for me too.

For whatever plan they had for me, I wasn't asked to stay for closing and I was sent home early. Sure enough, I got paid in cash, just like Victor had always done. No one had to tell me twice to get out of there. Looking over my back every step of the way to my car, I peeled rubber and couldn't get home fast enough!

I guess I was lucky they didn't let me finish out my shift. If they had, they might have had time to figure out a way to get rid of me permanently like they did with poor Victor. I'll never know how close I came to feeding the fish that night and maybe even joining my beloved boss in the mob's favorite burial ground--the Connecticut River. God must have been watching over me is the only explanation I have for them letting me leave there alive as I did.

The next day I was surprised to get a phone call from my grandmother. She sounded real nervous over the phone and that made me real nervous. She'd never done that before. She was always so in control of things. She was a tough lady and I was about to find out why.

"Your father is here and you need to come over right away," Gram said over the phone. I rushed right over expecting to find someone in our family had died. "Maybe it was my crazy cousin," I thought, but then I repented of it as quickly as the thought came to me.

When I pulled into Gram's driveway, I noticed my father's car too. There was that dark feeling again. It couldn't be. "Could it?" I asked myself. "No." I said almost out loud praying it couldn't be. No way could my own father be involved in this mess with the mob.

My father Pete usually kept to himself, which was why Gram and I never saw much of him. He was never known to just drop by for a visit with his mother, like he was doing now. Still shaking from my experience the night before with Skyball's crew crawling all over the Lounge, I hadn't suspected anything so I wasn't prepared for a sit-down, but that's exactly what it turned out to be.

It would be nearly six weeks before Victor's body would be discovered. Living in Agawam most of his adult life, I never suspected Dad might know about his town being run over with mobsters. It got me to thinking about my murdered friend Gary Dube who had been an Agawam guy himself.

If it turned out that Dad knew about Victor, like Al knew about Gary Dube even before a body ever turned up in the river, then this was a sit-down and it would explain that dark feeling I had.

"What is this?" I asked Dad as I let myself in the house without knocking. "Some kind of a sit-down, or what?"

When he looked up at me startled, it was the look of recognition on his face that said he didn't appreciate my using the mafiosa term "sit-down" that usually meant a meeting called to settle a beef.

To this day I am still not sure of what Dad's ties to the Springfield Mob were, except it was rumored he ran a bookmaking racket after he had quit boxing. Looking back, after the sit-down with my Dad and Gram, I can't help but think he had to have been more than a bookmaker in his day for what he was prepared to do for me, much less think he could pull it off and live to tell about it.

Gram was as much in the dark as I was when I walked in on them. They were waiting on me before getting down to the business that brought Dad to Gram's.

Family comes first but which one?

"No one's gonna kill any daughter of mine," he shouted angrily. "Wow!" I thought to myself, "Where did that come from?"

Poor Gram, from the look on her face, I thought she was going to have a heart attack. As for me, I still hadn't a clue about Gram's infamous gangster husband and a life in the mob much less that my own father had taken to the life too.

Dad immediately began telling Gram how he knew about the mob murder of my boss Victor DeCaro and, skipping over all the details, came straight to the point of the reason for his visit.

"We need to talk about what we're gonna do," Dad said, still raising his voice.

Honestly, I didn't know we had to do anything. I had a child to take care of and I needed another job, but I didn't think dad was here for that. And so, Gram and I just stared intently at him waiting to see what was up. Finally, searching for words to broach a taboo subject in our family, he just came right out with the "C" word. Back then, a contract was an old-time term referring to an order by the mob to murder someone.

"Who do they think they are that they can put out a contract on my kid?" Dad suddenly blurted out. My father just kept going on and on about how he wouldn't let anyone kill me. When I finally could get in a word, I stupidly uttered, "Why would anyone want me dead?"

Yes. I knew why, but I didn't know he did. Growing up Dad scared me. He was subject to fits of anger and I can still feel the sting of his belt on my backside. Well, looking at him now, he still had his belt on, so I figured I wasn't in for a strapping.

If looks could kill, I watched as Dad squinted his eyes and gritted his teeth, probably thinking how he was going to get me out of this mess if I didn't even have the sense to know I was in trouble with the mob. When I finally realized Dad was serious about my life being in danger, I spit it out….the unthinkable question I knew even Gram must have been thinking.

"Could anyone really stop a contract on someone once it was ordered?" I asked. My dad gave me the strangest look, one that I shall never forget as long as I live.

I was left wondering if Dad could read my thoughts. I couldn't stop thinking about how Gary Dube was murdered only a few weeks ago. Wasn't he just a witness to a mob crime too? Yes, he was and they killed him for no other reason than to protect themselves from going to prison.

Gosh, it seemed like it only happened days ago and now here we were talking about another mob murder involving my own boss and maybe even me now too.

Dad had my full attention now and I was really starting to believe it when he said I could end up dead like Victor. So, when my father asked me to tell him what I knew, about Victor's disappearance, it was more like going to confession and talking to my priest. You always felt so much better after getting it all off your chest.

When I told Dad about the guys taking Victor for his last ride and how I overheard Skyball talking the next night in the Lounge, he asked me if I had heard anything, and I said "Yes. Yes, I did." But I assured my father that I pretended not to have overheard their conversation about what happened to Victor. Judging by the look on my father's face, I knew I hadn't fooled anyone into thinking I knew nothing.

So, I asked, "If I keep quiet Dad, maybe they won't have any reason to kill me, right?"

Wrong! I tried to convince my father, but he wasn't buying it. He never gave up any names in our sit-down, but Dad reminded me and Gram how those who wanted me dead all had a history of killing their witnesses fearing they could testify against them. And as Dad pointed out, "you're a witness and now that makes you a threat to them too."

Listening to my father, I couldn't help but wonder if he was thinking about Gary Dube. He'd been into so many things that could've gotten him killed, it came as no surprise to me when I heard about it. But my father must've known.

If he knew about a mob ordered hit on me, he had to have known about why Gary was killed too. Didn't I read it on *masslive.com* while doing my research? Yes. I was reported how "Prosecutors maintained [Francis] Soffen executed the men

[Gary Dube] in cold blood to keep them from testifying against him about the bank robberies."

Sitting in my grandmother's living room, I remember how my father never dropped any names around us. But even today, as I write this memoir, I can't help but wonder what earned the mob's respect of my father enough to make him believe he could actually talk someone like "Skyball" out of killing me if they believed I could testify against them. Especially, if he could kill his own son-in-law, why not me too?

As for me, I was nowhere to be found in Massachusetts when news about the Feds linking Skyball to Victor's murder came out years later. As to who had put out a contract on me and ordered my death, my father never said. But in this whodunit, who do you think was behind it? And it really does matter because there were even more murders in Agawam involving me in the upcoming chapters.

But for me back then sitting down with Dad in Gram's living room, all that mattered, was the fact that my name was on a contract and my father could make it all go away.

I know that I am alive today only because my father risked outing himself to me and made a deal with the devil himself to save my life. I figured he had to have been involved with the mob at one time in his life. Heck, all I ever knew, and still now about my father is that he was a boxer, a bookmaker and then later hired on with the railroad and even got promoted as an engineer driving the trains. Looking back, I figured Dad was lucky to get out of the life alive himself—or did he ever get out of it?

According to all reports I've studied up on, no one ever did get out without giving up something. In any case, my father, like my grandmother before him, wasn't talking.

Before he left Gram's house that day, there were conditions of course and he made it clear what was expected of me to ensure he kept his word to "them." He warned me in no uncertain terms, "You're not gonna say anything to anyone about anything you saw or heard. Just forget it ever happened."

The "it" my father was talking about was the murder of my boss Victor. Well, either I was hypnotized to forget "it" or I experienced some type of blackout to the incident….all I know is that I did forget about the "it" after I agreed to Gram and dad's plan to get me out of the contract and let me off the hook. But it's what they came up with, that I had to do to save my life, that adds more mystery and clues to this whodunit.

A witness on the run

My grandmother and father asked me to leave the room and I could hear their voices getting louder as they argued about what would be the best plan right now for me, and my three year old son.

"You have to get out of Springfield," Dad says walking into the kitchen where I was waiting for the verdict to come down. "Take your son and go visit your mother in Texas." There, far away in Texas, they both believed I could be safe until my father makes "it" all go away.

When Gram came into the kitchen she was shaking her head as if wanting to remind him of how my mother had tried to get rid of me when they were married. "Assunta won't like this at all Pete," she kept insisting.

"Well, she's gonna have to take her kid in, and help her if she doesn't want her to turn up dead," Dad replied.

To this day, I still remember the look Gram gave my father. "You forget Pete, but I haven't," she said as she walked out of the kitchen. Poor Gram, I figured she knew something that I didn't and I was determined to find out what it was. So I stuck around after Dad left and we had a sit-down of our own, Gram and I, and that's how I finally learned about our family's own dark secret that I shared in Chapter 1.

My poor grandmother who was now worrying about me being wanted by the mob, must have been having flashbacks of the day when her own gangster husband had been in the same predicament as me. Knowing how badly that turned out for him, I am sure Gram knew the Springfield crew wouldn't stop until they got their man…or in my case….got their girl!

I was just a mixed up kid at the time the Genovese family put out a contract on me. Today, I am not so mixed up. I have a law background with years of experience holding public office fighting corruption and so I can truthfully give my honest opinion of the situation that took place all those years ago. The following incidents set up the clues for solving this whodunit.

Back in Agawam 1972, I never paid any attention to who Victor DeCaro's father-in-law was. Francesco "Skyball" Scibelli was reputedly a capo in the Genovese crime family, and boss of the Springfield crew. Heck, I was just a kid working in a night club minding my own business until someone had to go and knock off my boss.

As for Gina, I know she was honestly trying to do me a favor when she asked Victor to hire me on as a cocktail waitress, but it was a favor that just wasn't worth dying for. Still, for all her good intentions, thanks to my crazy cousin, I ended up a witness to a mob murder.

As a witness I could have testified against the Genovese family. Dad and Gram had good cause to worry. I wasn't forgetting what the family does to their own whom they fear might testify against them.

I took Dad's advice, I made plans to head out to Texas.

Like my gangster grandfather's own assassination, no one was ever charged in the DeCaro case either. According to *masslive.com* mobologist Stephanie Barry's online series of vignettes published 2011 and later updated in 2013, titled Organized crime in Springfield OC evolved through death and money: "The murder remains unsolved, but organized crime figures speaking on condition of anonymity said DeCaro had been warned about a nefarious relationship with another gangster's wife. No one was ever charged with the murder."

I was never called in for questioning even after Victor's body was fished out of the river. Agawam police and area law enforcement knew they had a homicide and I was easy enough to find if they wanted to. If no one was charged in Victor's murder, after his body turned up, then that's because no one wanted to make any charges. And, why not? It's not like they didn't have a witness right?

Everyone knows you don't conduct an investigation without interviewing the eye witness—and I was a star witness. Heck, I was their only witness! And no one came looking for me to tell them what I knew. Why not?

In any good whodunit, it begs the question--Did someone intentionally botch, or cover up, the investigation of the 1972 contract hit on Victor? All records, dating back from 1972 through 1979 (the year I sat on the Town Council), indicate the organized crime figures behind the mob presence in Agawam were all still active. As for the Mafia's reputation of avoiding convictions in most of its assassinations, it goes back a long way.

Back in 1921, who knows what the story was with my grandfather Tony? As for 1972, that's another story, and it's one that should have been told, but have faith dear readers, sometimes clues come from ghosts of the past like Agawam's very own Police Chief Stanley J. Chmielewski who died in 2015. Interestingly enough, Stanley was on the Agawam police force in 1972 when Victor DeCaro was assassinated. Stanley also served as its police chief from 1976 to 1994. So, why is this a clue in my whodunit?

In Chapter 9, as incredible as it sounds, I tell about an Agawam Police Chief named Stanley Chmielewski who had been ordered to make me an offer I couldn't refuse when the mob decided my time had run out while serving on the Town Council in 1979.

While I had no way of knowing whether or not the Agawam police were corrupted back when my boss Victor was murdered, I figure my father must have known and he didn't want to risk my life by going to the FBI or State Police. Normally, I would've been put in a Witness Protection Program, but looking back I don't think neither one of us would've been left alive if Dad had tried.

So what should you do if you suspect someone has put a contract out on you? In my case, Dad knew exactly what to do which remains a mystery to this day as to how he knew what to do.

God's Witness Protection Program

If my memory serves me right, I tried to get more answers out of my grandmother after Dad had left and we were alone.

"Who is he Gram, that my own father can stop a contract on me?" I innocently asked.

"Your father loves you despite what you may think," Gram said, ignoring my question.

"Do you really think I'll be safe in Texas, Gram?" I asked. "What if they change their minds and come after me?"

"If your father says they gave him their word, then they won't be killing anyone, not even you Elaine," she tried to assure me, but I wasn't so convinced seeing the heartbreaking expression on her face.

"Poor Gram, what had I done to her?" I thought to myself. I always suspicioned Gram knew what her son had done and why he could do what he had done for me. Like every other unfinished story, both of them took their secret to the grave with them. All I knew was that there was some honor even in crime families, like my father's, who everyone understood that when the talking is done and agreed to, there can be no death--no more talk of killing.

Mario Facione knew it too

Back then, I didn't understand the so-called code of honor among crime families. A former associate of the Detroit mob, Mario Facione, confirmed this code of honor in the Mafia when he was asked to get out of the mob after he was baptized into the Church of Jesus Christ of Latter-day Saints in 1981. His story is compelling and which is why I have dedicated my book to his memory.

In an excerpt from his own published memoir, Mario tells of the time he had to make a decision to get out of the life or stay in it when his new Mormon Bishop told him that he couldn't do both and serve the Lord too. "But you don't understand. They'll kill me," Facione responded. "You don't just walk away from the mob."

Obedient to the Lord and heeding the counsel of his bishop, Mario Facione, who died 2015 at the age of 76, shared his testimony of "Walking Out Alive" in a chapter of his own memoir, titled Mafia to Mormon: My Conversion Story. In his book, Facione tells of how his Detroit mob boss responded when he told them about his baptism and conversion and how he "needed to get out of the business."

The mob's organization leaders listened to him explain about his conversion to the Mormon Church. To his surprise Facione, the forty-two year old mob associate, recalls them saying they knew of the Mormons and they knew them to be "good people and they're trustworthy people."

To his sheer amazement, Facione listened as his boss assured him, "If you live the way they want you to live, I have nothing to worry about." "The conversation," according to Facione, "ended with a handshake" and it was only then, with that handshake, that he realized "I had done the impossible, escaped from the mob with my life."

Facione lived to tell his story just as I once did. And so it was, that unlike Mario's situation who had no contract on his head, my father had done the unthinkable too. Hadn't Dad talked his Mafia family into letting me get out alive just as Mario had done? The only difference, Mario got to hang around and stay put. Not me. I got exiled to Texas.

I am, after all this time, humbled by the fact that I was wrong about my father. I had always believed Dad had condemned me to a life spent running from the mob by brokering a deal with the devil himself--the Genovese family. I know Dad couldn't know it at the time, but I believe it was divine intervention that I witnessed what happened to my boss Victor.

Yes. My father may have thought he had intervened on my behalf but I know now that it was my Heavenly Father, God Himself, who rescued me from the mob and the life I had stumbled into as a young girl growing up in Little Italy.

Hoping to put the Genovese family behind me, unaware of God's plan for me, I naively believed I was under Dad's protection and I could move on and begin a new life in Texas—a second chance more or less. Sure, I had to promise never to return to Massachusetts again, but at the time it seemed doable considering my other option--sleeping with the fish.

However, I couldn't help but think how I was running away from the mob, while at the same time running toward a mother who had attempted to kill me twice already. I would've never had to worry though, if I'd understood God's Witness Protection

Program known for keeping his children, like me, safe from the enemy and changing lives.

I know God our Heavenly Father made it possible for me to go undercover until the day, like Mario Facione, I too would get a visitor from the Church of Jesus Christ of Latter-day Saints and find my way back home again.

CHAPTER FIVE:
GOD'S WITNESS PROTECTION PROGRAM

"Say hello to your grandmother," I said to my son, as I placed his hand protectively into my mother's hand.

"Welcome to Texas, Elaine," Mom said, none too excited.

My three year old son and I arrived in Texas in the summer of '72. We were met at the DFW airport by my mother, who reluctantly invited us into her home, only on the condition that I find my own place as quickly as possible. I knew she felt like this was deja vu all over again. The last time she got a call from Dad, she was in Germany and she was told in no uncertain terms that she would have to take me off his hands just like he must've done again when he called her after our sit-down with Gram.

The ride home from the Dallas airport gave me chills. It was so quiet you could hear a pin drop. I pretended to fall asleep hoping to make it go away. They must've thought I was really sleeping because I remember Boots telling my mom not to get too comfortable with me staying with them. If memory serves me right, their conversation went something like this.

"I want her out of that house as soon as you find her an apartment." Boots sure did sound agitated and I didn't like the sound of his voice.

I guess Mom didn't either. She got real excited like she always does when confronted with a problem. "This isn't my fault." She shot back. "Her father sent some money with her. You can find her an apartment can't you?"

When we pulled into the driveway, we all got out of the car and I looked around at my new home wondering how long I'd be staying.

"Don't get unpacked. You won't be staying that long," Boots said as if reading my thoughts.

Even though it was another awkward reunion for us, I had dared to hope that this could be a step to repair my relationship, with my mother, which didn't go so well for us in Germany. Under the circumstances, I wasn't sure how that would work out. Before, it was just the court ordering my parents to take my sister

101

and me off the state. Now it was an order from the Genovese family and I must confess, I never thought how frightened she must have been to be taking orders again from the mob. Isn't that why she left my father in the first place?

Looking back, I should have been more understanding of my mother's hesitation to take me in again, but I wasn't. I don't know why, but all I can say in my defense is that if I couldn't accept the reality of my own situation which brought me back to a mother who thought she had finally gotten rid of me, then how could I be expected to know how she was feeling? If my mother was alive today, I'd ask her to forgive me for misjudging her as I did.

Here I was expecting her and her husband to welcome me into their home without any consideration for the danger my very presence might be exposing their family to. Sure I was being watched, and I'm sure they knew it too. As for me back then, I never gave it a second thought.

After I moved out and got an apartment, I was always bothered by the fact that they'd never watch my son whenever I needed a sitter for him. It wasn't like they didn't want to do it because they always welcomed watching their other grandchildren, but never my son. It never dawned on me that they might've been afraid to invite any unwanted attention into their home after I had gotten my own place.

I'm sure Mom and Boots didn't appreciate Dad putting them in that situation. After all, hadn't his own father brought violence into his family's home when the mob tried to kill him and Gram? Looking back I am sure that's what Boots and Mom must've been thinking.

Heck, I didn't give it a second thought anymore once I touched Texas soil. If Skyball wanted to bump me off, he had time to do it before I got on the plane. And I knew I wasn't spilling the beans about what I'd witnessed back in Agawam, so I figured everyone around me was safe right?

I may not have been in a federal witness protection program, but seeking sanctuary in Texas and living undercover pretending to be a normal unwed mother working as a keypunch operator had to have been the next best thing. Once I'd started attending church again, it sure did feel like something the Lord might've worked out for me. Despite the fact that I was with a mother who had tried to kill me twice, I was okay with that too.

Thinking back on it all now, Was that what God's witness protection program would've been like? Why not? I'd like to believe that my relocation to Texas was no coincidence in how it all came down.

Trying to ignore the reason I'd suddenly been thrust on Mom and Boots again, I decided to take advantage of the moment.

Forget the past

"Whatcha doing, Mom?" I asked as I walked in the door after a day of apartment hunting.

My second day in and I figured I had as good a chance as any of getting some answers to the story behind my mother's desire to kill me so many times. We were alone, just Mom and me when I flopped into the comfortable chair in the kitchen where she was shucking beans. I should've waited until she put away that porcelain dish.

Nearly smashing a plate she had been holding in her hand when I stupidly broached the subject, she screamed at me in her thick Italian accent, "Your grandmother is a liar! She told you those stories to turn you against me."

"But why would Gram do such a thing?" I asked while making some space between me and Mom. "And what about the newspaper clipping she showed me when you attempted our murder-suicide?" She didn't like that question any better either.

I never did get an answer as she stormed off into her bedroom and slammed the door behind her. I let it go and never brought it up again while I was living in her house. A few years later, when we had a better relationship I broached the subject again. Like before, she became hysterical and I never did get the story out of her. My mother, who died in 2002, took her story about us and my father to her grave.

The life of a witness on the run

"I don't want you doing anything stupid while you're out here Elaine," Mom warned. I know she meant for me not to get

103

into trouble hanging out with the wrong crowd again like I did with Big Al and his gangster friends. I'd learned my lesson.

"To start," I said, "I'm not gonna make the same mistake of not attending Church anymore. I'll start going with you on Sundays Mom."

We were in the car and had been driving around and agreed on an apartment for me to rent. She must've been relieved thinking they were finally getting me out of the house.

Not sure she heard me correct she said, "Well, alright," Mom said hesitantly. "If you're serious about that, let's get you some decent clothes for church and I'll introduce you to our parish priest."

It was great going back to church and meeting new friends that lived normal lives. Awakenings, like coming out of a dream, sometimes take a while to set in. In seeking to save my life by running from the mob, I never imagined it would put me back on the covenant path to God where all truth seekers will always find a steady supply of blessings and help.

Since moving to Texas, known as the *Bible Belt* where Christian church attendance is generally higher than the nation's average, it didn't take me long to realize I wasn't running from the mob anymore--I was running to Jesus.

Seeking asylum in Texas while pretending my life was just fine and dandy in the land of cowboys and country music, seemed to work for me. I loved everything about Texas, but I was still licking my wounds from the life I had left behind in Massachusetts. My son missed his father Big Al and so did I. Without Al watching over us anymore, I found myself looking over my shoulder and ducking if I caught a stranger watching me. It didn't get past Mom, who took me aside one day, when were in the mall shopping for my new clothes.

Grabbing me by the arm, "What are you doing?" Mom asked in her annoying tone. "Stop it. No one wants to kill you out here."

It took me a while to stop ducking whenever I was out in public. Even to this day, when someone sneaks up on me from behind I still jump out of my skin. Church helped. I began feeling more peace to my soul after I found my way around my new Catholic parish. For me, getting away from the dark world of organized crime might've even contributed to my being more sensitive to the Spirit of the Lord and my prayers became more meaningful.

Bless me Father, for I have sinned

Starting over like I was, I had the same name but I seemed to take on a new identity with my renewed walk in the Lord. Oh, don't get me wrong. I was no angel for sure. I still broke a lot of commandments, but I loved the Lord and made confession regularly.

I felt safe as I welcomed the protection of the Holy Ghost and the angels as I did my best to obey God. I guess that's how people placed in a government witness protection program must feel too. You get a new life and move on. Yep. That was my story here in Texas. Only I had moved on with God.

I had forgotten how good it felt to live a Christ-like life as I had once done when visiting the nuns all the time. I recall growing up under the Christian influence of my grandparents, albeit only a couple of years, but it was enough to build a foundation that I could fall back on as I tried to rebuild my life in Texas. And that's how it happened that I soon found myself answering the call to deepen my faith through spiritual direction and the retreat.

Sounding the Retreat!

"What you need is to go on a retreat Elaine," my new parish priest wisely counseled.

"Isn't confession and attending Mass enough, Father?" I innocently asked.

"I know you're saying your prayers, but it's not always enough," Father counseled me.

Handing me a brochure for a Catholic Retreat, the grey haired gentle mannered priest read to me from it, "A spiritual retreat can help us find peace and purpose in life when adversity becomes overwhelming."

The *Catholic Encyclopedia* describes the necessity of such retreats "In the fever and agitation of modern life, the need of meditation and spiritual repose impresses itself on Christian souls who desire to reflect on their eternal destiny, and direct their life in this world towards God."

"Father," I said, "I think this is exactly what I need, but I have never been on a retreat before."

Looking over the brochure when I got home, I thought to myself, "I sure knew what it's like to retreat. Wasn't I running from the mob?"

According to *The Free Dictionary* by Farlex, "retreat is the withdrawal of a military force from a dangerous position or from an enemy attack. [Whereas], retreat can also be a place affording peace, quiet, privacy or security."

Farlex got that right. I was in retreat from the enemy and because of it I probably needed to go on a spiritual retreat. I guess I should thank Dad who couldn't get me into a government witness protection program. Never a day goes by that I don't think how my life would have been different had Dad gotten me into the feds program.

And yet, I know my story would've ended with this chapter if Dad had brought in the feds. Instead, my story continues and I am forever grateful I took my parish priest's advice for a retreat. It was the first step toward recognizing I was a more important witness to God's program than to the feds.

I made plans to go away for a weekend retreat soon after my parish priest introduced me to another communicant of his parish who agreed to accompany me.

When we arrived at the retreat, I happened to meet an angel. She was a nun who had also signed up for the same weekend retreat as mine. We hit it off spiritually and she soon became my new retreat companion over the next few months. She lived near me and I was delighted when her Mother Superior gave her permission to travel with me to more retreats.

Even though I found solitude and peace at those retreats I soon felt prompted by the Holy Spirit to visit other denominations. During the week I kept busy working a good nine to five office job. I had a nice two bedroom apartment and my son was adjusting better than I had hoped. We kept to our Sunday worship schedule even when I followed the prompting to visit other churches. I remember even visiting a Jewish Synagogue and taking a new Jewish friend with me on one of my Catholic retreats. I was on an amazing search for truth and didn't even know it.

"What is the purpose of life?" I asked Tamara one day as we traveled on our way to the retreat.

"You do know I'm Jewish right?" She asked, not wanting to answer my question.

"Sure," I replied. "But haven't you ever wondered what life is all about or what you're doing here on earth like this?"

"Maybe it's just to find happiness or to have a family," she said.

"No. That can't be it Tamara," I explained. "I haven't had much happiness in my life and I sure have no family that ever wanted me."

"What about God Elaine?" Tamara asked with genuine interest now.

"Yes. God is my Heavenly Father, but it's not the same as an earthly home or parent," I responded.

And that's how the *purpose of life* question got me going on a spiritual search that would last for the next couple of years. Ever since I could remember, I always felt I had no home on this earth. It wasn't just because I spent my entire childhood living with relatives and foster families who never wanted me. It was something more than that, and for the first time in my life, I found myself earnestly wanting to know why we are here?

Elvis Presley's Bible and mine

As if in answer to my question, my prayer was answered one day when I accepted a neighbor's invitation to attend Sunday service at their Pentecostal Church. When the congregation started speaking in tongues, as some Pentecostals do, I kept thinking, "I am a Catholic. What am I doing here?" I no sooner thought the question, when the Pastor holding up his bible called out to me from the pulpit.

It seemed God wanted to get my attention alright. Does everyone have a bible? Well, I never did. Despite my Catholic background growing up in the 50's and 60's, I never had a bible of my own. So I was surprised, when right in the middle of his

107

preaching to a large energetic congregation, the pastor calls out to me and, stepping down from the pulpit, places his own bible right into my hand.

I timidly accepted the worn out bible embossed in gold on a red leather cover. I liked how it looked-- so naturally worn from devoted use. Catholics didn't do that I thought—read and mark inside the margins of a bible like the one I had just been given. I remember seeing pictures of the bible Elvis had owned that looked very much like the red covered bible I was given by the Pentecostal pastor except his was black.

When I lived with Elvis I never saw him reading his bible that he'd gotten as a Christmas gift in 1957. We'd both been given our bibles as a gift on a very special day it seems. Like the pastor's bible I'd been given, I was surprised to see Elvis had the same habit of writing inside the margins of his bible too. There was a handwritten note in Elvis' bible: "There is a season for everything, patience will reward you and reveal all answers to your questions."

"I don't know what to say Pastor," I said after the service. "You've given me your own bible."

"Just promise me you will read it and pray about what you read," he implored.

Encouraged by the Pentecostal pastor's bible study plan, I started reading my new bible and marking inside the margins as prompted by the spirit. Just like Elvis must've discovered when pondering the scriptures, I too found myself getting closer to my savior Jesus Christ as I prayed to understand God's plan for me. It's a study habit I continue even today. I didn't know about Elvis' study plan but his notes intrigued me.

As evidenced by his own notes in his bible, Elvis knew he could receive answers to any questions about life and God. In the illustration depicted above, he wrote, "There is a season for everything, patience will reward you and reveal all answers to your questions."

Looking back on the days when I lived with Elvis in his Palm Springs Villa in 1969, I never knew he had a testimony of studying the word of God until I came across these file pictures of his bible. As for "every man can be tempted," as written in his notes, Elvis had been taught what to do to overcome temptation and make right choices in life—turn to God.

Known for being religious, Elvis even recorded some great worship songs. Unlike Elvis though, who towards the end of his life, I wasn't doing drugs. I chose to live under the influence of the Holy Ghost instead of the influence of drugs. Looking back we had something in common, Elvis and I, we both wanted answers to questions. I moved on shortly after my testimony of the bible experience with the Pentecostals. I had more questions and I felt the Spirit prompting me to investigate other churches.

When God calls get ready

As if heeding Elvis' own advice written in his bible, I was patient as I prayed continually for God to tell me what he wanted me to do. And then, one day just out of the blue, I acted on a prompting to reach out in service to some youth in my apartment complex where I'd been living for a couple years. This was totally out of the norm for someone like me to do. But I listened to the Spirit and obeyed.

I'd been studying in the Book of Matthew in Chapter 25 wherein Jesus taught, "Verily I say unto you, inasmuch as ye had done it unto one of the least of these my brethren, ye have done it unto me." Thus far in my life, the principle of serving others hadn't been a priority for me. As an unwed mother running from the mob, I guess I'd been too caught up in my own problems and just trying to survive. Busy as I'd been, I hadn't taken the time to worry about the needs of those around me.

Elvis, to his credit, did a lot of good for others despite his wicked lifestyle. I can't help but think he had a testimony of service that might've been influenced by the teachings of Jesus in the bible he had once studied. Well, whatever it was that had once influenced Elvis, it now seemed to be working on me too. Reading the bible, understanding the word of God, was working.

The years passed, I kept studying, reading my bible and continued investigating other denominations. With each church I visited, I hoped to find the answer to my question about life and why we are here. But I never did find it. And so, I stayed with the Catholic Church.

I remember the summer of '78, in Texas, as if it was yesterday. I was living in a nice apartment complex, near my son's elementary school, occupied by other single working parents like myself. There were no houses in my neighborhood, just lots and lots of apartments. Texas was the fastest growing place in the '70's and the small rural towns were ill equipped for the changes it brought.

Latchkey kids had nowhere to go after school, so they hung out unchaperoned looking for fun but usually finding innocent mischief instead. One day the loud noise of kids outside, roughhousing with one another in playful banter, caught my attention and that was all it took to set me on the path that God had called me to do.

"Hey boys," I called out from my porch balcony. "Whatcha doing?"

"Nothing much," one of the boys shouted back.

I joined the boys in the back field by my apartment and introduced myself. We talked and I had a chance to get to know them a little bit better. I felt impressed by the Spirit to get involved. Since I worked Monday through Friday, as did most of their parents, I prayed about what I could do for those kids.

"Can you do me a favor?" I asked my son, the next day, when I saw some of the latchkey kids hanging around our back field. "Can you go out there and talk with the boys and see what they would like to do for fun?"

I was delighted when he came running up the stairs, all smiles, ready to report back. "Mom. Guess what?"

"What's up son?" I asked.

"I talked with the kids like you asked me to do and all they want is to get out of this neighborhood."

And that was the beginning of our weekend campouts with fatherless kids for an entire summer at Grapevine Lake a few miles from where we lived. Growing up, my grandparents had gotten me and my sister in the Girl Scouts and I liked camping out. It was fun and I figured these latchkey kids would like it too. So, I bought a couple of sleeping bags for me and my son and a huge tent that looked like a small house. I didn't have enough

110

money to buy all the fancy camping gear, so I just used what I already had around the apartment that would work for a campout. I made up a signup sheet and hung it outside my apartment door for the fatherless kids to sign up for camp outs. I made everyone get a permission slip from their parents. One of the kids, excitedly showed up at my door later that day.

"I got my mom's permission," he assured me, as he handed me his signed slip. "And I told all the guys to get theirs signed too and get some sleeping bags so we can go camping this weekend."

Yes indeed. These kids were really excited and I was thrilled. My son, on the other hand, wasn't so sure, as he explained to me, "Mom. You don't know what you're getting yourself into. These kids are crazy."

That was a little detail my son failed to tell me when he volunteered me for the campout plan. My nine year old son, acting more like a big brother than a son, changed his attitude real quick when I suggested we bring his Honda dirt bike along on the campouts. Suddenly, the campout seemed okay now. And as it turned out, the dirt bike idea was a really big hit with those kids!

I had gotten the dirt bike for my son to have something to do after school and on weekends. Arlington, Texas had some great dirt trails for motocross racing and that's what we did in our free time. My young son even got his picture on the front page of one of those Motocross magazines for being the youngest racer to take a steep climb that only the best and more experienced riders ever succeeded in doing.

Weekend campouts with the latchkey kids sure was a lot of work on my part, organizing those weekend getaways, but the ten kids we took every week really loved it. Those campouts made me think of my weekend jaunts with Yvonne and my memories of Elvis and the Memphis Mafia. Somehow, it just wasn't the same.

For one thing, I wasn't being paid to do it like I had been with Yvonne's weekend trips. In fact, the campouts were costing me more money than I could afford on my meager budget, not to mention the sacrifice of my own time as I gave up my weekends.

And yet, through it all, I never ran out of money for my own food budget each month which, of itself, never ceased to amaze me. I hadn't yet come across that scripture about the widow at Zarephath who, in feeding Elijah the prophet her last meal of flour and oil, did have food every day for her and her house until the day the Lord sent rain on the land. (I Kings 17:9-16)

The tick that made me forget the Springfield mob

The summer campouts were uneventful. No one was injured or lost in the woods. We were warned about ticks and I got one that attached itself to the back of my ear. At the time, I didn't think much about it. Back then, in the '70's, no one knew much about Lyme Disease or about ticks passing it on to anyone bitten after feeding on infected animals like deer or mice.

I never saw the telltale sign of a bullseye rash what with it being behind my ear. But I did notice some strange flu-like symptoms over the next few weeks that began slowly worsening and developing into full-blown migraines that gradually increased over the next year.

It wasn't until after our summer campouts with the latchkey kids that my condition took a turn for the worse. Soon, the symptoms were so disabling that I couldn't hold a job for more than 3 months at a time and I would have to quit and stay home often bedridden for a month or more. I thought I was dying.

I didn't know I had Lyme disease and I sure didn't know it was the reason I was experiencing Alzheimer's-like symptoms at the ripe young age of 29. Besides bone crushing pain in my entire body I was having blackouts too. I recall experiencing severe memory time loss wherein I couldn't remember hardly any details of past events in my life anymore.

Up until the tick bite I remembered everything about what had happened and the reason my father exiled me to Texas--I'd been running from the mob and I was safe as long as I stayed put. But I no longer had any memory of that.

Doctors were clueless as to the cause of my life threatening symptoms. I thought if I was going to die, I wanted to go home to be with family. And that's how I found myself on my father's doorstep, with my nine year old son, in the summer of '78.

Everyone to this day still asks me, "Why did you ever go back to Massachusetts?"

Hello I'm back!

Sick as I was upon arriving in Agawam where my father had been living since I moved to Texas, I had no memory of the past and I didn't know why Dad was so upset to see me show up at his home like I did. Needless to say, he wasn't happy to see me.

"What's the matter with you?" Dad asked me as if he'd seen a ghost. Shrugging his head, he just blurted out, "Why'd you come back?"

"I need a place to stay Dad. Can I stay here with you for a while?" I pleaded.

After I explained my situation he wanted to know why I didn't just move back in with my mother. I was too sick to argue with him. Would it have mattered if I told him I had begged my mother to let me move back in with her? With my blackouts of the past, I was clueless that Boots still feared I would bring danger into their home if I did.

"Dad. You know Mom never wanted me to live with her and Boots. Remember?" Yes. I remembered that much about my past.

"Didn't your mother tell you anything before you just up and moved back here?"

"Nope. Actually, Mom seemed kind of glad to have me out of her hair."

His facing getting red like it usually did when he got angry, Dad was starting to worry me when he demanded to know why I was back in Agawam. "But why didn't you call me before just coming out here like this?"

"I don't know," I said as I took a few steps back from him and keeping my eyes on his hands. "What could I tell him," I thought, "if I didn't even know myself?"

"You can't stay here," Dad insisted.

"I'm sorry dad. I have nowhere to go. I need help and I need you to put me up for a while." I was so sick, but I didn't tell him. He'd find out soon enough I figured.

My father had a lovely three bedroom house in Agawam and he was living alone at the time. He was divorced from his third wife and his sons, my half-brothers, were all grown and living on their own. Thinking he was going to let my son and I have the spare bedroom, I was stunned when Dad carried our bags straight down to the unfinished basement of his house. It was kind of creepy down there and I didn't like it at all.

"You can stay down here until we get you settled in somewhere," he explained.

Looking back, I can only assume he was trying to hide me in case anyone came around looking for me. But I didn't know that at the time, and so I just thought it was incredibly mean of him to put us in the basement like that. Once again, like I had done with Mom, I misjudged Dad too.

After my son and I had settled in, I prayed Dad would change his mind about us staying with him, but he didn't.

Dad never had the talk with me, the part about why I should not have come back, or maybe he did and I just can't remember. All I know is that I never told my son about why we left Massachusetts. Heck, he was just a toddler at the time it went down and I never said a word to him or anyone else about my life as a witness on the run once I got to Texas.

Ignorant of the danger that I had placed us in, by coming back to Agawam, I prayed to get out of Dad's house as quickly as possible. The basement was creepy.

Besides dealing with sleeping in the basement, I was really sick and unsure of what to do. I couldn't talk about it to Dad and I worried with him acting so nervous around me. I didn't have long to worry about it when I heard Dad calling out to me to come upstairs.

"I got a friend who owns some nice apartments here in town," Dad said. "He's got a vacancy right now. It's yours if you want it and I suggest you take it." He wasn't asking. It was more like an order.

"I'm not sure if I can afford anything right now Dad," I replied. I was thinking of how I'd pay the rent if I didn't even have a job yet, much less feeling too sick to even try to find one.

"Don't worry about it. It's taken care of," Dad explained. "Let's just get you and your kid outta here so you can have some privacy."

"Sure. Let's do it Dad." I let him know I was good for it sight unseen. Heck, I didn't care what the apartment looked like, I was just glad to get out of the basement.

"Come on, I'll drive you over there," he said walking out the door wasting no time to move me out.

And that's how I came to live in a nice two bedroom apartment on High Street in Agawam. My new home was in a nice neighborhood and I was really excited about living only a short walk's distance from St. John Evangelist Catholic Church. I planned to make that Church my home away from home while in Agawam.

Little did I know how those church steps would lead me right back into the dark world of organized crime—the very family that I had once promised never to threaten again.

The prodigal witness returns

I soon found myself getting settled into my old life again and never gave another thought about why I had ever left Massachusetts in the first place. Looking back, whatever my father did before I left for Texas must have worked, because no one bothered me or my son in Agawam, at least not right away.

While I felt safe and had no reason to suspect otherwise, it didn't matter since every mobster has a story. Moving about town like I had no worries in the world, I was unaware of how my very presence in Agawam had put some mobsters on high alert. They were all around me and I hadn't a clue!

Mine is a story that was never told until now. Looking back, someone in Agawam knew I could finger them. Incredibly, the mob knew it was mine to tell-- if only I could remember.

And now I can tell my story because I do remember everything and because it couldn't be told until every mobster who ever wanted me dead was dead themselves. Understandably, you can't go around naming mobsters and expect to live to tell about it. As such, I've only protected the identity of those who are still living who are **not** suspect in this whodunit.

115

For now, let's get ready to go inside the dark world of organized crime as it really happened to me on the streets of Agawam shortly after I moved into my apartment on High Street in 1978. It is there that I come face to face with the truth about a mob problem in Agawam, Massachusetts.

CHAPTER SIX:
REVOLUTION IN AGAWAM – THE BEGINNING

"There sure are a lot of kids hanging around here Mom," my son called out as he was walking in the door.

"Yep. I've been noticing that myself. How was your day at school?" I asked, trying to change the subject.

"Don't go getting any ideas Mom," he warned.

"I don't know what you mean?" I asked.

"I know what you're thinking Mom," he said. "Don't do it. Those kids don't look anything like the ones you rounded up for our campouts in Texas."

I knew he was right. There was definitely an air of dangerous mischief lingering about the neighborhood. For some reason, it's what intrigued me about those kids ever since we moved into our new apartment on High Street.

"Don't worry son," I promised, "I got better things to worry about right now than some street kids."

I really meant it. I desperately wanted to focus on getting well so I could take care of my own kid and not think about anyone else's kids for the time being. As such, I had no immediate plans to do anything more than find a way to outlive this mysterious illness.

And so, I wasn't too surprised when another Good Samaritan miraculously came into my life to help me do just that.

It's all coming back now

So far, I still had no idea that Heavenly Father had a plan for me beyond bringing me home to either die or be healed. Looking back at my life in Texas, I always believed that I never had any intention of returning to Massachusetts. But I did return.

But alas, if that tick bite hadn't made me forget why I'd ever left Massachusetts in the first place, I wouldn't have a story to tell about how the Lord actually called me back to face my enemy--the very mobsters who had once wanted me dead.

Leaving my latchkey kids in Texas, I didn't leave the migraines behind. The migraines followed me to Agawam and I was definitely struggling to hold down an office temp job in Springfield where I'd just been hired. Thanks to a referral from a co-worker, I found Dr. Roger A. Proulx. Doc was a chiropractor, into natural healing, who had an office in West Springfield just outside of Agawam.

1979: Bonavita with Dr. Proulx in his Chiropractor's office.

Not yet diagnosed with Lyme disease, he was my first experience with a chiropractor and he was an answer to prayer for me. All the same, he knew what to do to get me well. When I didn't have the money to keep up the chiropractic adjustments twice a week, Dr. Proulx made me an offer I couldn't refuse.

"Don't worry about paying me. Let's just get you well for now," Dr. Proulx offered.

Another Good Samaritan I thought, as I sincerely thanked the Lord for bringing Dr. Proulx into my life. As the migraines eased up, and Doc's adjustments began detoxing and rebuilding my immune system, he accepted my offer to work part-time in his office to pay down my ongoing chiropractic bill.

It didn't take long for us to realize we were kindred spirits and we soon became good friends. Doc, who had never married, had a great story that intrigued me. Before he'd become a chiropractor, he'd been training for the priesthood.

Dr. Proulx, who died in 2016, had actually trained for the priesthood as a La Salette Missionary in the Catholic Church. In his obituary it even mentioned "he chose to leave the Order and train to become a chiropractor."

Looking back on how Doc had taken me in as a stranger I couldn't help but think that had been the mission of the La Salettes to provide economic and spiritual assistance to the poor. I was poor alright and definitely in need of his assistance. Doc truly lived the La Salette's mission.

When Doc told me about having trained for the Priesthood, I shared with him my own dream of becoming a nun. One thing led to another and I found myself telling him my story of how my dream got derailed when I found myself pregnant.

I hadn't noticed right away, but it didn't take long before some memories were slowly starting to come back. I even started remembering about why I ran off to California and my life with Elvis Presley. Doc's healing hands were doing something alright. I was remembering again.

As I got to know Doc better, I learned he was a staunch Christian conservative and quite active in the Republican Party. Up until I met Doc, I never gave politics a second thought. Oh sure, I identified myself as a Catholic Liberal Democrat because that's all I ever knew growing up.

Hanging around Doc, I found myself getting interested in politics for the first time in my life. In time, I recovered just enough to quit my temporary job and find something more permanent.

What I can only accredit to the Lord, I somehow stumbled onto an open 9 to 5 position near home working for a distant cousin of mine in the Data Processing Division at Johnson Insulation Corp. in West Springfield. I was starting to feel better than I had in a long time and feeling like I could take on the world again. And that's when I got my motor vehicle tax bill in the mail.

My Tea Party is a hit

I was still living in my apartment on High Street when I started making the news after I organized a Tea Party based on the original Boston Tea Party.

I was obviously feeling a bit better, thanks to Dr. Proulx, because I was well enough to spark a revolution in Agawam only a few months after my arrival in town. It all started when I got a $300 bill demanding payment for an excise tax on my vehicle right after I registered my pick up in Massachusetts.

Having lived in Texas, we didn't have a vehicle excise tax. So, I was surprised to find we had one in Massachusetts. I can still see my boss's face when I walked into work ready to drill him about my 1978 vehicle tax bill.

"What's this all about Jerry?" I asked nervously while waving a $300 invoice in his face.

He just chuckled and explained, "You pay the use tax on your car when you register it every year."

Still aghast while staring at my bill, I mumbled something like "Every year, I'm gonna get a bill like this?"

"Yes. Yes, you are," he confirmed, still grinning from ear to ear.

I didn't know how I was going to pay off this huge unexpected tax bill much less accept the fact I was going to keep getting this bill every year. "No way," I thought to myself. "If I couldn't pay it now on my small pittance of a salary how could I keep doing this year after year?"

It's all I could think about for the rest of the day. I quickly figured that I could literally end up paying the full amount of my sticker price on my '75 Nissan pickup truck I had bought new in Texas. I did my homework in the weeks to follow and decided to take action after Dr. Proulx encouraged me to take it to the people.

The first thing I did was take a poll outside the Food Mart on Springfield Street in Agawam. I polled the shoppers and asked if they favored repeal of the State Auto Excise Tax. Only nine out of 100 persons said they'd oppose repealing the tax. I didn't bother to ask why.

I had people actually coming up to me and wanting to give me their names and help me get that tax repealed. "Wow!" I thought to myself, "I'm not the only person incensed over this unfair tax." Still new at this political activist stuff, Dr. Proulx encouraged me to write a *Letter to the Editor*.

I did and it was printed in the local newspaper and that's all it took.

The next thing I knew there was a newspaper reporter with a photographer showing up at work and doing a story on me. Her name was Kim Hessberg and she had a photographer Mario Sarno with her.

"You want to do a story on me?" I asked in surprise.

"Yes. No one has ever challenged this excise tax before you," Hessberg told me.

The headlines in Hessberg's story read, <u>Irate Woman Seeks Way to Ax Income Tax</u>. Heck, I really didn't think I was all that irate, but I was incensed alright. Glad to have the free publicity, I used the opportunity to call for a town-wide meeting announcing my plans to get a bill sponsored to get the tax repealed. It helped to know that the excise tax was actually a war tax and was supposed to be removed after the war ended. But it wasn't and that's all I needed to fuel the debate in my favor.

The public response was swift and positive, except for the Agawam Town Treasurer who wasn't about to let me get my hands on their town's piggy bank funded in part by the yearly million dollar excise tax revenue.

Still suffering from memory time loss, I had no reason to be suspicious of him or anyone who held office in Agawam. No. I just figured it was politics and nothing more.

As the Treasurer Andrew Gallano explained to Hessberg, "the revenue from the excise tax goes directly to each municipality from which it is collected and that last year, Agawam received from $800,00-$900,00 from the tax." Yes indeed. Looking back on it all, that sure was a lot of money I was threatening to deprive them of.

Today there is evidence of how prolific organized crime became over the years in looting municipal treasuries. At the time I had no thought about our town treasury being a piggy bank for the mob, but as I got more involved in the politics of Agawam within the next year, I was stunned at what I would discover.

Having no internet back in 1978, I was quite anxious to go online today and see what other communities were reporting, and here's what I found.

One of the more interesting breaking news stories reporting on organized crime's influence in the looting of municipal treasuries involved the Town of Cicero in the Chicago Illinois judicial district.

Among the numerous indictments handed down in its infamous 2001 scandal, names included Cicero's former **Town Treasurer** and Assessor, to name a few town officials. According to a Washington Post story, titled <u>U.S.A. Says Mayor Looted Treasury of Illinois Town</u> by William Clayborne June 16, 2001, "They used their mob connections to turn the town of Cicero into a personal piggy bank," said U.S.Attorney Scott R. Lassar, who announced the indictments and early-morning arrests…"

In the same Illinois mob story, "Kathleen McChesney, special agent in charge of the Chicago FBI office, said she hoped the charges would "bring an end to a sad history of government for profit in the town of Cicero." She added, "The Cicero candy store is closed."

The statewide candy store

Back in 1978, there wasn't any Republican Tea Party movement around when I challenged the unconstitutional auto excise tax in Massachusetts. The idea of a modern day Tea Party rallying the people to action just came to me after a lot of praying and inspiration I guess.

Unlike the latter-day patriotic Tea Party movement organized by conservative Republicans in 2010, mine in 1978 wasn't for the purpose of electing pro-life and pro-constitution candidates. Actually, mine exemplified the political protest of a specific unconstitutional tax, much like the colonial tea tax with the Sons of Liberty activists whose original purpose invoked the Boston Tea Party in 1773.

According to *Wikipedia*, the Tea Party is a conservative political movement in the U.S. that opposes taxes and government spending.

As for Agawam and my little latter-day tea party group, if I had known the town treasurer's own brother Andrew Gallano was nicknamed after the original "Gold Dust Twins," which was a mafiosa moniker named after a real pair of notorious mobsters who'd been skimming union dues, things might've turned out differently.

I didn't know and it was a good thing, I guess, because I got a lot done that I might not have otherwise pursued had I known I was raiding someone's personal candy store right in my own back yard.

As it was, no one had bothered to warn me about the infamous Gallano brothers et al in our town's administration and I happily pushed on with my tax reform plan rallying the people. As for my son, he didn't mind all the publicity I was getting and he liked having a celebrity in the family.

"Mom. Did you see the newspaper? He called out. "You're in it again."

"I know. Thanks. I've been getting calls all day about it." I replied.

Among the latest breaking news, some of our local reporters were proclaiming me a "self-styled Caesar leading Agawam's fledgling anti-tax legion" while others dubbed me "the dark-haired firebrand."

Looking back, I wonder what "Skyball" Scibelli and Agawam's own resident mobster Adolfo "Big Al" Bruno must've been thinking watching me run around making so much noise while boldly violating an agreement to stay away and leave them alone?

Whatever they were thinking, I still hadn't a clue I wasn't even supposed to be back in Agawam much less running around tampering with their candy store. As it was, I unknowingly proved to be an innocent annoyer of the very mob that had once ordered a contract put out on me.

I still have the September 1978 news clipping of an interview I did with *The Morning Union* Staff Reporter Kelly Christman who did a story on me with our very own town treasurer David Gallano. I was quoted and made to look every bit the patriot.

"The power to make changes lies with the people, but it is often usurped by politicians who count on the fact people will stay in their homes and not fight. It's time for the people on the bottom to reach up and seek change," Miss Bonavita said. She decried public apathy, saying, "the pockets of apathetic people are being drained by manipulative politicians."

As for Agawam's town treasurer David Gallano, he kept right on giving interviews hoping to strike down my revolution, although it only seemed to fuel more public support for my Tea Party revolution that was growing by the day thanks to all the news coverage. Ever grateful to the Lord for answered prayer, I'd been blessed indeed. As it turned out, the more Gallano came out against it, the more support I seemed to get for our little tax reform plan.

Happily for me, all of the publicity I got with my Tea Party group had unknown to me made its way to Boston right into the office of another patriotic organization who called themselves Citizens for Limited Taxation (CLT).

My Tea Party goes statewide with Prop. 2 ½

"Hello. Is this Miss Bonavita with the Tea Party in Agawam?" a friendly voice inquired.

"Yes it is. May I help you?" I answered, thinking it was another news reporter.

I was surprised to learn it was the Director of Citizens for Limited Taxation, Donald L. Cassidy, on the other end of the telephone. He came right to the point of his call.

"We've been following your Tea Party's efforts to repeal the auto excise tax," he explained. "On behalf of CLT, we'd like to invite your Tea Party to join with us in our statewide tax reform Initiative campaign."

It seems that the Boston folks with CLT, had been following the news about my own tax reform efforts in the western part of the state and were impressed with my success thus far. Unknown to me, CLT had been preparing to place an Initiative Petition on the 1980 ballot to lower taxes statewide and they wanted to include my auto excise tax on what had come to be named Proposition 2 ½.

Anyone interested in finding more about this proposition can find it online today. For me, I really liked how they had modeled the Massachusetts plan after California's Proposition 13 which had been quite popular with their taxpayers.

"I'm in Mr. Cassidy," I eagerly volunteered when he offered me to be their Initiative's no. 2 signer.

"Just so you know," he explained, "it will be about a year before we take to the road and actively campaign. The Initiative will be ready to go on the 1980 ballot."

I was so excited to join forces with another group that Cassidy didn't have to ask me twice. I was thrilled to be a part of making history in Massachusetts. As for my auto excise tax, the passage of Proposition 2 ½ would set the rate upon the value of a vehicle at $25 per thousand as opposed to its current $66 per thousand.

The invitation to join up with the CLT group was a blessing indeed for a fledgling group like my financially strapped Tea Party. The document covered more tax cutting reform than just my auto excise tax, but to me that was the best part of Prop. 2 ½.

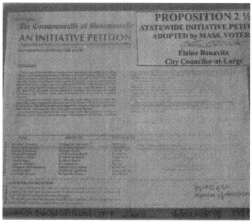

The Prop 2 ½ Initiative Petition with Elaine Bonavita as its No. 2 signer pictured reads in part:

> "It would impose a limit on state and local taxes on real estate and personal property equal to 2 ½% of the full and fair cash value of the property being taxed. If a locality currently imposes a tax greater than 2 ½% of that cash value, the tax would have to be decreased by 15% each year until the 2 ½% level is reached. If a locality currently imposes a tax of less than 2 ½%, it would not be allowed to increase the tax rate. In either situation, a city or town

could raise its limit by a 2/3 local vote at a general election."

When I signed on and joined forces with CLT, my little known Agawam tax revolution went statewide overnight. I went from a Tea Party organizer to being one of the ten sponsors of the now famous Proposition 2 ½. Suddenly I really felt like we were standing together just as the Sons of Liberty had once done in Boston so long ago.

Another voice and Prop. 2 ½ goes on the road

I'd been working full-time for my cousin at Johnson Insulation Corporation when I had the chance to take a temporary leave of absence for a paid position with the Proposition 2 1/2 campaign.

October 1979: Agawam Town Councilor Elena Bonavita and David P. Wilkinson confer during a forum on Prop. 2 ½ in Belchertown, Mass.

As the number two signer of Prop. 2 ½, I not only represented my own Excise Tax Tea Party group but I also joined forces with other conservative city councilors for our roadshow debates. I soon found myself debating powerful politicians like the former

Democrat State Senator Alan Sisitsky who vigorously opposed our attempt to lower taxes.

Like so many others committed to tax reform, I kept up a constant schedule of public appearances, giving speeches and debating critics. We decided to split up the state with Citizens for Limited Taxation (CLT), covering Eastern Massachusetts while I campaigned in the western part of the state. As the sponsors of Prop. 2 ½, we were determined to make the coined term *Taxachusetts* a myth instead of the reality that it was.

My legacy lives on in Massachusetts even today

"Did you hear the news?" Cassidy was calling to report in from CLT's headquarters in Boston.

"From the sound of your voice I take it we won?" I asked.

"Yes. I told you the people would see past the propaganda and lies despite our side being outspent by the state machine's war chest," he replied.

"I can't believe we really did it," I excitedly proclaimed. "We, the people, actually won a major tax-cutting ballot initiative? No more Taxachusetts now?"

"Well, we still have some work to do. I'm sure opponents of 2 ½ will find a way to turn public support against it," Cassidy was quick to remind me.

Cassidy had been right about that and it seemed like it was no time at all when local authorities threatened to cut vital services. The Department of Revenue and local municipalities may not have been very happy with the passage of Prop 2 ½, but overburdened taxpayers were sure glad. Those voters knew there were other options to cutting vital services and that's why 59% of them voted to adopt our tax cutting measure.

After the victorious passage of Prop. 2 ½, opponents fought back hoping to turn public opinion against our citizen sponsored tax reform measure. As it is even today, it wasn't unusual back in the 80's to see liberal school teachers using their classrooms for a propaganda platform.

It's the same today isn't it? But, thankfully, not all students were so easily brainwashed. I recall back in April 1981, getting a phone call from a courageous conservative Chicopee high school sophomore. His name was James Kendra and he invited me to give a presentation on my tax cutting measure after his school had sponsored a liberal opponent of Prop. 2 ½ to address them.

Kendra actually did his fellow students a great favor by reaching out to me, and I wholeheartedly accepted his invitation. After I addressed the student assembly, Kendra did an interview with Lori Woehrle a reporter for the Transcript Telegram.

"Miss Bonavita's presentation, was designed to balance a discussion held last month between the students and two Democrat State Representatives," Kendra was quoted as saying.

The Democrats were of course among the opponents of Prop. 2 ½ and they were not willing to let it go despite its passage the previous year. But what that brave lad, James Kendra, did stands as a witness of how one person, one student, can make a difference when they exercise their rights and voice.

One of the questions that I was asked by the group of comprehensive High School Social Studies students was on the effects of cutting essential services. Budget constraints under the tax-cutting measure fueled scare tactics, like threats of losing fire and police protection, which were absurd.

I relished addressing those kinds of issues. It gave me a chance to educate taxpayers on the real purpose of my tax-cutting measure while giving them ammunition to challenge their own local authorities.

I wasn't about to let opponents undermine the will of the people who had overwhelmingly approved Prop. 2 ½. Kendra gave me a chance to be a voice for Prop. 2 ½ that day.

Another question I fielded at Kendra's forum concerned the propaganda being spread about Prop. 2 1/2 and how teachers might lose their jobs. Sadly, that was atypical even after its passage.

"But don't you feel bad about putting all those teachers on unemployment?" one student asked me during the high school forum. I didn't have to ask where that question came from.

Woehrle accurately reported the entire exchange for her readers. "Miss Bonavita responded that more jobs may eventually be created for teachers if property taxes are cut and businesses are attracted to the area or expand because of low taxes. You've got to have businesses to survive," Miss Bonavita said. "A tax cut feeds the economy."

As my own readers might recognize by now, I believed in the **Laffer curve** whereas reducing taxes actually stimulates the economy. For example, when Prop. 2 ½ was passed, in fiscal year 1981, public sources reported, "Massachusetts ranked sixth among all states in the amount of state and local taxes residents paid per $1,000 of personal income.

Five years later, in fiscal year 1986, it ranked 14th. By 1990, it had dropped to 36th. Indeed, the voice of the people who voted for Prop. 2 ½ actually made this possible for Massachusetts. I learned first-hand about the simple genius of the economist Arthur Laffer.

According to the *Wikipedia*, the **Laffer curve** is a representation of the relationship between rates of taxation and the levels of government revenue. In other words, a reduction in tax rates only increases revenue if the current tax rate is higher than the revenue-maximizing rate.

I find it rather amusing how Massachusetts Governor Mitt Romney, the 2012 Republican Presidential Nominee, had actually claimed credit for lowering the taxes in Massachusetts. He claimed this throughout his campaign and I was disappointed that he never mentioned it was mostly because of our tax reform under Prop. 2 ½.

I only mention Governor Romney because of the historical significance of Prop. 2 ½. Lest we forget, this law is still in effect today, as of March 2017. Indeed, I feel Prop. 2 ½ is my legacy of a battle hard fought by its committed patriots inspired of God and with His help.

While researching my memoir, I reached out to a loyal supporter of mine when I was on the Agawam Town Council. Unlike most characters in my memoir, he is still alive but no longer living in Agawam.

Michael A. Cascella, who'd been a volunteer on my *Agawam Voice* newspaper staff that I published in 1981, made it perfectly clear he had no desire to talk about the old days in Agawam. He did however, give me permission to quote him in an email he sent me reminiscing about my work with Citizens for Limited Taxation dated September 21, 2016.

"Elena Bonavita was Agawam's most dedicated and sincere Town Councilor," Cascella said. "Her sole interest was her constituents and the issues that affected their daily lives. She was always available to hear their concerns and work with them for a solution."

My old friend Cascella, despite trying to forget about Agawam's dark past, was still excited and eager to talk about "the legendary Proposition 2 1/2." Almost sounding more like my obituary then an interview for my memoir, Cascella wanted my readers to know what I'd done for them in Massachusetts. He wrote more in his email and he asked me to share it here.

"It was the dedication and commitment of citizens like Elena that brought overdue tax relief to all, and most importantly, to our senior citizens whose livelihoods and dedication made the cities and towns what they are today, and deserved not to be forced from their homes due to out of control taxation."

And that's my story on Prop. 2 ½. Looking back, I had lots of other stuff going on while I'd been involved with my Tea Party group and the tax cutting measure. Despite my busy schedule since returning from Texas, I still managed to stick my nose in someone else's business. A "business" that was never my intention to stumble onto again.

I walked right into it

I'd begun to go into a type of relapse from overdoing it and I took Doc Proulx's advice to take some nice relaxing walks to beat off the stress from the politics of Agawam. I still hadn't been diagnosed with Lyme disease and it was definitely getting worse. I started taking walks around the neighborhood and that's how I walked right into another latchkey world again.

Having issues with memory time loss, I didn't seem to have any problem remembering the latchkey kids I'd left behind in Texas. I missed them and that's probably why I took more notice of those kids hanging around our church parish.

I guess you might say that's how I got started on another path of public service, in the small town of Agawam, after I innocently stumbled into it. They say service to your fellow men brings you closer to the Lord. I was soon to find out.

Being privy to that dark feeling usually warning me of danger ahead, I had no such warning when I came upon a group of latchkey kids hanging out on the church steps. Little did I know it would bring me right back into the dark world of organized crime and the very mobsters I should have been avoiding.

CHAPTER SEVEN:
TAKING IT TO THE STREETS OF AGAWAM

"Don't get involved with those kids," I was repeatedly warned by well-intentioned neighbors.

Some of the elderly neighbors in my apartment building confided in me on how they were afraid to go outside alone. When I asked, "What do you mean, you're afraid?" I was shocked at what they told me.

"It's those kids," one elderly woman shared with me. "They break the windows in our cars and slash our tires."

Sure, I hadn't noticed anything myself, but according to some of my neighbors, our neighborhood did indeed have some issues going on. It seems it all started when the kids were told to hang out somewhere else.

Of course, that didn't go over too well and some of the neighbors woke up the next day to find their cars vandalized. It continued to be a problem after that.

"When are we moving Mom?" my son asked.

"As soon as I can find us a safer neighborhood to live in," I replied.

In the meantime, thinking I had plenty of time before getting called in to start campaigning for Proposition 2 ½, I focused on trying to get well again. Doc Proulx had tried a few different things and I was feeling a tad better.

I hoped it was just enough to let me make ready to move into the new rental duplex I'd found on Walnut Street a short distance from my apartment. I was glad to get out of there, especially since hearing stories about the kids dealing drugs.

They weren't rumors. I got it straight from the elderly neighbors themselves.

"If what you say is true and those street kids are really dealing drugs, then why haven't you called in the police?" I asked my neighbors.

"You think we didn't?!" one of them asked in feigned surprise.

And that's how I found out about our town fathers, the men who sat on the town council who according to my neighbors knew all about the drug problem in our neighborhood. I couldn't get out of there fast enough after that.

"Has anyone tried to sell you drugs since we moved into this apartment?" I asked my son when he'd gotten home from school that day.

"Nope, but I don't get much of a chance to talk to any of them Mom," he explained. "Those kids always look like they want to start a fight and I stay away."

I started watching my street like a neighborhood watchdog after that. I was surprised to see boys as young as seven years old hanging out with the eighteen year olds. It made me get to thinking.

I worried that my own ten year old son might be enticed into joining their gang. According to the police today, the average range of age among gangs is seven to twenty-four.

Unlike other communities, committed to ridding their neighborhoods of gangs, I was never warned about the problem by the Agawam police when I moved into my apartment.

"Isn't it common knowledge," I thought to myself, "that the most susceptible, to gangs, are kids like mine who come out of single parent homes?" Yes, and I sure didn't want my son to end up in any gang.

Even today, police often educate their communities and remind parents why young people join gangs. Motivations for joining are varied, but usually fall within one of the following as explained on the *Official Site of the Los Angeles Police Department*: "Identity or Recognition, Protection, Fellowship and Brotherhood, Intimidation, and Criminal Activity."

To be fair to Agawam in 1978, the problem I ran into was nothing like the gangs in Chicago we hear about today. But some neighbors were, nonetheless, still scared.

Walnut Street

"How do you like our new house?" I asked my son after we'd moved in to our new duplex on Walnut Street not too far from where we'd been staying on High Street.

"I love the fenced in yard Mom," he said. "Can we get a dog?"

"It's all I can do to feed you," I jokingly replied.

"Have you seen any of those kids around here from our old neighborhood?" I changed the subject.

"Don't do it Mom," my son snapped back.

"What? I don't know what you're talking about?" I asked while trying to hide my thoughts from him.

"I know that look when you get an idea," he said. "Don't do it. Those street kids aren't anything like the kids we took on campouts when we lived in Texas. Leave 'em alone Mom."

In our new home, I did my best to forget about the street kids I'd left behind less than a few blocks away. But for some reason, I couldn't. So, I did what I always did when perplexed and seeking guidance—I prayed.

The Lord lays them at my feet in His house

It was a nice sunny day and I was on my way, taking a stroll through the neighborhood, to visit my parish priest at the St. John Evangelist Catholic church. I was a communicant of St. John's and lived within walking distance from my new home.

It just so happened, on that day, that the entrance to the church was blocked by those very same street kids from my old neighborhood. I hesitated because I liked to go inside and pray before visiting Father Huller in the rectory.

"Excuse me boys, are you waiting for Father Huller?" I asked while pretending to ignore the fact they were smoking and partying on church steps. Although I knew this was one of their hangouts, I'd never seen them here before.

Smiling and looking confident, I tried again, "Hey guys!"

"No answer. No smart mouths in the group either," I thought to myself, as I made another attempt to start up a conversation. "So. What y'all doing?" I asked in my best Texas drawl.

"Just hanging out," one of the older boys mumbled under his breath while checking me out to see if I was going to cause any trouble for them.

Well, one thing led to another, and we all got to talking. That's when I just blurted it out. "If you had a place of your own

134

to hang out, would you like that?" I asked while standing there wondering where the heck that thought came from.

They all just kind of looked at me like I was crazy. Until one of the younger boys, looking around to make sure he wouldn't get smacked up side of the head, dared to ask, "Just what is it you got in mind lady?"

And that's how the idea of a youth center in Agawam was born. Maybe it was the comradery I had formed with my Texas latchkeys kids, or some other hidden talent I didn't know I had, but one thing was certain, I was making headways with the very kids no one else wanted to mess with.

After that chance meetup, I often met with the kids on their turf making plans until one day they just showed up at my back door. I thought I was doing well, but I didn't realize I was creating another kind of problem in my new neighborhood.

"Do you know how long it took me to run these kids out of our neighborhood?" My neighbor lady angrily shouted at me.

"No," I foolishly responded. "Where did they go when you ran them off?" I asked stupidly knowing the answer even before it even came out of my mouth.

"Over to the High Street neighborhood," she angrily shouted back. "And now you brought them back here!"

"Yep. I saw them over there before I moved here," I cautiously confirmed.

Yelling at the top of her voice, she screamed as she stormed off, "I couldn't get rid of them until I took my shotgun to them and ran 'em off."

We never did get along after that probably because the kids started hanging around when we had our meetings usually in my backyard. Looking back on those days with my street kids, I am pleased to say that they never did harass anyone or vandalize property on my street, not like they'd been doing before they were run off.

Probably my favorite memory were the good times we shared whenever I took them camping with me and my son. Yes. I figured if it worked with our Texas latchkey kids, it just might do some good for these kids too, and I was right.

The first campout went just fine and as the boys got used to doing fun family recreation, I noticed their attitudes and outlook on life begin to change too. Encouraged by the change, we took up a vote one day and everyone agreed they'd like to do some fundraising to get a youth center or a boys club.

I was a curiosity in Agawam and that made me a good story for the local newspapers especially when the local police took notice of our fundraisers. Incredibly, my street kids actually looked forward to planning some fundraisers.

In no time at all we were making plans. First, we held a raffle with a TV donated by a local merchant, although some of the money didn't always make it back. Then, there were the car wash fundraisers. That's a story of itself.

All I needed was willing volunteers, a high-traffic location with good visibility and some attention-getting car wash signs and we were in business in no time at all.

"Here ya go," one of the boys said, as he proudly placed a medium sized coffee can wrapped in bright yellow paper in my hand. "I made a donation can for our first car wash. Can I handle the donations?" he asked, hoping I wouldn't suspect his eagerness to volunteer.

"Nice try. But I'll be in charge of the donations," I answered. "Nice donation can though!"

The kids pulled in the cars off the street and a few water fights were fun, but mostly I appreciated how the kids were there to make money. I just had to keep my eye on that donation can. At our first car wash I still remember a police squad car pulling into the parking lot.

"Everything okay officer?" I asked. "We have permission from the business owner to run our car wash today," I volunteered while praying we weren't in any trouble.

Instead of calling me over, the police officer stepped out of his car and walked up to me. As he took in the scene of street kids soaping down cars and hosing them off and playfully squirting each other too, I waited to see what it was he wanted of us.

"I can't believe what I'm seeing," the officer exclaimed. "What you're doing with these kids is amazing."

"Yes. It really was amazing," I thought to myself, "when you think about how some of the kids already had arrest records like the one who had taken an axe to his mother and here he was washing cars." I guess the police must've been pretty impressed indeed.

Bringing in reinforcements

I'd been making the news again, but this time instead of tax-cutting measures, I was getting recognized as an advocate for our Agawam youth. Looking back, I couldn't know how all the free publicity was threatening my personal safety.

I may have had no memory of why I ever left Massachusetts, but the Mafia never forgets and now here I was, for all they knew, rubbing it in their face bold as day, attempting to rehabilitate what many believed to be "their" street kids.

Sure, the mob thought I knew I was in their territory, but I didn't. All I had to go on was what the frightened neighbors had told me. As with any organization, even the mob often slips up when they get desperate just like they must've been feeling around me.

I never mentioned what I'd heard about a drug ring to the kids themselves, but as I got to know the kids more, I realized why some as young as seven years old, might have gotten pulled into it. Like my latchkey kids in Texas, these boys came from broken homes too. But unlike the boys in Agawam, the kids in Texas didn't have mobsters hanging around dark street corners waiting to recruit young boys into their drug running rackets.

Not yet sure how, or even if the town fathers were involved in any drug racket, I knew I was going to need some reinforcements if I was going to help these kids. After my run-in with the town treasurer Gallano, from my Tea Party days, I had a pretty good gauge of the political scene in Agawam. I wasn't so naïve as to think they'd be putting out a welcome mat for me.

In answer to prayer, I followed a prompting to contact our local college inquiring if they had any social work majors who needed to get a hands-on experience working with juvenile delinquents.

I was invited to make an appointment with the college counselor and I was surprised to learn my preliminary work with the street kids qualified me to have two students. I was offered two social work majors who would be assigned to assist me which would go towards their required hours of work experience.

I couldn't believe my luck and yet I had to remind them, "But I'm not registered as a non-profit organization." I figured that would shut me out for sure but it didn't seem to matter.

To my delight, she replied, "What you are doing is wonderful. And I think we can help you and our social work majors at the same time."

It seems that I qualified for the program based solely on what I had achieved in less than two months. I had indeed been busier than I realized since taking a break from my Tea Party and Prop. 2 1/2. True to their word, the college sent me two bright-eyed students who showed up at my door as excited as I was to get to work with my street kids.

As Chairwoman and founder of the North Agawam Youth Council, I was soon able to sponsor the Building Renovation Committee, Boys Club, and Recreation Center Studies with the Agawam Town Council's approval. I also petitioned successfully for the hiring of beat cops in those neighborhoods reporting vandalism by street kids throughout the town.

Up until this point, I had no reason to suspect the Mafia held sway over our police department. Heck, I'd always looked to police for protection. But this was Agawam and even though my father had to have seen what I was doing, he said nothing.

I had no one to take into my confidence and I wasn't sure I needed to just yet. Looking back, I should've suspected something was amiss when I lived on High Street and some well-meaning neighbors warned me the police knew about the drug trafficking yet did nothing about it.

The more I got to know the kids, the more I suspected they just couldn't be working alone. "If they couldn't figure out how to run a car wash," I thought to myself, "how the heck could they pull off a drug running racket so sophisticated that even the police left them alone?"

Two things happened right after my chat with the police officer at the car wash fundraiser that convinced me I was right about the police.

Surveillance incognito

I'd just come home from work one day to find my house had been broken into. I didn't have much but I was suspicious that my new television and record player weren't stolen. In fact, all that the thieves took was my full-length rabbit fur coat. What the heck, I thought.

I didn't say a word to my street kids. Instead, I quietly mentioned the break-in to the police to see what they would do. I only asked that they try to find the thief so I could get my coat back. I suspected it had to be one of my street kids but I didn't want them, I wanted their boss.

There was a story here and it didn't help that I was starting to regain some memories of my earlier run-in with the Springfield mob. It was only bits and pieces, but it was enough to make me suspicious and watch my back.

"Those kids wouldn't steal from you Mom," my son tried to reason. "They look up to you and trust you. I know, 'cause that's the word on the streets."

"Not unless someone ordered one of the kids to break in," I thought to myself, "and do something that had nothing to do with stealing anything either."

I didn't have long to wait to hear back from the police about my coat. Sure enough, a police officer showed up the next day with my fur coat in hand while refusing to tell me how they got it.

"But I don't understand how you found my coat," I told the officer. "How can you not know who broke into my house if you found the one who stole my coat?"

"You got your coat back and leave it at that," the officer said gruffly, as he thrust the coat into my open arms and walked out the door without saying another word.

After the police officer had left, I couldn't help but think about his strange response to the theft of my rabbit fur coat. I'd had a lot on mind at the time so that's the only reason I can come up with today as to how I could've missed the obvious signs.

For the sake of this whodunit, we must consider another reason for the break-in. Is it possible that whoever was behind the street gang might've ordered one of the kids to get in my home to do a job for them? And do it without anyone being any the wiser for it too?

At the time, it hadn't dawned on me it might've actually been a fake break-in just to give one of the kids a chance to plant some listening device in my home or phone. Who knows? I hadn't a clue at the time nor the sense to suspect anything either.

Looking back, it does kind of make sense given all the issues like those discussed in Chapter 10, which I would eventually have with illegal surveillance, unmasking and leaking of my every move and that of my informants as well.

Knowing what I know today, I think we can add another clue here for our whodunit. The police officer's response begs the question, what if the kid who broke into my home messed up.

In other words, what if the kid was supposed to quietly get in and get out and not touch anything except what he was told to do? Yes that would make sense. But what if the kid simply couldn't resist my fur coat and decided to grab it on his way out the door?

Even though the mysterious break-in should have been a red flag making me nervous enough to back off and stop what I was doing with the street kids, it didn't. I didn't back off even when the town council unexpectedly began withdrawing their support for my youth project.

As for council meetings that I'd been addressing on behalf of our youth projects, it was getting real ugly after the fake break-in. Seeing it as my only protection from an unseen enemy, I did anything I could to get media coverage. Up until the fake break-in, I'd been portrayed as a local hero working with street kids.

In the meantime, more memories of my run-in with the mob were slowly coming back. But it wasn't until I suddenly found myself being vilified in the media, by some of the more vocal council members, that I figured I was annoying someone--but who?

Someone was giving orders and I suddenly felt like I had a target on my back. The media had even started backing off from its coverage of me. There was that dark feeling again.

Surviving a home invasion

I was awakened from my sleep to find one of the older boys in the street gang leaning over me with a knife in his hand. I didn't scream. I didn't move. Despite the fear of the moment, I felt a calming spirit come upon me and I did not scream out. Staying calm probably saved my life.

Finally, when the boy said nothing, I simply asked, "What are you doing?"

"I knew this boy," I thought to myself, "he never came across violent around me, yet here he was holding a knife over me." Only seventeen, this man-child seemed startled at my calm reaction to him. I figured he had to be under the influence of drugs otherwise he wouldn't have done that to me. His eyes were glazed and he seemed incoherent as he mumbled the words I have never forgotten.

"I just wanna feel my knife twist inside your guts."

Whoosh. I didn't want to hear that. But the boy had said it. And I knew I had to do something to change his mind real quick. Recalling my response that night, I can't say enough about the importance of saying prayers before going to bed. Else, how could I have known what to do?

"How did you get in here?" I calmly blurted out without thinking and still half asleep.

That must've gotten his mind off of me, just long enough to distract him, because he sure looked surprised that I'd even ask such a question. He could've plunged the knife into my gut at any moment, instead he just stared at me while leaning over me holding firmly onto that knife.

What seemed like an eternity, lowering his knife ever so slowly, he surprised me when he answered, "I used my knife to cut through your back screen door and then broke one of the glass panes in your door so I could unlock it...then I just walked in."

The memory of it is as vivid today as it was the night it happened. Looking back, I don't know why my life has been

141

spared so many times, but I praised the God who rescued me from those who have sought my life through the years.

As if by some miracle, which to this day I still cannot explain, I watched as the troubled boy seemed to come to his senses long enough for me to ask him if we could go downstairs and talk. My ten year old son was in the next bedroom and I didn't want this to bring him into harm's way.

Incredibly, the boy still holding onto his knife, actually stood up and gestured for me to lead the way. We went downstairs to the living room where I sat down on the sofa and watched as he paced back and forth keeping an eye on me the entire time.

Not knowing what else to do at this point, I felt the Spirit prompt me to ask, "Can we pray?"

He was stunned. "You want to pray with me?"

"Yes. And you know why, don't you?" I asked ever so careful trying not to do anything to set him off. I had the sense to know he was under the influence of drugs but I wasn't sure if he could feel the influence of the Holy Ghost. So I waited.

I watched as he closed his eyes for a brief second as if thinking "what is this woman doing?"

When he didn't say shut up, I began praying out loud and he soon stopped pacing. How many times had I simply prayed out loud when I was in a similar situation like this before, and it worked? "Why not now?" I thought.

When I finished praying, I asked him if he needed to rest awhile before going home. As if by some miraculous healing to the boy, it was as if nothing had ever happened. Just moments before he'd broken into my home, he seemed bent on killing me, and here we were talking like mother and son.

He was still holding onto the knife, when I decided to make my move. I slowly got up from the couch and walked toward the front door. When he didn't try to stop me, I opened the door ever so slowly.

"I'm okay now," he said. "I gotta get home." And he walked out the door just as if nothing had happened.

But something happened to me that night - something that made me more afraid than facing an armed intruder in the dead of night. I began remembering again. Waking up the next day I woke up to more than the memories of the night before. I awakened to the memory of why I ever left Massachusetts in 1972.

I started having flashbacks of the night my boss Victor DeCaro disappeared. I suddenly found myself thinking the unthinkable. Had the same mobsters behind his disappearance decided to finally finish me off like they did with Victor?

"Merciful God," I thought to myself, "is it true that I am right back in Agawam—the very place I promised the Genovese family never to set foot ever again?"

For those participating in the whodunit, now might be a good time to ask who sent the boy to kill me, but he wasn't talking. And so, we continue our journey into the dark world of organized crime inside its Agawam faction to find out who sent this boy to kill me so we can get some idea of who was behind everything else.

Time to wake up!

"I can give him a good life," Al said, staring deep into my eyes.

"But why now after all these years do you suddenly want to adopt our son?" I asked genuinely wanting to know. "Is it because of what happened the other night?"

I didn't have to tell Al about the home invasion and attempted murder on my life by one of my street kids. Al always had a way of knowing things even before the police did.

Didn't Al know about his mobster friend Gary Dube's assassination even before his bullet-riddled body turned up in the river weeks after he was taken out by the Springfield mob?

Yes. I was sure Al knew who had sent the boy to kill me too. But like everyone else in my family, Al wasn't talking and like all the others, he took this to the grave too. The conversation that day went something like this.

"You got a lot of stuff going on around here Elaine," Al was quick to remind me.

"So you know what happened with the break-in the other night and you think our son isn't safe with me anymore, is that it Al?"

"They'll try again and I may not be around the next time. You've got to think of the boy now." He warned. "Let the boy come with me Elaine," Al kept insisting, but as always, it sounded more like an order, or in this case, an offer I couldn't refuse. He wanted to adopt our son and until I came along no one ever said no to Al.

"And you think you can keep him safer than I can?" I argued as I thought of all the times God had rescued me when no one else could.

"You don't know what you're talking about Elaine. Think about what you're doing," Al said as he walked toward the door to leave.

"Sure. I didn't know everything behind my troubles," I thought to myself, "but really, could Al keep anyone alive better than God Himself had done for me so far?"

Al had always been a man of few words. But I knew he loved our son. I'd only been aware of one other out-of-wedlock son he had with another love interest while I was in California. I really believed Al when he said he wanted to raise our son and I admired him for wanting to do that, but I had to turn him down.

The problem for me was that Al was still married and that alone remained a mystery to me. He never spoke of it ever. All I knew about Al was what I heard on the streets--he was a bodyguard for some mobster in the Springfield Crew. He was Big Al, and I just couldn't picture him ready to be a full-time father.

After Al left, I had time to reflect on his offer. And yet, there was another "boy" Al never mentioned--the boy who tried to kill me. A mere boy, just a few years older than our own son. A boy willing to take a life most likely to become a made member of a family he believed cared more about him than his own parents ever could. But I'll never know.

It was enough to know how organized crime figures used kids like him to run drugs and then let them work their way up in the family by becoming a made member after killing someone for them.

"My boy, our son, was safe by the grace of God," I thought to myself, "but what would've happened to that other boy if I had turned him in and gone public with the home invasion?"

Even though it all happened before I ever thought about running for office on the Agawam Town Council, I was still a public figure making news with my Tea Party and Prop. 2 ½. Looking back on it today, maybe I should have gone public with it, but I didn't.

Even now all these years later, there's the question of the botched criminal investigation into my boss Victor DeCaro's own mob assassination in '72. I am not forgetting how no one called me in for questioning despite everyone knowing I was the only eye-witness to the crime of his murder. I figure that must have been on the back of mind or else why didn't I go public with the home invasion incident?

It's no secret that the mob protects its own and silences anyone who gets in their way. And besides, say the boy had succeeded and really killed me. Does anyone think he would ever have been charged by the Agawam police if he had been ordered to kill me by someone in the Springfield Crew's own Agawam resident mobsters as I had always suspicioned? If the Genovese family wanted me out of the way, what better opportunity?

In Agawam, I've always suspected that my murder would have been the perfect crime given how the law handled the cover-up of DeCaro's murder. And, the Agawam police? What good is a whodunit without more villains? Don't worry. I leave plenty of clues to this crime scene when you get to Chapters 9 and 10. Keep taking good notes!

As for the teenage waif, the boy who laid down his weapon after I prayed with him and he let me live, I never said anything to anyone. I kept quiet mainly because I wanted to keep my word to the boy that I would never speak of it if he walked away. But I probably had another reason for keeping quiet.

I didn't need whoever sent that boy to harm me coming after me. I didn't want to go there again. Nope. I wasn't going to the police for the same reason I never did when I was witness to Victor's assassination.

In the meantime, unknown to me there was another Big Al running loose in Agawam and he wasn't in love with me. Just the opposite.

The other Big Al's home invasions

Since I'd experienced a frightening home invasion myself, I was curious while writing this memoir and decided to see if any of the Agawam mobsters had a history of home invasions. I found the Feds report online for the 1991 shoot-out involving Big Al Bruno's family in their barn in Agawam. But what about the '70's? Bingo! Agawam's resident mobster Big Al Bruno made the Feds list.

Interestingly, as reported by local mobologists, Agawam's Big Al Bruno was identified by the Feds as a known hit man who was himself behind home invasions in his earlier days in the mob. It was also reported how he drafted street kids into similar activities.

Reading like a real whodunit in Agawam, the clues get even better on the subject of home invasions and my own history with the mob. Take for example, the story of a soldier in the Genovese family named Anthony "Bingy" Arillotta.

As a youth once recruited by the mob, Bingy had been "running drugs, guns, scams, committing murders and other misdeeds virtually his entire life." This was reported, in one of a series of vignettes on the Springfield mob published on *masslive.com* by Stephanie Barry July 24, 2015. It was titled Greater Springfield mob, whatever happened to Arillota?

Does anyone remember when "Bingy" himself was once charged in another violent home invasion in 1993 in Springfield? According to Stephanie Barry's own report on organized crime, Bingy was even arrested in connection with "Big Al" Bruno's mob murder in 2010.

According to *Wikipedia*, it seems that Bruno (1945 – November 23, 2003) ran an organized crime operation in Springfield, Massachusetts and was even acquitted of attempted murder in an Agawam, Massachusetts shooting. As the story goes, Bruno shot convicted bookmaker Joseph Maruca in a barn owned by Bruno's brother Frank.

It's evident how **home invasions**, murder and running drugs could have all the elements of an ongoing crime scene operating under mobsters like "Skyball" and "Big Al" even in the little town of Agawam while I was living there. According to mobologists, Bingy was actually known to be Big Al Bruno's own protégé. Here's where the whodunit takes an interesting turn.

Although Bingy was only eleven years old when I survived one of my street kid's home invasion, why couldn't Big Al Bruno have also ordered another protégé of his, like one of my street kids, to kill me in a similar home invasion?

Everything about my life in Agawam after I returned from Texas begs the question of whether the Genovese's Springfield crew might've been operating covertly as an Agawam faction in a drug running racket with my street kids. Given everything I was stumbling into involving the police, town council and street kids, I felt like I was onto something at the time. As for Big Al Bruno, what was he doing?

Despite the memories that started coming back after I survived the kid's botched home invasion and I began suspecting who I was dealing with from my past, I still didn't know about Big Al Bruno running loose. Looking back, I thank God that I had the sense to wisely back off until I could come up with a plan. For all I knew, someone wanted me dead again, wasn't the mafiosa signature home invasion on my own life absolute proof?

Does the Mafia ever forgive and forget?

For mob fans familiar with the case of Bingy, I found it interesting, as did local mobologists who reported how the mobsters he crossed did forgive and forget and decided to let him live after he kept his nose clean for a while. Is this why the mob left me alone when I first returned to Agawam? Undoubtedly they were watching me and if the home invasion incident was any clue then someone most likely had decided I had worn out my welcome and along with it any hope of reconciliation with their boss.

According to one of Stephanie Barry's online organized crime updates on Bingy, rumors claimed that the city's so-called "new regime" had reconciled his potential return since Arillotta's testimony didn't cause trouble for any of them.

Barry's updates really work good for this whodunit don't they? After all, I didn't set out to intentionally or knowingly cause trouble for any of them in the Genovese family when I returned. Hadn't I kept my mouth shut like my father promised the family I would do if I was exiled to Texas? Thanks to the tick bite I did! So what if they didn't know I had lost my memory?

Looking back on it all today, I don't know whether I should thank that tick, or not, for infecting me with Lyme disease and giving me major memory time loss issues the way it did.

Heck, maybe that tick actually saved my life so I could return to Agawam for whatever purpose the Lord had for me. One thing was for sure, had I remembered why I was in Texas in the first place, I would never have returned to Massachusetts!

Wanted by the Mob again!

Anytime you get in someone's face, it's sure to bring those very people back into your life. It seems I did just that when I innocently tried to rehabilitate some street kids. One home invasion and a botched attempt on my life, was enough to convince me I was a wanted woman again. But who was behind all this?

Making more decisions from my knees, I came up with a plan to save a town, the street kids, and stay alive doing it. The Town Council stood out like a beacon in the night. Clues, more like red flags, were popping up all over the town.

One thing led to another and it was soon evident, to me, the mob held sway over our town leaders and its police. Yes. Agawam had a mob problem! But I wasn't running from them this time! I was taking a stand and with God's help I truly believed I would survive!

Miraculously, I did live to see the year 1979. Despite everything, I was surprised to find myself organizing another campaign. This time it was for me--the candidate. All signs pointed to the Town Council and that's where I felt the Spirit leading me. I only had a few months to prepare, since the elections were to be held on November 6th.

Still struggling with health issues from the undiagnosed Lyme disease, I ignored Dr. Proulx's order to avoid stress. Actually, I was supposed to be resting up for the statewide Proposition 2 ½ campaign that I was involved with at the time. So, I prayed a lot those days.

"What are you doing now Elaine?" Al asked during one of his father-son visits.

"I don't know what you mean." I replied, knowing full well he knew what I was up to in Agawam.

"Think of our son," he pleaded. "You don't really believe you've got a shot at getting on the council, do you?"

"All I know Al, is that this is my only chance to find out what's really going on in this town."

I tried to ignore his question but I knew what he was thinking. Before they'd let me get on the council, they'd kill me for sure. I knew too much and I was becoming a liability to someone.

Over the next few weeks, I reviewed everything I had done since returning to Agawam. I was really impressed with myself. For someone sick and dying half the time, I did quite a lot of good for the community and I had unknowingly built up quite an impressive resume.

I even surprised myself that I was actually qualified to run and hold public office. Lacking any education beyond high school, my community service made up for it. It even included my recent petition to hire beat cops. Kind of ironic isn't it? Yeah. Well, what did I know at the time?

Thinking back on it today, this could be another clue in our whodunit. Why, for instance, would the Town Council, approve my petition for beat cops in neighborhoods troubled by street kids? Given the budget of a small town, it might not have been approved unless it served a higher purpose for those who were watching me.

Having my memory back, I couldn't shake the feeling that maybe someone wanted the beat cops on the street to keep a closer eye on my street kids instead of me. When you try cutting into someone's business like I'd been doing, it's never a good thing. Either way, beat cops were hired thanks to my petition and it looked real good on my first and only campaign ad for my run on the town council.

I had my resume to put out to the community and the next thing was to enlist some volunteers to help me make campaign yard signs and get out fliers to the voters.

"You're gonna need more help than just me Mom," my son reminded me one day. "I got a lot going on after school."

"I know, don't worry I'll work out something," I answered.

No one had to remind me that I was still a single working mother with no budget for a campaign. I figured if I was to have any chance of winning an election in this town, I should make a city-wide run instead of a precinct. I decided to make my own signs and fliers. But I was going to need help.

Street kids volunteer

"What do you think about me making a run for the town council?" I asked the boys during one of our meet-ups.

"You sure you want to get mixed up with any of them the way they been treating you lately?" one of the older boys asked, showing genuine concern for me.

I knew what he was thinking. It was getting real ugly every time I approached the council over the past couple of months. Our town fathers had turned on me alright and it hadn't gone unnoticed by the boys.

These kids were street smart and I always made sure not to mention anything around them that I didn't want getting back to the mob. For now, my plan was to let everyone think I was still in the dark and not suspecting anyone was still after me.

"You're gonna need help making those signs." One of the younger boys surprised me when I mentioned my plan for putting out yard signs.

"Sure. Why not?" another boy volunteered while looking around to feel out the group.

The next thing I knew they were actually advising me on what materials I should get and even where to buy them at the best price. I was more impressed with how they were willing to knock on doors handing out my campaign fliers.

Given how this was a last minute throw together city-wide campaign, I'd been worried how I would get my message out through direct voter contact. I welcomed their help. Hey. What can I say? I was desperate! I couldn't risk having innocent locals walk the streets for me but I figured if what I thought was true about the street gangs, then the mob behind my problems wouldn't do anything to their own boys.

"What if someone asks us questions about you when we're going door to door?" one of the boys asked who volunteered to hand out fliers.

"Well, if they do," I replied, "just ask them to call me."

I wasn't sure what the boys might say. In their eagerness to get me elected, I feared they might get too pushy and scare off some voters. I may have been working with the kids for only a few months, but they definitely still were not rehabilitated as much as I would have liked.

"You sure got a lot of stuff to make plenty of signs," one of the boys said, as they made ready to put signs together for me.

We spent an entire afternoon working on the yard signs. I was pleasantly surprised to see the expertise these boys used especially in the spray painting. I didn't want to know where they had gotten the experience. I was just glad for the help.

I had lots of offers throughout the town to let us place signs in yards and I even got offers to put up a couple of my homemade billboards after yard signs started disappearing. To my surprise, a big supporter of mine, Charlie Avecci, volunteered for one of the billboards.

Charlie was a character indeed. He had a bone to pick with the town council and he loved me. I was his hero. He owned a farm and volunteered his horse drawn covered wagon he had used to deliver his eggs and other farm products.

He eagerly painted over the advertising on both sides of his wagon and turned it into a traveling campaign billboard for me. That was probably the best advertisement of my campaign. It was seen by voters every day as he traveled throughout the town of Agawam.

151

Not to be outdone by Charlie, another supporter of mine who also produced eggs in Agawam, came up with an idea for a hanging street billboard.

I had met Al Griffin of Springfield Street while organizing my Excise Tax Tea Party earlier in the year. He was a great patriot and I was thrilled when he contacted me with his idea for a billboard after he saw what Charlie was doing with his wagon.

Al Griffin and Mark Powers got together and painted my campaign slogan on a huge piece of wood they used for a billboard announcing, "Vote Bonavita Councilor-at-large". The billboard was strung up from Al's crane and they placed it in front of their home.

Now for me, that was great because it just happened to be on the busiest main street in Agawam. I don't think any traveler missed Al's billboard and it was the hit of my campaign among the voters!

Unfortunately, someone else saw our ingenious billboard and they didn't like it one bit. It didn't take long for Al Griffin to get a call from the town clerk Ed Caba ordering him to take down the signage immediately. It seems it was a violation of a local ordinance.

"We'll take it down Ed," I promised the town clerk, while indignantly insisting, "And I will win this election without it too." Those were my exact words and I've never forgotten it either.

We took it down. We had to, but it had been up nearly a week and it had done its job as far as I was concerned.

An unexpected whistle blower

It was the fall of '79 and I was wrapping up my campaign making ready for the town elections, when an incumbent councilor-at-large contacted me. His name was Floyd L. Landers and he was a feisty ole kind of guy that looked more like someone's overprotective grandparent.

As I recall, I was a bit suspicious of Floyd at first. Heck, I was understandably suspicious of anyone on the Agawam town council. So I was surprised when he approached me and asked to meet up with me somewhere private.

On our first rendezvous, Floyd mentioned how he saw I was in over my head right from the start when I came onto the Agawam political scene. To this day, I have never forgotten our talks. He seemed to be on a mission and always filled me in on the Who's Who of Agawam politicians.

The first time we met, he said how he saw something in me that reminded him of why he had originally wanted to get on the council. "I got on the council," Floyd told me, "so I could give something back to my community."

"Yes." I nodded in agreement, while asking a bit sarcastically, "Isn't that what everyone always says when they run for office?"

"I'm not here to discourage you," he replied. "I want to help you because I believe you can win this election."

Even the average voter knew Floyd's story. Isn't it really the same with most everyone who runs for any public office? In the November 1, 1979 issue of the Agawam Advertiser/News its publisher Rick Sardella wrote an editorial.

It was titled Council Elections – Lean Field, But Interesting:

"It seems that every two years the electorate is faced with making a decision on a variety of candidates who promise much but when the final tally is tabulated, much is lost in a mish-mash of controversy over the two year span."

Indeed history remembered Floyd kindly. In his obituary, printed October 19, 1979 by *The Daily News*, "Landers was recognized as an outspoken political veteran who usually took his own stand on controversial issues. He had served on the council since 1976."

At one time he was quoted in an interview as saying, "But it's been one of the most educational experiences I've had in politics."

In Floyd's obituary, he was also recognized for his sincere commitment wherever he lived in the many states throughout the country. "In nearly every community, he became involved in politics in some way and continued that interest in Agawam."

Reading through his obituary, I couldn't help but think how Floyd's ideals sounded much like my own. I guess Floyd saw that

153

in me too. But looking back, I don't think that was the reason he singled me out in all the field of rookie candidates that election year.

Floyd definitely knew something that he figured would most likely save my life, if I lived long enough to get on the council.

"Don't tell anyone about our meetings or me helping you," he often reminded me. "I get some things done on the council," he told me, "but I keep my mouth shut about what goes on behind closed doors."

The unmasking of Floyd

I got that dark feeling again when Floyd dragged me into his confidence the way he did. Yes. Floyd knew what I had walked into alright. I guess he wanted to pass on his legacy to me since he had already decided not to seek re-election. He saw me as his replacement I think. But what was his legacy? I had no way of knowing and so I had no choice but to take him at his word until I could figure out his game.

I agreed to Floyd's condition to keep our meetings secret. Looking back, I never thought out secret meetups were a matter of life or death for him or me. But here's where the whodunit takes a strange turn which makes it worth following very closely.

The question that still haunts me, today, is why Floyd ever thought no one would find out about our secret meetings? Obviously, Floyd knew it was dangerous to be seen talking to me because he even told me so. Poor Floyd, he desperately wanted me to know what I was up against and he was nervous as a mouse cornered by a cat.

For some reason, Floyd told me he didn't think I would survive in Agawam politics unless I fully understood who and what I was up against. Finally, I thought, I was going to put some names to those who wanted me dead.

It was right about that time that I thanked God I had my memory coming back. For if it had not, and had I not already known who the players in Agawam were before Floyd, I am sure I would've been scared by what that whistle blower was getting ready to lay on me.

"And you really think I can take your place on the council?" I asked Floyd one night hoping to get some encouragement to stay in the fight. Back then, Agawam politics was dirty as anything I've seen and taking them on alone, as I was doing, required a lot of faith.

"If you can fight off what they're going to throw at you, then yes I believe you can," he replied.

"What do you mean? What else could they possibly do to me before the election?" I asked.

He never got a chance to divulge everything that would get thrown at me over the next few months because Floyd died before he could tell me.

Floyd's death, just a few weeks before the elections, remains a mystery only because the cause of death was never investigated. I am partly to blame for that I guess.

While his obituary explained he died "after a brief illness," I never bought into that explanation. I didn't then, and still don't believe it today, only because of what Floyd told me right before he died. Until now, I have never spoken of it.

Even today, Floyd's death still haunts me. But I get ahead of myself again. In Chapter 8, I tell what really happened to Floyd only if his sacrifice may save more lives by somehow offering more clues for solving this whodunit.

The Good Aunt

Right after Floyd died I prayed to God for help. My mentor was gone. Like a Good Samaritan, taking me into his confidence the way he did, I figure Floyd probably saved my life.

Waiting in the shadows, was another Good Samaritan who came to me as if in answer to my prayers. She lived in Agawam and just happened to work in the town clerk's office.

She was my grandmother's niece, but we never got to see each other very much after I moved back from Texas. All the family lovingly called her JuJu as did I. So, I was surprised when Auntie JuJu pulled me aside one day while I was on town business in the town clerk's office. I had just announced my bid for election to the town council.

"I want you to take out an ad in the Agawam Advertiser/News," my auntie explained, as she stuffed enough cash into my hand to pay for an ad space measuring a fourth of a page.

"Thanks Auntie," I said as I testified to her how she was an answer to my prayers. Up until that moment, I had no money for an ad and I had been wondering how I could pull it off.

My auntie, who died just a few years ago, was a very religious and devout Catholic. She loved the Lord and I loved her for that. I have no doubt that she listened to the Spirit of the Lord and obeyed the prompting to give me the money for that ad like she did.

Working in the town clerk's office as she had been doing for years, she had to have known what I was getting myself into and she put herself out there for me. As it turned out, hers was the only newspaper ad I had ever taken out in my campaign.

Bonavita's ad placed in Agawam
Advertiser Nov 1, 1979

As I prayed about what to do for my one and only ad, I was inspired to go with a "wanted" theme. Thanks to Floyd, I had some idea of what my political enemies may have been plotting.

156

The police and the mob were up to something but I didn't have all the details. Floyd had died before he could tell me.

Ever praying, I recall how I had impressions of what to put in that political ad. I know it was from God, because of myself, I had no way of knowing what was lurking behind the scenes. Even now, after all these years, I can still have a good laugh on the boys in Agawam who had planned my political demise even before it got off the ground.

As memory serves me, the word WANTED, as in a fugitive from the law, just kept coming into my mind. I wasn't knowingly focused on any particular reason for using the WANTED theme for my campaign slogan. Who does that I thought? But for some crazy reason, I had the prompting and knew better than to ignore it. And besides, I think it was something that Floyd Landers had mentioned to me the last night I saw him alive.

"Wait Floyd, you didn't tell me about the campaign," I remember calling out to him as he was walking out the door.

"I gotta go. I'll talk to you later."

Wasn't it something about a "smear campaign" he tried to warn me about? Yes. That's exactly what Floyd had hinted of but never got a chance to finish telling me.

For anyone working this whodunit, you might want to keep track of all the characters who were behind all my troubles mentioned in this memoir. Who might've suspected Floyd had lived long enough to tell me what they were up to after seeing my *Wanted* ad in the newspaper?

Since I hadn't a clue at the time, I just assumed Floyd's warning had to have hinted of a corrupted political machine attempting to determine the outcome of Agawam's upcoming election. But since that was common to most communities with political machines, I wasn't worried.

Yep. I had no idea of any other plan by the mob involving me personally. I just knew I was wanted for something thanks to that inspired prompting from the Lord and I figured it was for all my good deeds that had incredibly qualified me for the town council. Boy, was I ever in for a big surprise!

CHAPTER EIGHT:
AGAWAM COUNCIL ELECTIONS

"Hey. That's us!" exclaimed my friend Dr. Proulx.

"I can't believe it!" I said in hushed tones so as not to be overheard.

"What are you whispering for Elaine?" Doc asked me. "You won and you should be shouting it to all the world!"

It was the night we had all anticipated and some of my supporters were hanging around town hall awaiting the council election results to come in when the town clerk announced the top three winners in the at-large council race.

"There's your name Bonavita," someone shouted out.

And there it was alright-- my name in black and white right up there with the three open slots for the at-large council seat I had prayed to win. It was close though.

Deforge ....3,958 at large	**Agawam Town Councilor**
Cincotta 3,160	**Election Results**
Bonavita 2,786 1979	*The Daily News*, Nov 7,

Candido 2,667

To this day some might say I had pulled off a miracle. Others might say the mob had something to do with it. Whatever it was, back then all I knew was that I had just barely beaten the political machine's own handpicked candidate Dominic J. Candido. I naturally figured the Lord had a lot to do with it. What did I know?

When a reporter from *The Daily News* flashed his camera right at the moment we started cheering and shouting hooray, it dawned on me that we hadn't thanked God for pulling off such a miracle. And so, right there in the lobby, we all stopped and took a moment to say a quiet prayer giving thanks to the Lord.

Political pundits all agreed it was the biggest political upset in the area and the media agreed. *The Daily News* even surprised everyone when it ran the little insignificant town of Agawam's election results on its front page.

The Daily News Nov 7, 1979: CHEERS FOR THE WINNER. Elaine Bonavita with her father Peter Bonavita is cheered by supporters with Dr. Roger Proulx in the background.

Besides my own election victory, several mayors in the area had won elections too, but to my amazement, it was the photo of me with my father and Dr. Roger Proulx that made the front page the next day.

The Daily News story by Carol Shultz, that featured my victory in its November 7, 1979 issue, sure did echo the excitement that swept through our community as did her front page headline, titled <u>Need for New Blood</u>. The story read in part:

"A surprise victory in the at-large council race went to Elaine Bonavita, who came in for a close third with 2,786 votes. She upset political newcomer Dominic Candido, heavily backed by some of the town's most influential members. Candido received 2, 667 votes. Ms. Bonavita,

159

a strong advocate of youth recreation centers, will be sworn in tonight to replace former Councilor Floyd Landers, who died last month."

As reported in *The Daily News*, and as if in fulfillment of Floyd Landers' dying wish, I found myself being sworn in the next day to fill his vacant seat on the council. Looking back, I remember it like it was just yesterday. This is not my story; it's Floyd's. I tell it to honor him, so that after all these years the real story can finally be told of why I ended up taking his place on the council.

New blood needed on the council or Floyd's blood?

Like everything else I witnessed, I never talked about the mystery surrounding Floyd's death to anyone except my beloved Big Al. Still, it begs the question even today. Was Floyd's death a homicide, and if so was it ordered by the mob?

There's nothing wrong with my memory today and I recall Floyd's story vividly. In fact, I couldn't think of anything else once I'd been sworn into office and replaced Floyd on the town council.

"What's the matter with you?" I remember Al warning me when I stupidly brought up Floyd's death. "Don't talk like that, it could get you killed."

"You know no one just ups and dies like that right after being warned never to talk to me again."

Knowing Al the way I did, I really didn't expect any answer from him. But he never denied what I suspicioned about Floyd's death either. After Al went home, I couldn't stop thinking about Floyd. Why did he contact me right after publicly announcing he wouldn't be seeking re-election to the council? Why me?

Up until I was seated on the council, I hadn't talked to Al about my suspicions involving Floyd's mysterious death the previous month. But for some reason, I couldn't dismiss what I was feeling every time I attended one of my town council meetings. It was as if the dead could really talk. More like something kept telling me not to forget Floyd's last words—the last words he ever spoke to me that sent chills up my spine and that I've never forgotten.

Surveilled and unmasked

"I've been warned," Floyd said. "They know I've been talking to you and they warned me not to come around here anymore. They said it would be my last time if I did."

"What do you mean?"

"I mean they'd make sure I never talked to anyone again."

"Okay. But who are *they* that threatened you?" I asked as if I didn't know. I began suspecting it was the mob but I wanted names from him.

Looking at me like I was an idiot, he blurted out, "It's best you don't know. It's for your own safety."

"Then why are you here now and why are you risking your life telling me this?"

I needed to know so I couldn't help asking. I was still hoping to get a name out of him.

"Because I believe in what you're doing," he finally explained. "And besides, I don't think they'll really kill me. I think they're just trying to scare me to stay away from you."

"I don't think so Floyd," I answered, while fighting off the temptation to tell him my own story of what had been happening around me in Agawam. But I bet he already knew. That's probably why he trusted me the way he did. He knew I could keep my mouth shut.

That's the burning question that stuck in my mind as I sat on the council in Floyd's place. If memory serves me right, Floyd was anxious about something and he wanted to warn me *before* the November elections. Like everyone else, I too had read *The Daily News* story about Floyd's announcement that "he would not run in the November election. He cited health problems and a business interest he wanted to pursue."

Yes. Floyd had plans to get out alright. According to him, those plans included me taking his place on the council. I guess that's why I never doubted he wanted to clear his conscious before anything happened to him. But after listening to him, I realized it wasn't his health that he was worried about. Was that the real reason behind why he wanted off the council?

Up until my talks with Floyd, I didn't have a clue what was going on behind closed doors involving council business or inside the town hall. Sure, I had my suspicions about the police but nothing more than that. Naturally, I wanted names of who had warned him, wouldn't anyone?

I never doubted Floyd knew. But he was dead and I didn't want to be next. I may have replaced him on the council, but I didn't want to follow him in death too! I was in over my head and one thing I knew for certain, I needed to more careful than Floyd had been.

I just assumed Floyd had to know what he was doing seeing as how he'd been on the council nearly two years. I guess he didn't know though, given how his career as a whistleblower sure didn't last long. I still recall his last parting words the last night I saw Floyd alive.

"Be careful Floyd," I told him, as he prepared to sneak away and disappear into the dark of night hoping no one would see him.

"Don't worry kid, I'll be okay," he said half joking, in a worried kind of way.

I watched as Floyd walked down the street and got into his car wondering if I'd ever see him again. Looking back, I wonder if Floyd ever knew about Agawam's own resident mobster Al Bruno who had been living right down the road from me.

The prodigal witness returns

Anytime I heard someone mention the name "Big Al" around me in Agawam, I always just assumed it was my Big Al, my son's father. Heck, how could I have known it was really Big Al Bruno who was my neighbor?

And I sure didn't know about Bruno's very own reputed partner in crime, Francesco "Skyball" Scibelli, who died in 2000 but was very much alive at the age of 67, when I returned to Agawam in '78.

By all the organized crime reports I searched online, Skyball was in line to become boss of the powerful Genovese family crew in Greater Springfield and eventually did take over as family boss after the death of "Big Nose Sam" in 1983. And wasn't it Skyball who had bumped off my boss, who I'd been running from in the mob all those years as a star witness?

162

These are great clues for our whodunit which begs the question, was it Floyd they'd been watching or me the witness? It had to be me, or else how could they have known about our secret talks at my place all the time? Only now, do I dare ask if my coming back to Agawam had actually gotten Floyd killed?

It had to be me and not Floyd that was on someone's watch list. Hadn't I violated the terms of reconciliation with the Genovese family? I did if by innocently returning to Massachusetts. To make matters worse for myself, how might they have reacted when I began nosing around the town they allegedly ran?

Today I know, but back then I was totally ignorant of the fact that they knew I knew who they were. Sounds kind of crazy, but thanks to my crazy cousin Gina who just had to have that affair with Skyball's son-in-law, and that doggone tick in Texas, I was walking around with a target on my back. But what about Floyd? What was his story?

I had just gotten home from the work the next day after meeting up with Floyd. The phone was ringing and there was that dark feeling.

"You'd better get over to the hospital right away."

"Why? What's going on?"

I will never forget that day when I got the call telling me that Councilor Floyd Landers was in the hospital and not expected to make it. If I wanted to see him, I had to hurry they said.

"What could have happened?" I asked myself. "He was healthy and alert when he left our meeting the night before. And now, only hours later he lay comatose in a hospital bed?"

I pulled myself together and rushed over to the hospital. I had to see what they had done to poor Floyd. He died but I had gotten to see him before he did. Flashbacks of another night in 1972 when I was the last person to see my boss Victor alive should've been racing through my mind, but it wasn't. I really couldn't remember.

I guess that's why I had such a crazy thought while gazing down on Floyd, as he lay comatose in his hospital bed. Every bone in my body had screamed it was the work of the mob. I tried to shake off that dark feeling as I left the hospital.

After I'd had time to digest what had happened to Floyd, I tried to convince myself that maybe he had really died of natural causes. Hadn't *The Daily News* reported he wasn't seeking re-election due to health issues? But that didn't work for me because I, and I alone, knew that Floyd had been warned not to talk to me anymore and when he did he ended up dying in the hospital.

Back then all I had were my suspicions and nothing more. But today I do have more. Who can forget the bullet-riddled bodies of my boss Victor and my friend Gary Dube, that had been pulled from the Connecticut River and my Dad and son's father knew about it even before it was reported? Weren't those mob killings out of Agawam?

Could the same mobsters that had exiled me to Texas afford to bring attention to themselves by killing another Agawam resident the same way? Nope. I figure a signature crime was not to the mob's advantage in that situation. Heck, what would that say about Agawam if the mob went around putting bullets in its politicians like Floyd?

Luckily, I got some answers to this question when I did some research online into some other murders in Agawam while I was on the town council. But I get ahead of myself. You can read about it in Chapter 10.

According to the Feds, the Mafia won't kill politicians like Floyd unless he was in bed with them. In November 23, 2013, Anthony Summers and Robbyn Swan reported on this Mafia code in an online article, titled <u>The claims that Mafia bosses Trafficante and Marcello admitted involvement in assassinating President Kennedy</u>. The following is an excerpt:

> "The Mob typically doesn't hit prosecutors or politicians," said former House Assassinations Committee chief counsel Robert Blakey. "You are all right....just as long as you do not `sleep with them,' that is, you do not take favors, either money or sex. Once the public official crosses the line, he invites violent retribution."

Even though I kept my silence after Floyd had died so mysteriously, I wanted to break my silence today in honor of

Floyd who reminded me so much of Mario Facione who had also chosen to walk away from the mob when he was just an associate in the Detroit crime family.

Which brings us back to the question--Was Floyd the victim of the mob's retribution? It's quite possible if he crossed them isn't it? And if he didn't cross them, then why would anyone bother to warn him to stop talking to me?

The fake affair

In Floyd's memory, I felt it my duty to keep serving the people just as he had hoped I would do and valiantly stand up to anyone who stood in my way. The election never haunted me, as much as Floyd's death, only because I had yet to know whether my father had intervened to save my life again. I hadn't suspected any foul play by the mob until years later when my crazy cousin Gina confessed the real story behind my election.

Speaking of confessions, I must confess something else behind Floyd's mysterious death. It's another clue that can help readers figure out this whodunit. It's true Floyd was married and even though we did not have an affair, it became evident his wife suspected we did.

I will never forget what happened the day I attended his wake. I was kneeling in front of the coffin where Floyd laid in repose. No sooner had I knelt down when Floyd's wife shot out of her chair, nearly knocking me over throwing herself on his coffin, and crying aloud in a feigned grief.

"What do you do with that?" I thought to myself, as I walked away from the coffin more embarrassed for her than me. I knew she was grieving, but there was something else going on there alright.

"What brought that on?" I asked a friend who, unlike me, had already figured it out and whispered it in my ear.

"Seriously? She thinks we were having an affair?" I asked, while trying to keep my voice down. "An affair?" I repeated. To which my friend nodded in the affirmative.

Sitting in the funeral home watching the parade of mourners viewing Floyd for the last time, I silently prayed to make sense of what just happened with his wife. "Was that their plan all along?" I thought to myself.

Why not? They make the wife think we're having an affair and get her to make him stop seeing me. Wouldn't that have solved the problem, and no one would've had to die?"

Sadly, there was no inquiry into Floyd's death and I regret I didn't call for one after I'd gotten on the council. But looking back, what good would it have done? The Agawam police were part of the problem and you can read about it in Chapter 9. And besides, if there was no investigation into Victor's own assassination back in 1972, why would I think anything would've come from my calling out Floyd's murder too?

As for the embarrassing scene at his wake, it still haunts me to this day because I figured if we were being watched, which Floyd said he was, then those doing the watching knew very well that we weren't having an affair. So, why did his wife suspect it, unless such a rumor was planted intentionally?

As for Floyd taking his wife into his confidence about our secret meetings, he was smarter than that. As for the warnings he'd gotten, I figured no one really wanted old Floyd dead. For this reason alone, I had to believe they hoped his wife would get on Floyd's case just enough to make him stop talking to me. But if that was their original plan, it didn't work.

For whatever reason, he didn't take the bait, or he wanted to let his wife think we were having an affair. Crazy? Not really. If she knew about Floyd's crossing the mob, wouldn't she become a liability, just as he had become to them?

We only have to look online to know that there have been politicians, even prosecutors, who got in the mob's way, often times been murdered along with their wives.

I had a lot on my mind as I was leaving the funeral home. I wanted to believe, with all my heart, Floyd would rather have his wife think we were having an affair, if only to keep her safe. But he never spoke of it to me, and I will never know for sure.

Will we ever know whether or not Floyd had become a liability that someone in Agawam could no longer control and had to eliminate? And were they simply forced to plug the leak in their crime organization as they are known to do?

166

Before anyone accuses me of being paranoid as to believe anyone might've actually killed Floyd, much less be proof of a mob presence in Agawam, hold your opinion until you read about my other informants in Chapter 10. Each of them all met the same fate as Floyd did.

The leak wasn't plugged

As for the other two incumbent at-large councilmen on the '79 ballot with me, Stephen R. Cincotta and Robert R. DeForge, both were easily re-elected. I have no doubt Floyd would have too, but for some reason he didn't want to stay in. He took his story to his grave.

With Floyd's at-large seat left vacant by his death, it paved the way for me to be sworn in immediately to take his place. With Floyd gone, I didn't have a mentor anymore. Who would show me the ropes and keep me alive, so I could do my job serving the people instead of the mob? I promised Floyd I would do that didn't I? Looking back, I guess poor Floyd thought he'd be around to counsel me in his stead.

Ask and ye shall receive. I believed in that promise of the Lord and so I prayed like never before. Like so many times before whenever I prayed, angels showed up. And that's how I met Anita.

In 1975, she was the first woman ever elected to the town council, at least before I came along. Anita M. Davilli, who died in 2007, contacted me soon after winning my own council seat.

Similar to Anita's claim to fame, I too, was once again the only woman on the council, only I had set a precedent as the first woman ever elected to an at-large seat which meant I was elected citywide.

Sadly, for the people of Agawam, Anita was defeated in her re-election bid by Frederick Nardi in the 1977 Precinct One council elections. Normally, good people like Anita don't last long in politics unless you play ball with the big boys. And I couldn't envision Anita doing that.

I'd heard she was a champion of the people serving on the council and I noticed she still continued to attend and speak at council meetings long after she lost her bid for re-election.

167

As for Anita, she was 56 years old when I met her, and while she could've been my mother, she soon became more like a mentor to me right after Floyd's death.

After I was sworn into office, Anita tutored me in the dos and don'ts just as Floyd himself might have done if he'd still been alive. Of course, Anita didn't know about me and Floyd. No one did. Well, no one except for those who warned him to stay away from me, I guess.

So, all Anita knew was what the media reported on Floyd's death and nothing more. I didn't want to get her killed and I figured she was better off with my not bringing her into my confidence.

Heck, I never even confided in my own father about Floyd. Thinking back, maybe I should have. I might've avoided what I ended up walking into but Dad wasn't talking to me those days.

I sure did appreciate having Anita for a friend. I still recall how excited she'd been about my surprise upset election, even weeks later when the subject came up again. Numerous theories were floated around town as to how I could've upset the political machine the way I did.

As for Anita, she never let anyone forget it either. Like most political junkies in Agawam, Anita had her own theory about my unexpected victory. Some memories never fade. Our conversation went something like this…

The fix is in

"Everyone's still talking about what Joe pulled off with Nardi," I remember Anita saying, while visiting with me one day. "Haven't you wondered what really happened?"

"What are you getting at?" I asked, hoping to get some answers. I'd already been suspicious of why a kid like Joe Rolland, or anyone in town, would risk going up against a powerful politician like Fred Nardi. There was a story there for sure.

"I really didn't think you would win either," Anita admitted. "No one did!"

"Well, it sure wasn't a well-funded campaign that put me over the top," I said, not wanting to get into any discussion after Floyd.

"You know Anita, I had no money to get my name out there. Maybe it was my *family* name," I coyly suggested, waiting to see her reaction. But Anita didn't do mob talk with me like Floyd did.

"You don't know the power Nardi has in this town," she went on to explain. "He has a voting block that guarantees him, or anyone he backs, a seat on the council. So what you and Joe did was a surprise upset alright."

"So you think the voters just happened to pull this off now, even though they couldn't do it to re-elect you, an incumbent who was popular with the voters?"

I hoped she might've had some insight as to why a kid like Joe and me both with no political experience and new in town, could do what she couldn't do herself. Nardi ran up against her in 1977 and she lost to him. So why didn't Joe?

The Mafia "thought" they had a deal with me

"Hey cousin, whatcha doing?" I texted Gina while writing this memoir and glad I still had her phone number.

I knew my cousin had always been real close to my father. For some reason he favored her over me and I never knew why. I guess that's probably why she had been so excited about my campaign and offered to help. Maybe Dad wanted her to keep an eye on me for him.

Wanting some answers for my real time whodunit, I thought Gina might have some thoughts about why I won the election like I did, and boy, did she ever! Here is the actual text message conversation I saved on my cell phone to use for this chapter:

> *My text to Gina*: "You were in Agawam with me in 1979 when I won the council election remember?"

> *Gina's text reply*: "Yes, but you don't believe the reason you won."

> *My reply*: "Why do you think I won? Did Big Al Bruno and Dad help me?"

169

Gina: "It was fixed, like most of what was done [in Agawam] and you won because they thought as your father's daughter they would have your vote on things they wanted. When they realized he couldn't influence you, they told him that they only had mercy on you because of the respect they had for him and that's why you ended up moving back to Texas again."

For starters, I never discussed with her why I moved out to Texas after her lover, my boss Victor was murdered. I sure didn't confide in her anymore after my election either.

Heck, I'd always assumed any mob business in the family was just between me and Dad. Besides, Gina never brought up the subject around me and I never bothered asking until writing this memoir.

Getting back to the reason for contacting Gina--Was my election rigged? According to my crazy cousin who had my father's confidence, yes it was. This was news to me!

Gina had jarred my memory with all her texting and it got me to thinking about some unusual things I noticed on Election Day, while handing out literature at my precinct polling location. Now as I look back after texting my cousin, it makes a whole lot more sense.

"Hi. I hope you'll vote for me Elaine Bonavita for town council." I said as I greeted the voters.

Using my best campaign face, I greeted the next voter approaching me. He was in his fifties, but I couldn't shake the feeling of how he reminded me of someone from my past.

Flashbacks were becoming more common lately and I bristled as the thought of guys packing guns and acting tough suddenly filled my mind.

I hesitated, but decided to ask for his vote anyway. When I handed him one of my handouts, his response surprised me. It is imprinted in my memory even today.

"Yeah, yeah. I know. You're Pete's kid," he said abruptly dismissing me, but not before he made sure to say "You got my vote."

I was met with similar responses throughout the rest of the day. As I checked several of them out, I thought to myself,

"Wouldn't this be great if it was happening all over town?" I started wondering how many of Dad's friends from the old days were still in Agawam.

I can't for the life of me figure out why it didn't register at the time. It sure did after texting my crazy cousin Gina. Didn't she say something about my election being "fixed?"

It begs the question then of who was really backing my election? More importantly, why if they wanted Floyd dead so he couldn't blow the whistle on them? Why want me on the council in his place? What did they think I would do? And that's where my crazy cousin Gina's confession is starting to make sense.

The deal made in proxy

I was troubled about something else that probably distracted me from Dad's buddies from the past. I had been keeping an eye on my strongest competition for an at-large council seat. It was Fred Nardi's hand-picked boy named Dominic Candido.

Everyone knew that my opponent Candido was backed by the town heavies—the political machine, Fred Nardi, etc. That's why I couldn't help wondering why Dad's buddies were suddenly supporting me right out in the open like they did on Election Day.

Sure they should've all been voting for Candido, unless someone had told them otherwise after talking with my father. And yet, do I dare believe Dad would have done such a thing? But didn't my crazy cousin Gina say so?

As so many other politicians have been known to do, even presidents including John F. Kennedy, it's not so hard to picture my own father brokering a similar deal with the Mafia. If Dad promised I would go along with the mob once before to save my life, couldn't he have done it again with my own election?

I couldn't think it at the time because thinking about it today and knowing how it turned out for President Kennedy and his own brother who were assassinated after inviting retribution by the mob, the thought was chilling.

Dad never said a word to me about the elections. But what happened after I got on the council convinced me someone had done something and no one had bothered to tell me.

Back then, I didn't have Gina to tell me what my father had done to get me elected. Looking back, I know I was truly inspired by the Holy Ghost to do what I did with my "wanted" ad. As it turned out, that one strange ad might've contributed to collateral in case I went rogue and unintentionally crossed the mob again.

My cousin might not have been so crazy, after all, with her disclosure of the election results. It all started making sense if my Dad knew what the mobsters whom I'd been running from were up to, like he did before when I witnessed my boss's murder.

Making deals, behind my back might have been getting to be a habit with Dad. I just wished he would have clued me in so I would have been able to stay one step ahead of the game. I can understand how he might've meant well if he planned it all to save my life again, but at what price?

What did my father promise this time in exchange for my life? I had survived that frightening home invasion a few months before I got on the council. Were they going to try again? If they meant to kill me, Dad would've known about it for sure.

Is it conceivable that my father would have dared to make a deal by convincing someone I would do their bidding if they put me in Candido's spot on the council? Dad's not alive to confirm it, but don't we have my crazy cousin's confession as proof?

I pray Dad never anticipated the danger he put me in by not telling me of the deal he made. As it was, is there any doubt today that I would inevitably invite the mob's retribution once I got on the council and started annoying them?

Wanted again!

"Mom, did you see this?" My 10 year old son came running into the house grabbing my hand, while holding onto the evening newspaper. "You better come in and sit down, it's not good."

"It's okay, son," as I took in the front page headline. "I expected something like this might come up once I started stirring things up on the council," I tried to assure him. "It's gonna be okay. Don't worry." But I was. I was real worried.

True to their code, the mob didn't waste any time coming after me. You can read more about it in Chapters 9 and 10.

172

Holding the newspaper my son had brought in, I slowly read the story that made breaking news on the illegal dissemination of my Arrest Record. It had been sent out to the media and every member on the town council had gotten a copy of it except me.

It seems that my past had gotten someone's attention before the elections but I didn't know about it at the time. I guess my "wanted" ad surprised the heck out of someone who had planned to blackmail me. Whatever my Dad did must've put it on pause. All I know is that right after I'd called for and gotten the resignation of our Town Manager, my Arrest Record was mailed out and that's how I found myself on the front page-- a *wanted* woman.

Just my luck, our town manager Peter Caputo must've been one of the mob's most valued associates in Agawam because someone apparently didn't like what I did at all and made sure I got the message!

To be fair, it's possible the mob thought I knew about their deal with Dad. But thanks to my father not bothering to mention it to me, it was soon apparent that the Agawam faction was operating under the misguided belief that I had sworn loyalty to protect and serve their interests, not the town.

In keeping with that line of thought, I guess it looked like I had crossed the line by taking out one of their associates and thereby had invited retribution. Leaking my arrest record was a good clue I'd made their wanted list again. But as with Floyd, they weren't so quick to come right out and kill me. This was the first warning. I guess I shouldn't have ignored it.

Who's behind it all?

Back then, I couldn't know about the other "Big Al" in Agawam, but today I do know.

To begin with, Adolfo "Big Al" Bruno reportedly was no stranger to gangland slayings. Based on his own and now very public criminal record, Big Al Bruno had killed a mobster named Antonio Facente in 1979 the same year I was elected to the Agawam town council and the same year my arrest record was leaked by someone in the mob.

173

Big Al Bruno, according to the Feds, managed to botch a gangland slaying in his own hometown of Agawam shortly after that too!

The Agawam Town Council and the mob

Getting back into real time with this whodunit, I looked up a persistent mobologist on *masslive.com* by the name of Stephanie Barry.

She piqued my interest when I came across an outdated spoiler alert of her next organized crime (OC) assignment, which popped up online under *The Republican* Editor's Note, announcing how the local mob landscape had changed in Greater Springfield. It seems there had been much speculation as to what had become of organized crime in the area, prompting Barry to publish a series of vignettes "on former and current players in Greater Springfield mob figures: **What ever happened to ...?"**

As a former publisher and newswoman myself, having published two conservative newspapers since being elected to the Agawam council, I know a thing or two about exposing corruption in government. I did it right up until my retirement after I moved back to Texas in 2011.

Like any good investigative journalist, I know about the news that doesn't make the news. Today it's called fake news, kind of like an interview Ms. Barry had once done for a local television program. In the video I pulled up online, she was defending her theory that the Mafia was inactive. And that's what gave me the idea to contact her while researching for this memoir.

It was personal for me at this point. I wanted to do it because of my own experience with the very mobsters she was writing about. I knew they just didn't go away over time as she wanted her audience to believe the Genovese crime family had done.

They'll never let go, no matter who dies or retires, even though times change the mob adjusts to those changes accordingly. Indeed, I really wanted to believe things changed in Agawam today, but thanks to what happened to me after I contacted *The Republican* and spoke with Ms. Barry herself, I know different now.

174

But I get ahead of myself. You can read about what happened to me after I got off the telephone with Ms. Barry in Chapter 16. It's not pretty, I can tell you that much!

For now, I'll only be introducing you to some of Barry's more interesting updates on my favorite mobsters like Agawam's Big Al Bruno and his partner Skyball Scibelli.

In a 2011 article, Barry mentions the late Big Al Bruno, "...other factors paved the way for Bruno to officially assume power of the "Springfield Crew" of the Genovese family in 2002, according to court testimony." Bruno was acquitted of attempted murder.

I am listing a few of the online highlights of his profile below for the purpose of proving that Big Al Bruno was quite active in the mob while I lived in Agawam.

> **PROFILE: Adolfo "Big Al" Bruno**
> **Hometown: Agawam, Ma**
> **Died November 23, 2003 at age of 58**
> Bruno wore over-sized eyeglasses and favored Hawaiian shirts and cigars, and liked to highlight his charitable efforts such as bringing toys to the Shriners Hospital for children at Christmas ... He rubbed elbows with politicians and played racquetball with the late Hampden County District Attorney Matthew "Matty" Ryan.
> **Last rank held:** Capo, made member of Genovese crime family
> **Criminal history:** Gambling convictions in 1981 and 1984; twice accused and twice cleared in connection with a bungled Mafia shooting [1991] behind his brother's barn.
> **Status:** Bruno was fatally ambushed by a paid gunman on Nov. 23, 2003 outside the Our Lady of Mount Carmel Social Club, exiting his regular Sunday night card game.

I sure do wish I had known about "Big Al" Bruno, who died in 2003, back when I had a few run-ins myself with his pal Hampden District Attorney Matthew "Matty" Ryan while I was on the town council.

In fact, this D.A. did everything in his power to cover up two insidious crimes involving Agawam authorities. This included protecting its police chief, who, acting on orders from the mob, sought my demise while I sat on the town council. More on that in Chapter 9.

According to mobologist Stephanie Barry, in another vignette published July 20, 2015, Big Al actually rubbed elbows with politicians and even played racquetball with the late Hampden County District Attorney Matthew "Matty" Ryan. It seems that Mafia informants told police that Bruno "had bragged to his colleagues that he had killed [Antonio] Facente in 1979 to allegedly cozy up to then-Hampden District Attorney Matthew J. Ryan."

At this point into the whodunit, some might be wondering whether Bruno and D.A. Matty Ryan were associates while I was in Agawam even before I got on the Agawam council in 1979? And the answer is yes!

I was only thirty years old at the time, so Bruno would have been thirty-four years old, having been born in 1945. So far, the timeline adds up. Thanks to Barry's own updated report, linking Bruno to Ryan in 1979, the year of my council election, it appears to be a match made in the mob. More proof they could've easily conspired to leak my Arrest Record and protect the Agawam Police Chief who leaked them too!

Reading about Bruno and Ryan in Barry's OC vignette, isn't it possible to assume that the same mobsters coming after me might also expect a favor from the Hampden District Attorney's office as they had both done before in other cases?

In Chapter 9, this whodunit explores two scandals that I had been framed for while I was on the town council, which ultimately landed on Ryan's desk in the D.A.'s office. Even now, I am still all amazed at how I survived repeated acts of retribution by the mob despite the blatant protection of the D.A.'s office.

Maybe this is a good time to bring in another alleged mobster to introduce into our whodunit of Agawam politics. He's someone that I got to know real well and whom I introduced to my readers earlier in this chapter.

Who's the boss?

"You don't mess with the *godfather*," a veteran councilman, half-jokingly reprimanded me.

"Nardi's not going to get away with it," I muttered under my breath, as I walked away from another council meeting fraught with violent outbursts after I'd just called for our Town Manager's resignation.

Town Councilman Frederick Nardi, who died in 1997, was a high profile politician who was the invisible face of the Agawam faction. He and his associates originally backed my opponent Candido, so I never knew if Nardi was happy I won, or resentful Candido lost.

You need to remember, I couldn't know at the time what someone had done to interfere with my own election. I only later confirmed it when texting my crazy cousin Gina.

To all appearances, Councilor Nardi was an honest businessman who kept a low profile on the town council and never gave anyone reason to suspect otherwise. But to political insiders, Fred Nardi was known as "the Godfather" of Agawam.

The question was whether it was because of the way he ran the town, for he did it in such a way that he could easily pass for a very real *boss* in organized crime to the trained eye. Either way no one was talking for the record.

Hanging around the South End of Springfield, I'd always been intrigued by monikers used to give nicknames to gangsters or made members of the Mafia. Nardi's title of *godfather* naturally intrigued me. Was his nickname the real thing? Was it a moniker, a Mafiosi nickname, Nardi preferred as did other councilor members like Richard Theroux and Andrew Gallano who were themselves known as the *Gold Dust Twins*?

According to *Wikipedia,* the Mafia in Sicily and America usually has a boss of all bosses – also known as the capo di tutti capi. The boss can also be referred to as "the capofamiglia, capo crimini, representante, Don or *godfather,* who is the highest level in a crime family."

A dance with the boss

"Don't be going back there councilor," one of the assistant town clerks in town hall called out. "If you need something Miss Bonavita, just ask me."

Serving alongside the one called the *godfather,* I couldn't resist turning into a sleuth. I soon found myself snooping around town offices under the guise of researching council business. I didn't know what I'd find, but since I couldn't go snooping around the police chief's office like I wanted to, town hall would do for a start. I guess that's how I ended up doing what I did.

Nardi, was a handsome man albeit your typical Catholic Italian hypocrite. He was married but as I soon discovered, he cheated on his wife. As I remember, he liked young girls but his reputation was more known for the power he wielded in our community than a playboy.

Nardi's own online obituary is evident of how corrupted politicians operate under the radar without anyone suspecting a thing. I looked up his to see what I'd find after all these years. Frederick Nardi died August 29, 1997. His obituary confirmed his life history that did not read like your average mobster who had served on the Agawam town council for eight terms.

Back then, there was no internet to do research on monikers of real life mobsters like we have today. Still, I could picture Nardi as a real godfather. It was his council sidekicks, the Gold Dust Twins that I didn't know why they had taken those monikers. I only found out recently the original mobsters with that moniker were made famous for skimming money from union dues. Now it makes perfect sense.

Today those clues work great for a real time whodunit, since one of those Gold Dust Twins is Richard Theroux and he is back on the council again as of the writing of this memoir. His Gold Dust Twin Andrew Gallano is no longer living.

Looking back, I guess I know now why the latter-day Gold Dust Twins, Theroux and Gallano, always tried to shut me up whenever I questioned big money items and union issues that came before us for a vote. It made for some interesting debate on the Agawam town council!

I sure am glad I kept a lot of those newspaper clippings. I've reprinted some of them in Chapter 15 thinking it might set up the real time whodunit quite nicely.

It was a set up but not a hit

I was only 30 years old when the 59 year old *godfather* started flirting with me. I was taken by surprise the day Nardi asked to meet with me alone.

"Please, not again," I thought to myself. "What if he wanted to take me into his confidence like Floyd had done? Wouldn't that bust a hole in my theory about him being a real *boss* in the mob?"

I knew Nardi liked young girls--really young girls. So I knew I wasn't his type, which made me wonder, "What could the man called the *godfather* possibly want with me?"

I knew it wasn't to set me up and put me in any danger. So, believing I was safe, I agreed to let Nardi pick me up in his car for our first meetup. He wasn't alone. He had a driver and we sat alone together really cozy like in the back seat.

I had flashbacks of the night I watched as my boss Victor get into a car with a driver in the front and one in the back. I guess that's why I was a bit nervous at first around Nardi but once I got to know him better, he was a real Don Juan when alone with a woman.

I figured I had to be safe with him. Heck, hadn't he put me in the back seat with him instead of putting us both in the front seat with his driver in the back? If he had, I was ready to make a run for it. That set up was my last view of Victor and I didn't want it to be my last ride either.

It was when Nardi put his arm around me and didn't try to strangle me, that I figured he really was coming onto me instead of trying to kill me. Oh sure, I knew what he was up to, of course. I wasn't that stupid to think he was hot for my body. I was a little cutie, but I figured there was more to it than that with Nardi.

He wanted something from me alright and I went along for the ride that night to see what it was.

"What do you want from me?" I asked feeling a little too comfortable in his arms.

"Shhh. Don't talk," he said, as he pressed his lips against mine.

We both knew I'd become a liability to Nardi since calling for his town manager's resignation, but I must admit, I never figured he'd seduce me to recruit me. We kept on seeing each other on the side and opposing each other at every chance we got at council meetings.

Ours was a strange relationship indeed. It was a dance with the devil and I didn't know it at the time. I was not thinking good for sure.

It was only after I'd been calling for, and getting, more resignations of their key players in the administration that I began wondering if Nardi might actually risk outing himself. It seemed reasonable, especially if they wouldn't have to get rid of me like I suspicioned they had done with Floyd.

But as it turned out, I never got the chance to find out. "God forgive me," I remember praying out loud. "I was not going down this road."

After a hot and heavy date with Nardi the night before, I needed intervention and called my mentor Anita the next day. We met for lunch. Up until then, I had never confided in her about me and Nardi.

I remember she said something like, "I can't believe you even risked being alone in the same room with that man much less get in the car with him."

It was more like a motherly rebuke, so I assured her nothing happened. Anita didn't know my story and I wanted to keep it that way. I figured she was safer not knowing too much.

Although Anita never let on she knew about the mob problem in our town she had heard about Nardi's reputation with the young girls. I guess that's all she meant by my being alone with him. At least I hope so. Maybe she was trying to protect me like I was doing with her.

"Poor Anita," I thought to myself, "If only you knew how many times I came face to face with death from mobsters more dangerous than Nardi."

But instead, I decided to tell her a half-truth. I lied about me wanting to get information out of him, and she bought it. At least, I think she did.

I can still see Anita nodding her head and pointing her finger at me, firmly insisting, "You stay away from that man, young lady."

Who I was I kidding? I really was attracted to Nardi. I couldn't tell anyone and I never did. But I never got past the guilt of knowing who he was and the fact that I didn't care. Nonetheless, Anita made me come to my senses and I stopped seeing him.

I would've been dreaming if I had thought what Nardi and I had shared together would let me off the hook with anyone watching me like they had been doing with Floyd. Nothing ever changed for me on that end.

Nardi and I finished with our flirtation when we both realized neither one of us was talking. I knew he was the boss alright only because he found someone else to keep me in line when we moved on. What happened after that was chilling.

Every boss has an enforcer

As in any mob whodunit, there's got to be an enforcer. Back in 1979, desperate to handle me and keep me in line, Agawam's own police chief came out of the closet literally.

While around me, the police chief began acting more like a soldier, enforcing rules for organized crime, than a police officer sworn to enforce the law.

According to *Wikipedia*, it seems that a "**mob enforcer** is a member or associate of an organized crime or corrupt political organization that is responsible for handling those who do not go along with organization policies, rules and deals. It often involves threats of violence, beatings or murder."

What can I say? I was never more convinced that Agawam had a very real mob problem, once the police chief stepped in to take Nardi's place with me. And trust me. It was no love affair!

CHAPTER NINE PART ONE:
THE AGAWAM POLICE CHIEF

"Hello? Miss Bonavita?" An unfamiliar voice on the other end of the telephone continued talking when I confirmed he had the right party.

"This is Officer Brown and I think I can help you with the problem you're having with the Agawam Police Chief," he explained.

"You're a police officer here in Agawam?"

"Yes ma'am I am."

Officer Brown's cold call was to be the first of many, in my short career on the Agawam Town Council, involving the town's police chief, Stanley J. Chmielewski.

First, it was the illegal dissemination of my Arrest Record intending to end my political career. Next, it was an ingenious set-up of an assault and battery charge falsely brought against me that could've put me away for ten years. As incredible as it sounds, these were all orchestrated by Agawam's very own police chief.

There were more of these felonious attacks against me while I served on the Agawam town council, but none so blatantly obvious as when I was made an offer I couldn't refuse by Chief Chmielewski, himself ,whose boss ordered him to control me or else.

You can read about it in Chapter 11. For now, you just need to get some idea of what I walked into, when I called for and got the resignation of our town manager that led to the leaking of my arrest record by an Agawam Police Chief.

The whistleblower

On February 20, 1980, *The Morning Union* ran the story about a whistleblower in the police department reporting that an Agawam patrolman charged Police Chief Stanley Chmielewski had circulated my arrest record and mug shots among his officers and that he later took the materials back.

Officer Brown had a history of ruffling feathers with his superiors in the police department. Listening to him tell his story,

I knew he understood what it felt like to be a victim of retribution himself.

He was a whistleblower for sure. It seems he'd been set up by the police chief for nothing more than a quarrel he'd had with a neighbor while off-duty. "If the chief of police sends one of his hench-boys to this woman to get her to press a complaint, you can see where I stand in their eyes. I'm not one of their boys," Brown said, in an interview with Suzanne McLaughlin of *The Union* Staff.

This story about Officer Brown made breaking news shortly after the illegal dissemination of my Attest Record went public. Little did I know at the time, when I was busy getting arrested in my younger days, that I was leaving footprints for anyone in the Mafia to blackmail me into serving them instead of God and the people whom I was elected to serve.

I'd just been on the town council less than a month when it happened. Despite a note signed by Brown that was mailed out with copies of my Arrest Record and mug shots to all the media and town council members, the officer stuck to his story. He claimed he was being set up.

The Arrest Record mystery

I believed Officer Brown had been set up and I still do today. Why wouldn't I? Who in their right mind would sign their name to an illegal act as to what Brown was being accused of doing? All fingers pointed to the Agawam Police Department for obvious reasons. Who else could get their hands on someone's arrest records and mug shots without going through proper channels to do it as had been done with mine?

As told by Officer Brown, *The Morning Union* also reported, "He charged that the "group" responsible for the dissemination of Ms. Bonavita's records is "quite concerned" that he will tell what he knows to the grand jury."

"They know I'm not the kind to shut up," he said. "What I know, I'm going to say."

Going public, like Brown did with McLaughlin's interview, only raised more questions than it answered. For example, who was the "group" Patrolman Brown mentioned in the interview?

183

All of this came at a time when I was trying to make of what was going on with Fred Nardi once I'd discovered he relished the moniker of "godfather." Didn't they have enforcers working for them in the Mafia? Isn't the Mafia or its associates who work for them a kind of "group?"

Thoughts about my street kids, the break-in involving the cop who mysteriously returned my stolen fur coat, and the surreal home invasion only made me more suspicious after hearing Officer Brown's own story.

Convinced I could trust him, Officer Ronald Charles Brown, who died in 2014, was an answer to prayer. Whether he was a good cop or bad cop, one thing was certain. He wasn't in their good grace anymore and he was ready to blow the whistle on his boss the police chief. At this point, that was a good enough reference for me in that town.

After that infamous interview, no one ever doubted for a minute that Brown was set up by his own police department to make it look like he had mailed out copies of my Arrest Record. As Brown later testified to a grand jury and repeated to the local media, "someone forged his name" on the note attached to the Arrest Record copies illegal disseminated.

Who's the boss?

Everyone has one in their communities. If you have a police department, you have a police chief. In 1979, when I was elected to serve on the Town Council, his name was Stanley J. Chmielewski who died in 2015. He joined the Agawam police department in 1956 and was sworn in as Police Chief in 1976.

In 1994, Stanley retired after thirty-eight years on the Agawam Police Force. Eighteen of those years he served as Agawam's Police Chief. When Stanley retired, Robert Campbell was sworn in as Police Chief.

I'd like to think Stanley started out on the Agawam police force wanting to make a difference in the quality of life that policing provides. Yes. I'd like to think he started out wanting to serve and protect Agawam's citizens. Maybe someone knows his story, but I never did.

Given how newly appointed police chiefs participate in a ceremonial swearing-in by taking an "Oath of Office," Stanley had to have known what was expected of him. Perhaps, this is why the International Association of Chiefs of Police recommend taking such oaths in the first place. Their website has the *Law Enforcement Oath of Honor* which reads:

"On my honor, I will never betray my badge, my integrity, my character, or the public trust. I will always have the courage to hold myself and others accountable for our actions. I will always uphold the constitution, my community, and the agency I serve."

Interestingly, this *Law Enforcement Oath of Honor* is even recommended by the IACP as a symbolic statement of commitment to ethical behavior. Like Stanley, I too took an Oath of Office when I was elected to the town council. But I took mine seriously and which is why I have a mob memoir published and he didn't.

The police are sworn to protect us aren't they? As for the police chief himself, I never suspected anything at first. Heck, I didn't want to believe it even after Brown's story went public.

Following in Officer Brown's footsteps, I too went public with my own police story and it got ugly real fast. I couldn't believe how I was being handled by the Chief. Heck, hadn't he done it to Brown? Who knows how many others before him?

For me, going public was insurance. Go public and watch the rats scatter and hide. Speaking of rats, the media descended on our little town smelling blood. Thanks to me, corruption allegations of our police chief made the news non-stop over the next few months.

Acting more like an enforcer for the Mafia than an honest police chief sworn to uphold justice, Chmielewski kept his mouth shut. Evidently, he was more afraid of what his boss could do to him than those calling for an investigation.

Instead of wanting to solve the crime of the illegal dissemination of my Arrest Record, our police chief did everything in his power to cover it up. Why would he do this, if he wasn't guilty of anything?

The Morning Union newspaper, after receiving a copy of my Arrest Record, couldn't get anything out of our police chief even after Patrolman Brown accused him of the crime. *The Union* must've been disappointed. I know I was!

As the story goes, there must have been some type of blue flu in the Agawam police department, because no one was talking other than Brown. Meanwhile, no one, not the media, or even the grand jury led by Big Al Bruno's pal, D.A. Matty Ryan, ever questioned whom the "group" was that Patrolman Brown fingered as "responsible for the dissemination" of my arrest records.

Up until Brown mentioned the ones behind the corruption in his police department in his *Morning Union* interview, I'd never heard of the Mafia being called the "group," as he did. It does, however, make for a good clue in this whodunit if we follow the line of succession after Stanley retired.

Ensuring a line of succession is critical to their survival wherever politicians and police are being controlled by the Mafia. You always see this whenever any organized crime holds sway over its police and politicians. This is the main reason for discouraging in-house promotions whether corruption is suspected or not.

Looking back, it's interesting to see that there have been two other veterans "tapped," from Agawam's police force, to serve as its police chief since Chmielewski retired in 1994. This alone deserves mention in our whodunit.

The line of succession protecting the "group"

According to the foreword in the *North Las Vegas Police Department* policy manual:

> "The integrity of the Department rests with the actions of its members. This manual is a guideline to assist with the regulation of conduct. Our community's perception of the Police Department is based on the competence and ethical deportment of our officers and staff. These policies will help to ensure that public trust is well placed."

An article in *The Republican*, published online in 2013 by George Graham, begs the question, was the "public trust well placed" in Agawam's situation? I only ask, because back then search committees were responsible for appointing its police chiefs, much like they would normally do for replacing city managers. A new police chief, Lt. Eric P. Gillis, was appointed by the mayor. According to the story, Gillis replaced Chief Robert Campbell, who served the department for over 40 years and had been sworn in as Chief in 1994 when Chief Stanley Chmielewski retired.

After my experience with Chief Chmielewski you would think I'd be relieved to know that he retired and moved on to other things. Unfortunately, knowing this today I don't have any confidence with an in-house promotion.

It is incredulous how a 40 year veteran of the Agawam Police Department like Robert Campbell could be named as Stanley's replacement only to be replaced a few years later by another 16 year veteran of the force.

When Stanley retired, if the "group" had anything to say about it, wouldn't his replacement have to be someone committed to his own legacy of unethical behavior thereby guaranteeing the line of succession?

It's a sure bet that everyone in the department, including Campbell, knew what Chief Chmielewski had been doing when I was on the council. This was especially true given how he'd Chief Campbell had been on the force "40 years before replacing him." Hadn't anyone ever bothered to question what was going on in that police chief's office after I left Agawam?

Another police chief joins our whodunit

Does anyone remember Police Chief Romeo Borgatti? I was around at the time, but I wasn't familiar with the situation that prompted his "early" retirement in 1978. Rumors were floating around and as memory serves me, everyone was asking "Who would replace him?"

I didn't have any run-ins with Chief Borgatti probably because I'd just moved to Agawam when he retired. I was busy with my Tea Party and organizing the Massachusetts statewide tax reform measure Proposition 2 ½. It wasn't until after I was on the council and had started up my own hometown newspaper, *The Agawam Voice*, that Chief Borgatti's retirement got my attention.

As it turned out, I was a natural born snooper. I never needed any schooling in detective work or even as an investigative journalist once I got on that beleaguered town council. The experience actually bolstered my career as a reporter once I began publishing my own weekly town newspaper in 1981. Besides covering the news, I also uncovered a lot of insider corruption while wearing two hats—a member of the media and a member of the town council.

I hadn't given much thought to Borgatti's replacement until I had run a story on Sgt. Robert Rossi in one of my Employee of the Week Spotlights. Rossi was a good kid and good kids don't qualify for police chiefs in Agawam unless there's no line of succession for the Mafia to protect. The kid got my attention.

Given what I know about the office of the Agawam police chief, I have long suspicioned the "good" Sergeant just didn't qualify for the "group's" unofficial job requirement of an enforcer. Maybe being passed over for the promotion, saved his life for all I know.

If Rossi had been appointed chief of police in '78, I just couldn't see him going along with the "group," much less following orders to do to me and others, what my pal Stanley never hesitated to do as a police chief himself. Nope. I couldn't envision Rossi as an enforcer for the mob.

Apparently others on the police force shared my opinion of Rossi as well. In my former newspaper *The Agawam Voice* May 7, 1981 edition, I went public with Rossi's story when my pal Stanley finally found a way to get rid of his competition permanently.

I ran a front page story, titled Chief's Competition Demoted. Speaking on behalf of Rossi as one of his co-workers, Sgt. Frank Evangelist said, "He (Rossi) usually puts his heart into what he does."

I interviewed Kenneth Grady, a former Police Chief from the past, in the same story so I could get his comment on Rossi too.

Chief Grady agreed "Rossi has got what it takes to be a good chief saying, "He's got the background and education. Yes, he could qualify as a good chief."

In other words, Chief Grady's recommendation meant something those days. And it says a lot I think about why Rossi was passed over the way he had been if the "group" was protecting its line of succession.

Suffice to say, you will find out soon enough, and in real time, how I know the line of succession continues even today in Agawam. Remember I told you I was a natural born snooper on the Agawam council. Well, I still am! But you can read about what Chief Gillis does to get his name in this whodunit when you get to Chapter 16.

Never fear the past

The phone rang. I picked it up and recognized the voice as one of the news reporters assigned to Agawam politics. "Hey Jack what can I do for you?"

I was getting a lot of phone calls that day from the media. Jack Flynn was a city hall reporter with *The Daily News* and he had a front page story above the fold that he was anxious to get out.

*The Daily News breaking news story
after a botched blackmail attempt
on Bonavita went public in
December 1979.*

189

When he called me for a comment about the illegal dissemination of my arrest records, I already knew what I would say. Heck, blackmail was commonly used to keep politicians in line, it still is. And I was sure I was on someone's hit list, even more after I had won the election.

So Jack's phone call was no big surprise. Actually, I had been waiting for this day ever since Floyd Landers warned me of a smear campaign. He never said what it was. He died before he got a chance to tell me.

I wasn't surprised when Jack called me, but I did have a flashback while on the phone with him of the time I followed a prompting to use an unusual theme for my one and only campaign ad, titled <u>Wanted to serve time on the Agawam Council.</u>

At the time, I never knew why I did that, but looking back, it sure must've spooked the mobsters behind all my troubles. If not, why did the leaker sit on my arrest record until *after* I got on the town council? In case you've forgotten, go back to Chapter 8 and re-read the part about my father making another deal with the mob to save my life by promising them I would do whatever they wanted if they put me on the council instead of their chosen candidate.

Now keep in mind, I didn't know anything about that deal and I never did, until I contacted my crazy cousin Gina while doing research for this memoir.

Inviting retribution and totally unaware of it

Before Jack's phone call, I'd been making headlines regularly in the local newspapers right after I called for and got the resignation of our Town Manager Peter Caputo. Now this alone, should tell you that I didn't have a clue about any so-called deal with the mob. Who in their right mind would take out a known associate of theirs like the town manager?

What must've seemed incredibly stupid to the mob, who knew I'd been a star witness for them in my boss Victor's assassination, I naively jumped right in and led the call for our manager's resignation only after I went public with a bribery charge against him. In what reminded me of sit-down, I was called in to his office after I had stumbled onto some evidence of his own corruptive practices in the administration of his duties as town manager.

Expecting a warning, or a threat to back off from any plans I might've had to expose him, Caputo stupidly instead attempted to bribe me for my silence. Normally, I would've overlooked it because of the line of succession rule that might've been in play even with city hall. I'd rather stick with the devil I knew then have to break in a replacement brought in by "the group" in charge.

I decided my best option was to go public with a bribery charge and send a message hoping to get the attention of the real "boss" in Agawam. It got someone's attention alright. But not the way I hoped it would.

Since my fellow councilmen couldn't ignore the bribery charge once I went public, I managed enough support on the council to get Caputo's resignation. I was feeling pretty good about myself right about then. Score one for Floyd I thought.

Even though I'd always suspected Floyd Landers had been permanently silenced by someone in the "group" associated with the Mafia, I hadn't counted on what happened next. It was retribution at its best and I was its victim this time, not Floyd!

Headlines screamed the breaking news out of Agawam: Meeting Set on Arrests. My arrests! It seems that my call for Caputo's resignation triggered the order to release my Arrest Record "in-waiting" only a couple weeks after I was sworn into office.

Associates and members of the Mafia all have one thing in common. They cover each other's backs. On that thought, I just have to throw in another syllogism here for our whodunit.

If Caputo was brought in as an associate for the mob, and his job was to cover up the ongoing city hall corruption, then they hired an idiot. Poor Caputo, he was in over his head with me on the town council watching his every move, eh?

Undoubtedly, he should've let the boss deal with me instead of trying to bribe me himself. The mob's own soldiers and handlers were much better in that department then inexperienced associates. At least that is my opinion from my own experience with mobsters.

As it turned out, Caputo was a man with a past that he didn't put on his resume. The mob is real good at finding people with a past and he must've qualified for our town manager job perfectly. I, on the other hand, surprised them all by calling Caputo out as I did. After all, didn't I have a past too?

After I'd called for Caputo's resignation, his fake resume issue resurfaced again. At that point, the media couldn't ignore two investigations anymore. I got lucky. Caputo was history.

It seems that an earlier news story about Caputo's doctored resume before I was even elected to the council, by Suzanne McLaughlin with *The Morning Union*, produced evidence it was "largely a work of fiction."

There was another work of fiction that someone in the mob, who had once wanted me dead, must've decided to produce with the hope of getting rid of me again.

A work of fiction makes for good fake news

I was a woman with a past and I had just gotten the resignation of another soul with a past. But unlike Caputo, my fellow members of the town council couldn't call for my resignation simply because of my past arrests which had all been dismissed.

Under the law, there is a stark difference between arrest records and a criminal record. For example, if charges are dismissed or a defendant is found "Not Guilty," then there is no criminal record for that person, and the document in question simply remains an "arrest record."

Reportedly, there are also serious legal risks should anyone in a local law enforcement agency, like the Agawam Police, attempt to use an arrest record to harm or harass an individual. If so, then why wasn't anyone ever charged and disciplined within its police department? Particularly when one of its own police officers testified what had been done to me, in a hearing and grand jury?

So, when the reporter Jack Flynn called me right after Christmas, wanting my response to the latest scandal in town, I was glad to have the holidays behind us. Christmas was no time to be dealing with this kind of a mess.

With the holidays over, I wasted no time hiring an attorney and calling for a meeting of my fellow town councilors. Unbeknownst to me, each of them, along with members of the media, had received my Arrest Record in the mail less than six weeks after I was sworn into office on the Town Council.

If it wasn't for *The Daily News*, I wouldn't have found out about someone leaking my arrest record to my fellow councilors. Wouldn't you think the council president would have raised a public outcry upon discovering such an illegal document in his mail, not to mention mailed out to all of the other council members too?

As clues go in any whodunit, this fact alone pointed to a collaboration between the police department and city council. The way I figured it, shouldn't the council president himself had contacted me, or at least warned me of what was up, so it could be investigated? But he never did. Why?

I never did find out why anyone held onto my arrest record until I called for Caputo's resignation. It remains a mystery to this day, even though others claimed knowing about this even before I was elected to the council. However, I am hoping to figure out this mystery when someone solves this whodunit.

So, who was the council president when all this was going on?

Enter the Gold Dust Twins

Until *The Daily News* contacted me, no one was talking about my leaked arrest record, not to me and not even to the media. Everyone was waiting to see what I would do first. I'd only heard that someone had finally sent out my Arrest Record, with my mug shots, to all of the other councilors. But heck, I never even got a copy of it in the mail for myself.

To this day, I have never even seen my own Arrest Record, but everyone else did! And it's not like I didn't try to get it either. Even while researching for this memoir, I contacted the proper authorities back east to get copies of my arrest records and mug shots. Guess what I was told?

Massachusetts authorities could find nothing in their records about any arrests of mine. All the charges had been dismissed, but if there had been an actual Arrest Record with my mug shots for the Agawam police to illegally disseminate, it was long gone.

Richard Theroux was council President when I was sworn into office two months early in order to take Floyd's place on the council. It was Theroux who aggressively spearheaded a cover-up despite my having the legal right to call for an investigation into the police department affair.

For that reason alone, Theroux was suspect in my books. Albeit I was a rookie councilor, but it didn't take a genius to know we needed new leadership on our council after that Arrest Record mess.

As I get more into the whodunit, we should start putting together some names for the "group" that Officer Brown held back from naming. I'd like to but I can't. Brown, who was 71 years old when he died in 2014, never gave out any names. I guess that's why he lived as long he did.

I, on the other hand, do have some names important to the whodunit for this chapter on the police chief though. So far, we have an Agawam Councilman named Fred Nardi who went by the moniker of the "*godfather.*" Whether it was merely an insider moniker or a real mob title, I never knew.

Next in line, we have a character who appears to be the "*enforcer*" named Stanley Chmielewski. Then, acting more like wannabe associates for the mob, I'd throw in two infamous members of the town council curiously nicknamed "The Gold Dust Twins"—Richard Theroux and Andrew Gallano.

Interestingly, both were named after two reputed mobsters known for skimming union dues among other crimes also involving other people's money. Hmmm?

I don't know why, but I never publicly mentioned anything about the "*godfather*" or an "*enforcer*" while I was on the council, even though I once absently name dropped Theroux and Gallano's moniker in my own newspaper *The Agawam Voice*. I'm glad I did name drop it or else I would've never remembered to mention it in this whodunit.

I just wish I'd have known why they were nicknamed for a pair of mobsters. Had I known, I could've used that in my column too. But I get ahead of myself. Chapter 15 is devoted entirely to

194

the Gold Dust Twin, Richard Theroux, and you can read all about his activity in Agawam today in real time.

Everyone has enemies on a town council, even the good ole boys. I got lucky when I figured that out. I managed to effect some change in Theroux's control over the council when I pushed for a change in council leadership after I saw how he intentionally mishandled my Arrest Record investigation.

I figured with a new president on our council I would have a better chance to garner support for an investigation into our police department. But it was a humbling experience for me, a rookie politician, as I quickly learned something about the line of succession even on city councils. Nothing got any better for me after Theroux was replaced as president.

That's why, when I got a call from Jack Flynn at *The Daily News*, I was ready to talk. I needed to take my case directly to the people. I was a quick learner if nothing else.

I knew that no matter who was council president, I would never stand a chance of getting any in-house investigation into the illegal dissemination of my Arrest Record.

The Daily News Jan 2, 1980
Bonavita Arrest Record Front
Page Story. Note Jack Flynn's
misspelling of my nickname. It
should be spelled "Elena."

In his breaking news story, Jack reported, "After speaking with 10 of the 14 other councilors about the circulating copies of the records, Ms. Bonavita said she decided to call the meeting 'to take some kind of action on this.'"

As I recall, Jack was always pretty decent with me as far as liberal news reporters go. I was sure glad he didn't have any more questions because I was running out of answers. Before cutting off the interview, I readily agreed to make a statement only after promising to quote me verbatim.

Going back on the record for the interview, Jack kept his word and quoted me as saying, "People in public office must never be afraid of their past, no matter how bad it may be. For once this is known then you have done more damage not only to yourself but to those people whom you serve. By allowing those weakest, yet strongest, in vulnerable positions to control you, you are adding to that awesome chain of power and corruption that exists and is allowed to exist in most communities."

As memory serves me, I felt impressed to go off the record to remind Jack, "You can't let anyone control you like that Jack, you gotta take it to the people and trust them to do the right thing and get behind you."

Looking back on my conversation with Jack, I am proud to say, the people did indeed get behind me, or I would not have this story to tell today.

While I couldn't say anything to Jack, I'd like to think that I had broken one of the "group's" line of succession within in its own associates on the council by replacing Floyd as I had just done.

According to my crazy cousin Gina, hadn't my father's own associates in the mob believed that I was actually securing the line of succession as a replacement for Floyd when they switched and backed me instead of their own boy, Candido?

Yes. Looking back and knowing what I know today it had to have been the plan. I'd sure like to think the "group" lost again when I chose to be a voice for the people, instead of the mobsters who thought they controlled our town. But to be fair to Agawam, this kind of thing goes on all around the country even in Iowa where I had the dumb luck to run into the very same problem again!

I think this might be a good place in our whodunit to take a break from the mob problem in Agawam and go back to my days on the school board in Waterloo, Iowa. Don't worry, we'll get back to Agawam after a brief trip down memory lane involving another crime family that was so bold as to take a page out of Agawam's politics exposing my past and leaking my arrest record.

It's what was done to a friend of mine, who I helped get elected as mayor, that deserves mention in this chapter about the Agawam Police Chief.

CHAPTER NINE PART TWO:
AGAWAM JOINS THE BATTLE OF WATERLOO

"How do you like your new office Al?" I asked my friend the new mayor of Waterloo.

"They set me up with a desk in a closet sized space in city hall until I get sworn into office."

"Give me a call when you get settled in after you get sworn in and we can go over your campaign promises like we talked about doing after you won your election."

"Yeah. Sure thing."

But I never got that phone call from the new mayor. Not when he got sworn into office and not any time after that either. I watched helplessly, as my friend the new mayor of Waterloo quickly abandoned his vow to clean up city hall. Instead, he decided to carry on the dark legacy left by our outgoing mayor almost as soon as he took office.

Everyone has a past that they wish would never have happened, especially when you try to leave it behind you. So you can imagine my surprise, when the same thing surrounding an arrest record happened to a friend of mine whom I helped get elected as mayor while living in Waterloo, Iowa.

It was in the year 1991 when I was elected to the Waterloo School Board and it involved a good friend of mine who ran for the office of mayor. He was my age and inexperienced in holding office but his heart was in the right place. Otherwise I never would have offered to manage his campaign as I did.

Like so many others, my friend believed he could make a difference if he got elected as mayor. As his campaign manager, I believed him. I prayed and we organized a grass roots campaign like I did with my own campaign that won me a seat on the school board just a few months earlier thanks to the help of my Heavenly Father. No one knew who this guy was until we hit the streets.

To everyone's surprise we did it! His election was a major political upset. But no one was more surprised than my friend. And so, I wasn't prepared for what happened next. Heck, I was too busy celebrating the most amazing victory in Waterloo. It even reminded me of my own mysterious political upset when I won my election to the Agawam Town Council in 1979. Who could know that history was set to repeat itself in the dark world of organized crime?

I should have suspected what was going on when my friend the new mayor for no reason shut me out on day one of his taking office. He wasn't himself anymore. He made it quite clear that I wasn't welcome around the mayor's office and he acted like a man with a gun to his head whenever I tried to make contact with him. I even got that dark feeling just like I'd had in Agawam whenever I had been targeted and threatened by the mob.

"What's going on with that mayor of yours?" a loyal supporter of mine had asked shortly after my friend had gotten settled into his new job as mayor of Waterloo.

"He's just trying to get a feel of the job. We gotta give him more time I guess."

What else could I say? I had asked my supporters to get behind the candidate I supported and I didn't know what to make of his betrayal myself when he seemingly went dark on us as quickly as he had done.

I was mystified as were so many of his supporters. He was an embarrassment to those who, like myself, had trusted him to keep his campaign promise to make the mayor's office more transparent and accountable to the people.

As it turned out, my friend the mayor was being blackmailed and threatened with an arrest record from his own past. To my disappointment he never confided in me and he never went public with it as I had done when I was in Agawam. Instead, he caved as so many other politicians often do.

It was only after his term as mayor had expired that I discovered why he did what he did. It seems that his past mistake was too painful for him to endure going public. So he allowed himself to be blackmailed into doing exactly what his predecessor had been doing as mayor. Whatever that was!

I never knew who was behind the blackmail and threats he'd gotten since his election because he never gave up any names, kind of like what everyone else in Agawam had done around me when faced with the same situation. Only the Waterloo story goes much deeper than that.

As the story goes, shortly after I'd been elected to the Waterloo School Board in Iowa, I began making headlines keeping all of my promises I'd made when I campaigned as a Pro-life Christian Conservative advocating the return to the 3 Rs in our public schools. I made no secret of my plan to keep doing the will of God and not the will of the liberal group who ran our schools.

As you can imagine, that did not go over well. It didn't take me long to make enemies in a school district whose liberal agenda was determined to take God out of our schools. I had originally been interested in what was being taught in the classrooms and so I had a chance to meet teachers, administrators and parents. And that's how I got wind of two sets of books to get past any audits of our district's operating budget which I think was over $60 million in 1991.

Naturally, it was inevitable that I would have a deja vu experience in Waterloo that felt like I was reliving my former life in Agawam battling the same demons with another kind of "group." Only I couldn't blame the Mafia for my troubles. Or could I?

The Iowa crime family

To my utter surprise, my enemies in the school district lost no time digging into my past after I started asking questions about two sets of books I suspected were being kept with our school Superintendent's knowledge. Someone had done their homework and had even contacted my enemies back in Agawam who were only too happy to accommodate when contacted by a *Waterloo Courier* news reporter.

It never dawned on me who might've tipped off the *Courier* and who might've had enough influence to pull off that type of unwarranted in-depth investigation of an elected school board director as was done to me.

It was with Agawam's cooperation, that the Iowa *Waterloo Courier* newspaper put out a front-page "prize winning" story reporting on my town council days that took up nearly two full

200

pages! No stone was left unturned and it was the arrest record scandal from my Agawam days that was the hit of the story.

Until the writing of this memoir, I never really gave that *Waterloo Courier* story of mine a second thought. It was ingenious I guess—the idea of someone in Waterloo's "group" using the same blackmail tactic on our new mayor that had been used on me by the Agawam Police Chief. Until now, I had always assumed the order to hang me out to dry hoping to turn off my loyal supporters had originated from the *Waterloo Courier* Editor's desk. But it obviously didn't.

It begs the question of why anyone would risk so much to keep control of its elected officials as had been done to me in Agawam and again to the both of us in Waterloo. And yet, why the similarities to both Agawam and Waterloo as I have discovered? Time to check it out on the internet again.

Agawam's own Genovese Family and the Iowa Family

On October 6, 2013, Kenny "Kenji" Gallo's website, the *Breakshot Blog* dedicated to The truth about Organized Crime and the American Mafia came out with a stunning insight on the Iowa crime family. A Mafia in Iowa was all news to me and I wish I had known about the Iowa Family and the history of its mobsters when I was on the Waterloo School Board, but I didn't.

I was on oxygen 24/7 and struggling to stay alive with the yet undiagnosed Lyme disease. Thanks to that doggone tick in Texas, I still had been experiencing memory time loss issues since leaving Agawam in 1981. That's the only reason I can think of why I wasn't thinking about the mob problem in Agawam when I up and married an Iowa boy whom I had met while living in Texas in the mid 80's.

Had I known about the Iowa crime family at the time, it sure would've explained a lot about my déjà vu experience in Waterloo. Like the time when someone had the power to pull the plug on my cable conservative television talk show while I was on the school board and it took the Iowa Civil Liberties Union to sue the City of Waterloo, Waterloo School Superintendent and the cable company itself to put me back on the air.

Praise the Lord I won the battle of Waterloo and the right to stay on the air which I did for seven years. But there were so many others like that battle, just like what I'd gone through in Agawam. It was as if someone in the Iowa mob was reading straight out of the Agawam Police Chief's own play book.

I should've told the world my Agawam mob story when I had the chance to do it in that despicable interview with the *Waterloo Courier*, and yet I said nothing about the Mafia or the Genovese Family. At least, not until now.

I guess that's why I was intrigued with Kenji Gallo who did a blog on Iowa's own problem with organized crime in 2013. According to Kenji, "Everyone knows that the Mafia is in Chicago and New York (the Genovese crime family), but most people do not know that there were 26 Families around the country....The Iowa Family is one of those La Cosa Nostra Families. It was based in Des Moines, Iowa and the first recorded boss was Charles "Cherry Nose" Gioe who was put in place by Al Capone."

Kenji also mentioned how Lou "Cock-eye" Fratto "would become boss of the Iowa family based in Des Moines in 1936 owing to a "sizable Italian population in Iowa at the time." As I recall, when I lived in Iowa in the 1990's there was still a "sizable" Italian community in the area. So where was the Iowa Family while I was on the Waterloo School Board?

According to Kenji, the Iowa mobster Lou "Cock-eye" Fratto's brother named Frank "one ear" Fratto "was his number two man so he stepped up to handle the family business until his death in May of 1996 at the age of 81." Did I mention that I was in Waterloo in the 90's too? Actually, I served on the school board from 1991 to 1994 and stayed around till I went on to Texas Wesleyan law school in 1999 after my divorce. Yes. Waterloo's "group" took its toll on our marriage. Small town country folks like my ex-husband's family didn't appreciate the on-going public battles I'd been dragging their good name through.

What happened to me in Iowa is another story or another mob memoir which you can read about when it comes out. But for now, I'll keep to my story in Agawam and its own mob problem.

As we compare what happened to me in Agawam and years later in Waterloo, it begs the question of what in the world is going on today with Organized Crime? Better yet, why do so many public servants, like my friend the mayor, end up giving into such corruption? The answer is they **fear their past** whereas I did not fear mine and I guess that's the difference between public officials like me and my friend the mayor of Waterloo.

Looking back, no one ever knew or suspected why my friend the mayor went dark like he did. It broke my heart to lose a friend that way. Had I known at the time that the Iowa crime family was still around and very possibly behind all our troubles, I might've had more sympathy for him. As it was, I didn't suspect anything and my friend the mayor never made any breaking news about it like I did in Agawam when I invited retribution and paid for it when the arrest record leak went public.

As for my friend the mayor, today in 2017 I just assume that he did what someone most likely in the mob wanted him to do and if that's what truly happened then he was not wanted by them because of it. Unlike me who fought them in Agawam, my friend the mayor would not have invited retribution. Understandably, he didn't seek re-election.

As memory serves me, my friend didn't do too bad for himself as a former mayor. Before his election, he was a poor working guy in a bakery, but after he left city hall, he opened up a nice little money-making franchise in town. Hmmm. That reminds me of some other politicians like a few of the characters from my Agawam days written up in this whodunit.

Agawam's own "good" associates

I dedicated this chapter to the Agawam Police Chief to highlight a problem in most communities whether or not they have a mob problem like Agawam did. It's the same reason I gave honorable mention to my friend the mayor's story.

But when it all comes down to it, isn't it really about the line of succession with its police chiefs and politicians? I'm sure we unknowingly broke a cog in the political machine's control of its politicians when my friend amazingly beat out the incumbent Mayor of Waterloo.

As one experienced in managing campaigns and investigating vote fraud in local elections, I know rigged elections are only suspect when an opponent is a serious threat to the powers that be. They don't take chances. So I just figured my friend, an obvious outsider an unknown to politics, got past someone's radar and was swept into office by the true will of the people and God almighty Himself.

As for what these do-gooders do, once they surprise themselves and get elected, is another story. Whether it involves police chiefs, or politicians, isn't it really just about well-intentioned men and women who **fear their past** and allow themselves to be blackmailed or bribed into violating their oaths once they get into office?

Playing on that rule of thought, no one likes to think such betrayals of public trust go on inside our very own police departments, right? As to why anyone in law enforcement would end up working as associates for organized crime, which is commonly reported throughout the country, there are many reasons besides succumbing to threats.

Some take bribes, and those who don't probably wished they had, given what happens to anyone with a past lacking the courage to face it. Agawam's Police Chief Stanley Chmielewski lived to be a ripe old age. He never talked and he lived a life in the public eye just as if nothing had ever happened. That's a story of itself in any police mob whodunit.

Maybe that's why being a police chief he achieved so many honors and positions despite everything he did. Public awards and rewards, to those who've been publicly accused of corruption, are really the opposite of retribution. It says a lot about those public officials whose actions often demonstrate protecting the powers that be instead of doing God's will and serving the people they've been sworn to protect.

I have observed, that even when caught red handed in the act, the Mafia's most loyal associates will stay in office or on the job. For example, after the illegal dissemination of my Arrest Record, I called for the resignation of another suspected associate of the mob who was Agawam's appointed Town Solicitor.

Agawam's solicitor Lambert Ollari stayed on the town's payroll despite failing to advise the council of a well-known law about using an arrest record, mine, to harm or harass an individual.

The U.S. of A. Criminal History Checks website verifies this rule, which is filed under <u>Criminal Conviction Records, Arrest Records, and a little bit of US law</u>. It reads as set forth:

> "In US law…Using an arrest record or non- conviction police record as part of a decision to hire, fire or otherwise harm or harass an individual is wrong, and also opens you up to huge legal risks.__Typically, criminal history information is first generated by law enforcement agencies such as your local police departments. Local police departments, sheriff's offices, and other police agencies usually maintain their own internal databases…and until an actual criminal conviction for say a felony offense is made, there is no criminal record."

It's the law but not for Agawam

In a story printed in *The Morning Union* by Staff reporter Suzanne McLaughlin, she quoted my lawyer Arthur Serota after our Town Solicitor did everything in his power to protect those behind the illegal release of my Arrest Record. "We consider that the information [Arrest Record] was disseminated illegally. The fact that she [Bonavita] was not convicted makes it that much worse."

As I explained in Chapter 4, both charges in my arrests were dismissed meaning I had no Criminal Record. But I did have an Arrest Record that would follow me all my life and right onto the Agawam Police Chief's desk shortly after I arrived in Agawam in '78 as Officer Brown testified to a grand jury.

After the release went public about my Arrest Record, I remember a conversation with my newest mentor former councilwoman Anita Davilli. As memory serves me, our conversation went something like this, when she dropped by to see how I was holding up.

"We don't know who's behind it until you can get your attorney to push for an investigation of the police department," she said. "In the meantime, watch your back and keep your eyes and ears open at all your council meetings."

"You know I will Anita," I replied. "I just wish someone would name Chmielewski's boss so we could know who ordered him to release my arrest records."

But she just shrugged and shook her head. Then she surprised the heck out of me when out of the blue she said something like, "You been hearing talk about Theroux and Nardi in any of your council meetings?"

"Yep. Not much I can say right now. Still keeping a look out," I replied.

From the look on Anita's face, I could tell she wanted to say something, but didn't want to worry me. Even though I prayed she would come right out and confide in me and tell me what she knew, I was quick to remind myself of what happened to Floyd. Did I really want her talking to me?

They wanted me dead but the Chief was safe!

Unfortunately, it is my personal observation that people like police chiefs and other known associates of the mob, who know where all the dead bodies are buried in corrupt administrations, never get fired or sent to prison unless it serves the common good of those they serve.

Sure, you might end up dead if someone fears you will turn evidence against them, but that didn't happen to our Agawam Police Chief Stanley Chmielewski. The fact that his bullet riddled body never turned up in the Connecticut River is a story of itself. Life in the mob is a reward to those who serve them. For people like me who fight them, it's retribution at its meanest.

For everything illegal that Stanley did to me, it only convinced me all the more that he had to be the "enforcer" in the "group" especially since he seemed determined to handle me and keep me line during the entire time I served on the Agawam Town Council. All evidence thus far points to such a conclusion, but if not him, then who?

Who do you think?

Solving any whodunit requires sufficient clues. One more thing about our Agawam police chief begs another question. Who escapes indictment by a grand jury like Chmielewski did if he didn't have the protection of the mob? What about Officer Brown's testimony to the grand jury?

Adding to the suspense in this whodunit, we need to consider another town hall character who is suspect in this Arrest Record case. Thanks to our Town Solicitor's suspicious behavior, I was able to identify another rat in the nest.

As I mentioned earlier in this chapter, it grieved me when Agawam's part-time Town Solicitor Lambert Ollari betrayed me. Back then, I couldn't help but think how he knowingly risked his law career protecting Chief Chmielewski and whoever his boss was. But given who he must've been working for, did he really risk anything?

I'm sure as a town solicitor, Mr. Ollari thought about Floyd Landers, maybe even me, and decided it was safer to break the law than to break from the mob and invite retribution. As I'd done with others, I didn't hesitate to go public questioning why Ollari would knowingly sabotage any investigation which was within my right to do as a town councilor.

Sure I was upset with Ollari. He set me up and brought me into harm's way by protecting those who wanted me dead or gone. To make a long story short, I had no choice but to call for his resignation. If for no other reason that the people had the right to see who their town solicitor really was!

Headlines in *The Morning Union* newspaper announced, Councilor Bonavita urges Ollari to quit by *Union* Staff reporter Suzanne McLaughlin. Even our acting manager Town Clerk Edward Caba was quoted in the *Union* story as saying, "Ollari gave us the wrong advice." Caba was no fool, he knew what to say but why didn't he fire Ollari if he knew?

Of course I had my suspicions about Ollari back in those days, but I hadn't known about Skyball's influence in our town as of yet. It wasn't until the time of this writing that I did an online search of my old enemy. I had to know if Ollari had ever been connected to Skyball Scibelli. Oh boy! Where was the internet for me when I was in Agawam?

Bingo! I got lucky and found it. One of Ollari's law partners was none other than a Scibelli! I couldn't resist reprinting the Law Office contact information in this chapter. Here it is:

SCIBELLI & VIVENZIO, PC
1120 Main St., Springfield, MA 01103
Industry: General Practice Law Office
Doing business as: SCIBELLI, **OLLARI** & VIVENZIO, P
Ollari, Lambert R
Registration: Dec. 28,1987

Looking back, I am very pleased that I had called for Ollari's resignation despite nothing coming of it except he was shamed publicly. It was another breaking news story in my Arrest Record scandal and I had the satisfaction of knowing he was outed for the rat he was. But whose rat was he? That's who I really wanted and who I still want to identify today. Is his law firm partner a clue for this whodunit?

What's with lawyers and the mob?

Betrayed by our town solicitor, Lambert Ollari, I approached another attorney sworn to protect and serve the public. Thinking I could expect justice if my case went before a grand jury, I naively believed I could trust the District Attorney's office. Was there no one in Agawam to clue me in to the fact that we had been taken over by the mob so I wouldn't be running to them expecting help like I had done?

Heck, I thought that because I had so much evidence, including Officer Brown's own testimony, how could I lose? Yep. I could see the indictments rolling in now.

Oh boy, was I in for a big surprise. I soon learned, even the District Attorney's office is not immune to organized crime's influence. Just like Ollari had misled my own town, the Hampden District Attorney's Office under "Matty Ryan," blatantly misled the grand jury and his pal Chief Chmielewski walked.

The mob drove the Senator insane but not me!

"I enjoyed our little debate here tonight Miss Bonavita," Senator Sisitsky said with a twinkle in his eye.

"I appreciate your respect for our position even though you don't want to see this approved by the voters Senator."

As it turned out, State Senator Alan Sisitsky was an old nemesis of mine who opposed Proposition 2 ½ and he might've helped me out had I known his own story before I debated him when I was campaigning for my citizen initiative tax reform.

It is only because Senator Sisitsky's bizarre story seems to be linked to my own that I am compelled to share it with my readers. It makes for a best ever clue in this Agawam police chief whodunit.

On May 20, 1981 Senator Sisitsky asked the Massachusetts Supreme Judicial Court to investigate Hampden County D.A. Matty Ryan. And what do you think he accused Ryan of doing?

According to *Wikipedia*, Senator Sisitsky accused Ryan of "abusing his office by using the indictment process for intimidation, **protecting mobsters**, and protecting a close friend who was charged with shooting at two police officers."

According to all reports, the Mafia came after Sisitsky big time. Sort of reads like my own story and it is chilling to say the least. If anyone is interested in finding out what the Mass. State Senate President William Bulger's brother, reputed mobster Whitey Bulger, did to his fellow Senate member Sisitsky you can go online and check it out.

Suffice to say, his experience in the State Senate parallels my own experience on the Agawam council. The only difference between the two of us is that I didn't let them drive me insane as they reportedly did to poor Senator Sisitsky.

By all reports, he'd been seen "roaming the halls of the State House unshaven and in wrinkled or dirty clothes, making short, bizarre statements to anyone who came within a few feet of him."

As the story goes, the mobster Whitey actually had his associates threaten the senator's staffers and even threatened to kill him too. I can't help but wonder if Senator Sisitsky ever cried unto God as I had done myself so often? Maybe that's why he went insane and I didn't. The power of prayer and faith is unbeatable and I prayed the Mafia back in Agawam had gotten that message thanks to how I survived everything they ever did to me.

What do you think?

Going back to Floyd Landers, a member of the Agawam Town Council, who was threatened with his life just like Senator Sisitsky, we might now have an idea or proof of how mobsters operate in politics. If it was the Mafia like Whitey's own associates, according to the Feds, who threatened Sistsky, then why not do the same thing with Floyd who was a well-known politician just like the Senator?

As for the mobsters like Agawam's own Big Al Bruno who Senator Sisitsky had publicly accused the D.A. Matty Ryan of protecting, I'd say it's safe to assume Sisitsky's list included those very mobsters who repeatedly sought my life and those of my informants, including Floyd.

The Agawam Police Officer said what?

Despite everything pointing to a serious mob problem in our town, no one ever spoke the "M" word in public, especially at town meetings. It seemed as if the word "Mafia" was banned from public discourse until, one night, when something happened.

I never dared utter the word "Mafia" in public. Not even in my weekly newspaper that I eventually ended up publishing my last year on the council. I knew better.

You can imagine my surprise when the "M" word finally slipped out at a public meeting and it wasn't from me either. It appeared to be from someone in the "group" right inside our Agawam police department. Here's how it went down.

Wearing my hat as a news reporter with *The Agawam Voice*, I'd planned to report on a liquor license application that came before our town's three member Liquor Licensing Commission. Despite strong neighborhood opposition the license was approved 3-0. It should've never been approved and that's a story of itself.

Here's where the story gets real interesting. It seems that one of the Liquor License Applicants' husband was an Agawam

Policeman by the name of Sgt. Robert Swikalus. On the day of the hearing for the Swikalus application, you could hear a pin drop when another Agawam policeman came forward to address the commission in support of it. The following is an actual reprint of an excerpt from the story as it appeared in *The Agawam Voice* May 14, 1981 edition:

> Addressing the Commission in full uniform, although off duty, was Officer Norman Nardi. "To listen to everybody you'd think we have a Mafia in the town. I don't ever recall responding to one call outside a package store or barroom. I'm in favor of this as a business venture regardless of the nature of his business," he said. Following the meeting, Wayne Henderson an opponent said, "I can't come before a group in a government uniform because it would influence the audience."

Did you catch the name of that police officer? Norman Nardi. Yes. His name was Nardi as in the nephew of "*The Godfather*" Fred Nardi who was a member of the town council at the time. And this was his own nephew who had definitely used the "M" word in public!

To this day, there was speculation that Officer Nardi intentionally appeared before the commission in his uniform simply to intimidate the three member Liquor License Commission. Why not? Even one of our locals, Wayne Henderson told me so after the meeting.

As opponents of the Liquor license had hoped, their attendance might've pressured two of the commissioners to feel safe enough to deny it. Rather than risk losing the vote, it appeared that the godfather's nephew was sent in all decked out in uniform as a backup for its supporters.

I don't know about anyone else. But I sure got the message from Nardi's presence. The problem was I didn't know how to bring it up for public discussion. Oh wait. I had a newspaper didn't I?

As I contemplated running the story, I wish I knew then what I know today about one particular commissioner. Doing research for this memoir I looked up some past allies of mine.

On a prompting I decided to call a former Agawam council candidate who had run against the "godfather" and was defeated the same year I was elected. I got nothing out of him on the first cold call. But when he called me back a few days later warning me to leave it alone, he spilled the beans. He'd been drinking and he wanted to talk this time. I got lucky and grateful that alcohol loosens tongues.

The Godfather has a Lieutenant

Fred Nardi was dead and I figured this fake whistleblower wouldn't have a problem talking about him after all those years. But he did. While the guy begged me to leave Nardi's family alone out of respect to Fred Nardi's memory, he didn't feel any such allegiance to the "Lieutenant" he named.

To my surprise, I know he didn't intend to, but he came right out with a story about one of the commissioners being Fred Nardi's Lieutenant who'd been on the Liquor License Board when Officer Norm Nardi showed up at the Swikalus application hearing in full uniform and called out the "**M**" word.

Spoiler alert! In the organizational structure of the mob, it is common knowledge that a Lieutenant is the Captain of a division within the Mafia.

According to Nation States by Max Barry, "The capo, is the captain or **lieutenant** of a division within the Mafia. He heads a crew of soldiers and reports directly to a boss or underboss, who hands down the instructions. He ranks much higher in the hierarchy of the Mafia. He is also in charge of handling most money."

From my personal observation in the world of organized crime, a Lieutenant is much like a CEO of a company making all the important decisions in the hierarchy of the Mafia crime family. The fake whistleblower named the liquor license commissioner over the phone and it all started to make more sense to me with what Officer Norm Nardi had done.

Fearful the crowd might pressure his two fellow commissioners to deny the liquor license, wouldn't a Lieutenant call on the godfather's own nephew Officer Norm Nardi if that godfather was really the Lieutenant's boss?

In the hierarchy of an alleged Agawam mob it would appear that the idea of an active Lieutenant fits. These kinds of titles, along with known Mafia monikers, whether real mafiosa or merely wannabe associates of the Genovese crime family, I'm told were worn like a badge of honor in closed circles. So what was with the mafiosa attitude similar to that of those from the real Mafia that I was observing in Agawam? And why were the police tracked right into it too?

If there was no active Mafia in Agawam going around threatening me, my informants and killing them as I suspected they were doing, then who was behind it? It's not like high profile politicians were playing some kind of a game. Those weren't kids, like my street kids or the one who pulled a knife on me in that home invasion I survived before I got on the council. Heck, people were dying around me in Agawam and that was no kids' game!

Aside from the fancy Mafia titles and monikers, what about the Mafia's associates, like Mario Facione, who are not actual members of the Mafia? Were they around in Agawam when I was on the council? I think they were. Those who earned a place in my memoir sure do seem to fit the bill and that's why I have a mob whodunit instead of just a plain ole' mob memoir.

Max Barry also explained, "Associates are not actual members of the Mafia but rather anyone who teams up with them on a criminal enterprise of some kind." So far this describes what Mario Facione did for the mob. What about Agawam's associates?

Barry also describes associates as "someone who does business with the mob, including money-laundering bankers, crooked cops, lawyers, politicians, drug dealers, etc. Associates are also fair game on the streets, they are not protected by the organization. Anybody can be an associate in the Mafia, however only Italians and Sicilians can be made."

Wondering why a Lieutenant would waste his time on a Liquor Commission, I got to thinking about some under the table bribes that I'd been offered on the council. I know bribery is common to politics even today, but I found it most interesting to witness it firsthand as I did. You can read all about it in Chapter 10.

Keeping it all in the family with the Nardis

The meaning of "family" took on a whole new meaning for me when Officer Norman Nardi stepped into the picture. He's my cousin by marriage. Until that commission hearing, the only family I had to deal with in my council business was the Genovese crime family.

Like all Italians, I had a lot of relatives in Agawam on my father's side. In fact, a close cousin of mine was married to Norman and they lived in Agawam. That made me nervous. Thanks to Norm marrying my cousin, I was kind of related to the mob again on the side of Fred Nardi's family this time.

I didn't want to upset my cousin who was married to someone whose uncle was known as the "godfather" of Agawam, but I couldn't let that get in the way of my plan to clean up Agawam. I quoted Officer Norman Nardi and ran the story with the "**M**" word and waited to see what would happen.

It didn't get past the boss of Agawam when word got out how his own nephew had publicly used the word "Mafia" at the Liquor License hearing. But you know, it's the darndest thing how the Lord provides when you pray for help to out the boys behind a mob problem as I had prayed to do.

Risking outing themselves, I was stunned that after I ran the story with Officer Nardi's quote, most of my 3000 papers of that edition of *The Agawam Voice* were stolen. You can read all about it in Chapter 12. It's a fascinating story.

I should mention that it was the only edition ever stolen and destroyed by hoodlums. It was confirmation I was on the right track. I reprinted the entire edition the following week including the same Liquor License hearing story with Officer Nardi's Mafia comment.

When something like this happens, it leaves little doubt as to who wanted that edition taken off the street. Of course, I had to explain why I was reprinting the entire edition the following week, but I never mentioned the "**M**" word as the reason.

Who else wants to keep the "M" word secret today?

I researched several online mobologists for my memoir. I finally settled on *masslive.com*'s organized crime timelines, offered by Stephanie Barry, to chart my own organized crime hierarchy in Agawam. So far, this whodunit was really coming together. The characters were just jumping off the pages begging to be identified thanks to slip ups like my cousin Officer Norm Nardi had made.

From here on in, the whodunit takes on the role of disproving *The Republican News* mobologist Stephanie Barry's theory that the Genovese crime family has gone inactive in Massachusetts today.

Thanks to mobologists like Barry, the very mobsters who sought to kill me so many times, while always staying under the radar, were finally getting the publicity they justly deserved. I just am uncomfortable with her attempts to convince her readers the Mafia is no longer active because some of its members are dead.

How many mobsters and bosses were killed off in my grandfather's timeline? And did the Mafia go inactive? Just the opposite, they became stronger as they got smarter in staying under the radar.

Isn't that how Satan operates? He wants God's children to think he doesn't exist and that's how Satan can get away with wreaking havoc in our lives eh? It's the same with secret combinations like the Mafia who are under the influence of Satan.

Trying to stay under the radar myself while living in Agawam, I looked for any connection to the Springfield crew that I could make after the home invasion I survived and especially after the mysterious death of Floyd.

I couldn't believe my luck when I came across some of Stephanie Barry's 2011 and 2015 updated organized crime series of vignettes dating as far back as my own family's Mafia lineage I shared in Chapter 1.

"Greater Springfield mob figures: What ever happened to ...?"

Stephanie Barry's published OC online vignettes on reputed Agawam mobster Adolfo "Big Al" Bruno is enlightening. But even more enlightening is how she presents her readers a timeline for his criminal activities. These revealed Bruno's association with the Hampden D.A. "Matty" Ryan and reputed mobster "Skyball" Scibelli who each have a big role in this whodunit!

Amazingly, Barry's OC timeline walks readers right into my own story of the Agawam Police Department. These included two mob assassinations going back as far as 1972. One involved my former boss Victor DeCaro and again in 1979 with the case of my Arrest Record when I solicited the aid of District Attorney Matty Ryan, who was Bruno's buddy.

In one of her organized crime vignettes, Barry presents Bruno as a cold blooded killer who kills someone to win the favor of the D.A. "Matty" Ryan. Interestingly, Bruno who lived in Agawam the same time as me, murdered another mobster named Antonio Facente in 1979.

Did you catch that? The year 1979 was the year of my election to the town council and that was also when the Agawam Police Chief was accused by Officer Brown of leaking my Arrest Record. I've taken the liberty of sharing a few lines from Barry's vignette that fits rather nicely into this whodunit.

According to an online source dated December 11, 2011 *The Republican News* offered Stephanie Barry's organized crime vignette, <u>Organized crime in Springfield evolved through death and money</u>. The vignette described how Antonio Facente's "bound corpse" was found in the trunk of a car in 1979. Bruno had apparently bragged of killing Facente to "cozy up" to Matty Ryan.

It wasn't until years later, long after I resigned from the council and left Agawam, that the friendship between Ryan and Bruno went public. Nonetheless, what's important is that the friendship existed at the time I was being harassed by the Agawam Police Chief, who had clearly been protected by the D.A. Matty Ryan.

Hadn't Max Barry writing for the Nations Stakes website described an associate as "someone who does business with the mob, including crooked cops, *lawyers* and politicians?"

The Stanley Standard

As I questioned earlier on in this chapter, Police Chief Stanley Chmielewski's protection by the D.A. Matty Ryan begs the question of how anyone gets away with breaking the law when a grand jury is involved, as one was in my arrest record case. It's simple, and as so many conservative commentators often remind us, "corrupted political insiders use the law to help their friends and hurt their enemies."

Clearly as all evidence thus far would indicate, I was their enemy and Stanley was their friend. Just look at the "Hillary (Clinton) Standard" wherein the 2016 Democrat Presidential Nominee got a pass from the FBI and DOJ involving her private server email scandal. Associated Press headlines read, <u>FBI director: Clinton extremely careless with email; charges unlikely</u>.

Similar to my own situation with the District Attorney's office who protected my pal Stanley, the AP story reported how "the FBI used their office to protect Hillary Clinton's campaign for President. Instead of rightfully indicting Hillary on criminal charges, she was vindicated of any wrongdoing. Republicans even say she created the "Hillary Standard."

In the case of Police Chief Chmielewski, it appears we had a District Attorney named "Matty" Ryan who did pretty much the same thing as Director Comey. Incredibly, D.A. Ryan also recommended no criminal charges be brought against Stanley despite having enough evidence to do so. Maybe Hillary could have used the "Stanley Standard" as a defense had she known about it at the time of her own possible indictment.

I found Chief Chmielewski's December 10, 2015 online obituary after I was prompted to look it up one day. I'd been waiting a long time to tell my story. It's been 37 years since Chief Chmielewski was ordered to handle me and had gotten away with it.

Although he's deceased, I still savor being able to say, "And now Chief, I get to disseminate **your** records!" The following is a reprint of his obituary I found online.

Stanley J. Chmielewski
Passed away on December 10, 2015

Stanley J. Chmielewski, 81, passed away Thursday at the Holyoke Soldier's Home surrounded by his loving family. Stanley was born in Feeding Hills on April 4, 1934 to the late Michael and Julia (Beckiel) Chmielewski. He was a lifelong resident of Agawam and was a graduate of Agawam High School. Stanley was a police officer in the town of Agawam for 38 years, 18 which he was the Chief of Police. After retirement Stanley worked for Attorneys Cooledge and Lauro for 10 years as an investigator. He was the President of the Western Mass. Police Chief Association, and a member of Mass. Chiefs of Police Association, New England Police Chiefs Association, Member of the Southwick Lion's Club, belonged to the Masonic Lodge in Agawam, Knights of Columbus and Sacred Heart Athletic Association.

Looking back, I am still amazed as to how he was allowed to keep his job as Agawam's police chief for 38 years if Agawam had no mob problem. It further begs the question of how he ever won enough support to become President of the Western Mass. Police Chief Association. Did the mob own enough police chiefs in Western Massachusetts to give them control over their own association? Just asking!

I only ask because of the Law Enforcement Oath of Honor that Stanley took as police chief. The oath is supposed to be a symbolic statement of commitment to ethical behavior. But in whose organization?

Thanks to Barry's organized crime timeline in one of her many online vignettes, it's not a stretch of the imagination to place "Skyball" and Big Al Bruno right in the middle of the arrest record incident. If Skyball and Bruno were known killers then what was to keep them from ordering an Agawam police Chief to leak my arrest record?

SPOILER ALERT! What we do know is that as Agawam's Police Chief he finally outed himself to me as an enforcer for the mob in 1981. But you can read all about it in the upcoming chapters.

In the mid 1980's, a federal prosecutor reportedly dubbed Big Al Bruno "second in command to Francesco "Skyball"

Scibelli." Add to that the District Attorney "Matty" Ryan's personal relationship with Bruno and it only leaves the question of who was Skyball's enforcer in Agawam?

Thanks to Stephanie Barry's organized crime timeline, it reads more like evidence in a mob whodunit. For starters, Stanley J. Chmielewski had to know about my past long before I ever served on the town council. Wasn't he on the police force in Agawam when I was a witness to a murder that happened in Agawam in '72? Yes.

The D.A. Matty Ryan, who died in 2009 at the age of 91, was another harassing spirit in my life while on the Agawam Town Council. So what happened to the District Attorney named Matty Ryan who threw me to the wolves too many times that I can remember? "Matty" Ryan's forced exit from politics in 1990 was finally disclosed in another organized crime vignette published August 2009 in *The Republican* by mobologist Stephanie Barry.

The fake assault charge and the Police Chief

Never one to give up, Chief Chmielewski wasted no time in coming after me again shortly after his arrest record caper failed to get rid of me or control me as they might've wanted to do. To their disappointment, my popularity with the people did not diminish as my detractors had hoped. So, what Stanley did next was totally unexpected.

Sure, I expected some type of personal retaliation from the Police Chief after vilifying him as I had done, but I naively assumed that was the end of anymore outrageous scandals originating from the Agawam police. Boy, was I ever wrong!

I guess I was naïve because I still had some measure of faith in our police like Officer Brown. Unarguably, revenge is a mafiosa commandment not to be taken lightly especially in Agawam.

To this day, I wonder why no one in the Agawam populace ever made such a connection, especially when all hell broke loose right after I called for and got Caputo's resignation. Editor's note: (Pardon my French)

My story now reads like something out of a television script from Matlock. But it makes for a great whodunit. Instead of the chief being charged and getting hauled into court for his role in leaking my arrest record, it was me!

Time to bring in another character who I am sorry to say, had to have been either threatened or bribed into doing what he did to me to get me hauled into court by the Agawam police chief. His name was Michael Shibley. He had his moment of fame when he made breaking news with his own fake assault charge against me and so he earned a place in this whodunit along with our Agawam police chief.

In the 1979 council elections, Michael was one of the underdog candidates for one of three at-large seats open on the council. Whether by luck, or brought in for such a job by the mob, Michael was known to be a slow witted young man. Looking back, I guess the poor kid was the perfect patsy for a job with the mob.

It was no surprise to anyone when he came in last in the field of candidates on Election Day. The surprise was that he got as many votes as he did. Naturally, I thought that was the last I would hear from the kid after he lost the election.

I was still reeling from the arrest record scandal I'd survived when I was notified of a criminal lawsuit filed against me for assault and battery. It was none other than the Shibley kid who had filed the complaint with the Agawam police.

This was no laughing matter either. The court record on file cited the <u>Offense as Assault and Battery by Means of a Dangerous Weapon</u>. The Chief sure wasn't messing around this time. I was facing ten years in prison if found guilty.

It seems someone had gotten Shibley to claim I assaulted him while campaigning in a neighborhood that I'd been canvassing as a council candidate. The boys in the "group" must've been sitting on this as a backup. Else why bring in this kid after their plan to get me off the council failed with the Arrest Record caper?

I knew I was innocent of the charges brought against me by Shibley. However I also remembered Chief Chmielewski, being guilty of disseminating my Arrest Record, and getting off scot-free thanks to "Matty" Ryan's tampering with the grand jury.

220

Guess who was handling my case for this one? Yep, "Matty" Ryan was assigned my case. And any chances of my getting off looked pretty grim.

Heck, if I'd known "Big Al" Bruno was around and the fact that he actually killed someone as a favor for Ryan, I would have been a whole lot more worried. But I didn't know all that at the time.

Earlier in this chapter, I included one of Stephanie Barry's organized crime vignettes on Bruno who had bragged to some Mafia informants how he killed Facente to cozy up to D.A. "Matty" Ryan. It read in part, "In 1979, Antonio Facente's shot and similarly bound corpse was found in the trunk of a car."

To know that Big Al Bruno was killing people in 1979 and 1981 while living right down the street from me is disturbing to say the least. But isn't a great clue for this whodunit?

Had I known all of this back then, I would have had a sit-down meeting of my own, or a come to Jesus meeting with my father who, by the way, was conspicuously absent. So was my crazy cousin Gina. And there was no internet back then for me to look up anything either.

Agawam Police Chief partners with the Gold Dust Twin

Getting back to Shibley and his newfound police buddies, I recalled a similar scheme employed by Chief Chmielewski and our Town Council's former President Richard Theroux alias the Gold Dust Twin.

The Agawam police officer who had testified on my behalf against Chief Chmielewski, made some headlines of his own when he tried to implicate Councilor Theroux and the Police Chief in a similar situation as mine.

Officer Ronald Brown made his remarks to *The Morning Union*, "after learning that President Theroux had urged a tenant of Brown's [after being evicted] to file an assault and battery complaint against Brown with the Agawam Police Department." Hmmm. Sound familiar?

Thanks to Officer Brown going public to testify on my behalf about the leak with my arrest record, I was alerted to another Stanley standard. It was when Officer Brown's own run-in with the Agawam police chief and Gold Dust Twin got my attention after the "group" tried to use it on me a few months later. But unlike Brown's situation, the Chief's trumped up charges against me carried a ten year sentence!

I remember being shown a picture of Shibley that was on file with the police who claimed to have taken it after I allegedly assaulted him. In the photo I could plainly see Shibley had a huge gash on his forehead. A wound he claimed I had made when I struck him with a rock. Since I knew that I did not smack him with a rock, I wondered who did.

I pictured Chief Chmielewski having someone hit the poor kid to make it look like I had really assaulted him. Whatever the story was, I never found out. As usual, no one was talking.

Getting ready for my trial, I thought it was interesting that my case actually went through the entire trial process. I figured it would have been thrown out for lack of evidence before it ever got to a jury. Looking back, I'm sure they would've killed the poor kid if Shibley had refused to go along with their scheme.

In my trial by jury, the only evidence provided against me was by witness testimony. In other words, it was going to be up to the jury to decide the true facts from what was said by each party and each witness. And that's where my trial got real scary.

In a true mob courtroom drama, the two witnesses were brought in from out of state. Two witnesses, both driving cars with out of state license plates, both claiming they'd been driving down the street and just happened to witness the assault (that never took place).

Incredibly, the two of them both decided to go on their own to the Agawam police to report the alleged assault. Well, the mob has a reputation for coming up with these kinds of fake witnesses who'll lie for them for the right price or a favor owed. And the mob has judges in their pockets too. It sure wasn't looking good for me.

I wasn't forgetting how the D.A.'s office that was prosecuting my case was in their pockets too. Watching this drama play out as I did, I was more convinced than ever that our town had a really bad mob problem. What kind of a police chief and D.A. bring in fake witnesses from out of state?

As reported in breaking news, my case was set for trial in Superior Court on June 27, 1980. The incident allegedly occurred in October 1979 one month before Agawam council elections. The boys were playing hard ball and I needed a good lawyer so I turned to my lawyer friend Arthur Serota whom I thought I could trust. He hadn't done much for me with my arrest record case, but he was all I had and he took my case pro bono.

Everyone has a past, even trial lawyers

Normally I change the names of those who are still alive at the time of this writing, unless their story had already gone public. And that is the story of my lawyer who shared headlines with me several times during my stormy days on the Agawam Town Council.

Arthur Serota of Springfield started out as a man of integrity with a reputation as a good criminal defense lawyer who assured me he wasn't afraid of the Springfield mob. Yeah, right.

Everyone has a past and sooner or later it will catch up with you. It is especially true if you stand in the way of the Mafia. And Serota unfortunately, acting as my defense attorney hoping to get me off of a ten year sentence, was definitely standing in someone's way.

At trial, the Commonwealth's argument was that the defendant, yours truly, engaged in an unprovoked attack against Shibley. I pleaded innocent and I soon found myself a defendant in a trial by jury that made breaking news overnight.

My trial counsel, Arthur Serota, set up my defense and I give him credit for showing up for the pretrial phase. But before I was due to appear in court for the trial, Serota backed down.

With eyes downcast, Serota quietly informed me, "I can no longer represent you. I am so sorry."

To which I stupidly asked, "And why not?"

I admit I already knew what he was going to say. I had heard it so many times before. But I just wanted him to say it. And he did.

"They got something on me," he said. "Something I thought no one would ever dig up." To which he explained, "Everyone has something in their closet. They found mine."

Now, I just want to say this on Serota's behalf. He was an honest man and might have been a good defense lawyer. But I didn't have a chance to find out. Serota only had a chance to do some of the preliminary work on my case before someone had gotten to him.

Trying to make me feel better, or merely easing his conscience, this defeated man standing in front of me told me how much he admired me for what I was doing in Agawam. Yes. Serota knew my story.

He never gave up any names though. Like Floyd Landers, no one ever rats on who threatens them, at least not around me they never did.

"Can't you tell me who threatened you Arthur?" I pleaded with him before he walked away from my case.

"It's best you don't know," and that's all he would say.

I had heard those words before from my mentor and former Agawam Town Councilman Floyd Landers the night before he died. Unlike Floyd who had the courage to keep talking to me after being warned not to, Serota was more cautious than to tempt fate. Floyd risked his life while Serota only had a reputation from the past to lose.

I couldn't' believe that Serota caved the way he did. Here I was being quoted in all the news as saying, "Never fear your past," all the while Serota had been representing me on my Arrest Record case. I guess my testimony didn't stir him in the least.

As for my sharing Serota's story, it's not like no one suspected what had happened. One day he was all over the front page news as my lawyer and the next day in court I'm sitting there all alone defending myself. It didn't take a genius to figure out why Serota had dumped me.

I admit I was frightened to find myself suddenly alone without any legal representation. Here I was a single unwed mother with only a high school degree and I'd never represented myself in the courtroom before. I hadn't yet gone through law school which I didn't do until 1999.

I thought I was alone in that courtroom, but I wasn't really. I was still praying and seeking guidance from my Heavenly Father and I knew He was listening. Now, I just had to remember

224

all the times God rescued me from death and other perils every time I prayed.

Still it was scary standing alone in the courtroom facing a judge and jury. I knew my ship was sinking when I saw the list of witnesses who were lined up to testify how they had supposedly witnessed me "picking up a huge rock and smashing it into Shibley's forehead."

It didn't seem to matter to anyone that none of the witnesses were locals of course. I knew they were prepared to perjure themselves, because no one could have witnessed something I never did.

Calling in favors was another favorite tactic of the mob and people will often risk perjury charges to lie through their teeth when called upon to do so by criminals in organized crime.

So I did what I always did best. I got on my knees and I cried unto God with all my heart and soul pleading with Him to tell me what to do. I can't explain it, but after praying, I felt impressed not to try to find another attorney. I felt the Spirit compelling me to defend myself.

And that's how I showed up at my next court hearing completely alone. My enemies must have been salivating at the expectation of my spending the next ten years in prison.

Proving my innocence

Recalling the words to a favorite hymn I'd learned in Texas, I kept repeating, "My God is a mighty God." As I called upon the name of Jesus Christ, I could feel the angels putting up a hedge around me as if to keep the devil himself at bay. By the grace of God, I built a simple yet powerful defense which I could never have done by myself.

Truth be known I had no defense. The prosecution had their witnesses lined up to perjure themselves and my accuser Shibley who stuck to his story throughout the trial. What happened that day was a miracle as I walked out a free woman.

I know it was a miracle because there no other explanation to have a jury find me not guilty. Looking back, my defense seemed more like a television legal drama and I was in the title role of a criminal defense attorney like the famous Ben Matlock.

Courtroom drama was at its best when I took to the floor to cross-examine one of the out-of-state witnesses. She had claimed to see me smacking Shibley up side of the head while she'd just happened to be driving down the street.

The judge did something amazing himself when he let me pull off a scene right out of a Matlock movie. Attempting to prove my innocence, I managed to unmask the plot of the prosecution when I stepped out of my high heeled shoes with the permission of the judge.

The judge sure did help me out that day when he ordered Shibley to step down from the witness stand so I could do my little demonstration. Standing next to him barefoot, I proved how his so-called witness had perjured herself.

Shibley was too tall for me to ever be able to take anything, much less a rock, to smack him up side of the head as witnesses claimed I had done. When the jury saw that courtroom drama unfold, they had no choice but to acquit me.

You better believe the first thing I did, when I got home that day, was to fall to my knees and thank my Father in Heaven for winning me my freedom that day. Yep. I lived to serve another day on the Agawam town council --much to the chagrin of my political enemies.

Moving this whodunit along, we need to ask where my father was. Conspicuously absent throughout the relentless attacks on me by the police chief, he never once stepped in to rescue me like I knew he could do.

Yep. My estranged father who once saved my life from the most powerful crime family in the country was nowhere to be found. Now that I think about it, he slipped under the radar right after I got elected.

Who knows, maybe he was watching from a distance. Isn't that how it seemed to go down when my boss Victor was assassinated in Agawam in '72? I'll never know if Dad might've been ordered to stay out of it and just left me to the mob.

Maybe Dad had agreed with his mobster friends that it was better for me to spend time in prison then to let them kill me.

226

Apparently Heavenly Father didn't agree that I should go to prison.

Unknown to me, another father had been quietly watching over me and his out-of-wedlock son. Despite his conspicuous absence during the trial, I figured he also must've known what had been going on around my house.

Someone else was watching me and it wasn't Dad, that's for sure.

CHAPTER TEN:
BRIBES, THREATS AND MURDERS

"Hey Al. What are you doing here?" I said, as I opened the door to let him in.

I was surprised to see my son's father "Big Al" standing on my doorstep. It was the middle of the week. He usually only showed up on weekends to visit with his son. He was sure good that way given how he was still married.

I knew why Al was here today. He knew everything. He always did. He just never bothered to keep me in the loop. I figured he thought it was safer for me that way.

"What do you think they'll do to me Al?"

"What's your plan for our son?" He asked while ignoring my question.

"He won't be any safer with you and so far he's never been in any danger with me," I reminded him.

Watching Al get up from the table and take a look around the house, it reminded me of another time he showed up unexpectedly.

It was right after Floyd Landers told me he'd been warned to stay away from me or else. It was the last time I saw Floyd alive back in October of '79 and things were never the same again after that.

I never got over how Floyd stubbornly chose to ignore their threats and ended up paying with his life for it. Now I was on the council in his place. Were they watching me now too, I wondered? I thought so. If not, then why the sudden visit from Al?

I figured if my political enemies knew the whereabouts of Floyd Landers, enough to warn him to stop talking to me, then someone had to be doing some high tech surveillance. But Floyd died before he could give up any names to me and he left me alone to deal with the arrest record mess. I thought I had dealt with it and it was over--until the surveilling started up again.

After what I had done to the Agawam Police Chief when he leaked my Arrest Record, I had expected to be surveilled and even tailed like what had obviously been done to poor Floyd. But I wasn't sure if the police chief's brothers in blue had seen me do anything to get their attention again after the arrest record mess settled down.

Were his brothers in blue surveilling my neighborhood hoping to catch more informants like they did with poor Floyd? Sure, I didn't know who was behind Floyd's death or if I was next on their list, but when my own "Big Al" showed up when the surveilling started up again, it was none too soon for me.

I never said anything about what I suspected happened to Floyd. Not even to Al. After all the commotion with the arrest record mess, I suspected he already knew. I wondered if he knew about the police cars that had begun trolling my neighborhood lately. As if reading my mind, he just came right out with the reason for his unexpected visit.

"I heard a few things had been going on around here. Are you okay?"

"Yeah, so far."

"I'm gonna be hanging around here for a while," Al said, with his back to me as he looked out the window.

True to his word, every day just as the sun went down, Al would show up like clockwork. The first thing he would do is open the curtains and shades in every room on the first floor of my two-story duplex home. Then he'd turn on all the lights in the house.

"What are you doing?" I asked him the first night of his watch. It was a ritual he performed each time he came by.

Al said nothing as he stood in front of the bay window in our living room facing the street. He just stood there looking out as if expecting to see someone come walking up to the door or something.

"Don't you want to sit down or have something to eat?" I asked.

"Elaine," Al said under his breath. It was more like an order for me to shut up and go about my business so he could do his. Al never used my nickname of Elena ever since I'd started using it after becoming a star witness to a mob murder.

229

When Al and I first met in 1968, I hadn't yet learned about the story behind my name from my grandmother. It wasn't until 1972 that she told me. After that, a lot more than my name changed for me when I found myself on the run from the mob.

Al was a man of few words. He never talked about his private life or what he did for a living. All I knew was that he'd been a heavyweight boxer and suspected he was involved in the Springfield mob married to a woman who owned a night club.

We never talked about what he did until now. A whole lot started making more sense to me after our little chat. It seems Al was a bodyguard for the very mobsters who wanted me dead or most likely wished I'd stayed put in Texas. He had to have been worried or else I don't think he would've even said that much about himself.

According to Richard Warner, writer and researcher on organized crime, "Bodyguards do exist, but not as formal positions. Some bosses have selected certain soldiers to act as their bodyguards when needed."

Walking back into the kitchen looking every bit the part of a bodyguard, satisfied the house was secured, he gave me his jacket to hang up.

"Nobody's gonna try anything while I'm here."

"Sure Al. But what about when you're not here?"

"I'll be hanging around for a while. Like I said, no one's gonna bother you."

Just like the time a few months earlier when Al stepped in worried about me after Floyd's mysterious death, I never saw any other suspicious surveillance activity for a while. No more police cars hanging around my street and no more noises at night either. Like my father, Al was a mystery of himself. Watching him standing there looking out the window, I wondered how could he make things go away like Dad did?

I knew Al had spent a brief time in prison, but he never told me what he had done to get sent up and I didn't want to know. As for him being a bodyguard to the mob I had been running from, I didn't want to know that part of his story either. And you won't hear it from me today either!

I always suspected, even today, that Al knew who'd been ordered to keep an eye on my every move when I got back in Agawam. He always knew just when to show up, didn't he?

Big Al, meet Big Al

Looking back, I can't help but wonder how Agawam's reputed resident mobster, Adolfo "Big Al" Bruno, was handling the news that someone in their own organization was now my bodyguard. What are the odds of that? It makes for a great whodunit though!

As the story goes, I never suspected that my son's father might actually be protecting me from another Big Al running loose in Agawam. Back then, I was clueless, although I guess my Big Al wasn't.

Even now, as I write this memoir, I am still stunned to realize for the first time how a known killer for the mob named Big Al Bruno had been living right down the road from me.

Could it really have been someone like Big AL Bruno behind the surveillance the whole time I was in Agawam? And if so, then was it him who had been giving orders to the Agawam Police Chief too? Or was it the godfather of Agawam, Fred Nardi, who was really behind it all?

I knew the godfather really good, even dated him as I reminisced in Chapter 8, and I just couldn't see him having people killed like what Bruno had been doing. It had to be someone else. Was it Skyball Scibelli? Heck, hadn't he ordered his own son-in-law's assassination and most likely mine too if not for my father's intervention?

Within any hierarchy of the Mafia, there are always associates. So who were theirs in Agawam that could've pulled off such high tech surveillance all around me and my informants while I was on the council? I suspected the Agawam police chief. Go back to Chapter 9 if you don't agree.

I called the state police and when they did nothing, I called in the FBI. Heck, I was a public official and I was hoping they'd take my complaint more seriously. But they didn't. No one did until my Big Al stepped in and kept watch over me and our son.

And even today, I can't help but think how the FBI had to know who was messing with me. Why didn't they investigate my complaint? As a public official, I reported what appeared to be some type of surveillance activity outside my house reminding me more of a stakeout.

By its very definition, 'when police watch a suspect's house, keeping an eye on who's coming and going, they call it a "stakeout." Everyone knows that a stakeout is an honored police tradition. Back then, I soon learned it's also a tradition of organized crime.

Well, whatever my Big Al did or who he talked to, seemed to do the trick because I never heard or saw anyone around my house for a while after he showed up. Nope. Nothing got stirring until I stirred the pot myself and brought them all back again.

Surveilled, unmasked and leaked again

It all started right up again after I'd begun meeting with some informants secretly. Yes, they were whistleblowers just like Floyd had been. And like Floyd, they too risked their lives to help me in my undercover work on the council. Was I being surveilled again? Someone was out there watching or else how could they have known about my informant again?

Al had run off the police chief's brothers in blue once before after I'd tangled with him involving my Arrest Record a few months earlier. But after that threat eased up, he was nowhere to be seen for a while. At least not until one of my informants told me he'd been warned to stay away from me or they'd kill him. Shortly after that, Al suddenly appeared as if out of nowhere.

As before, Al did his own stakeout. He kept to his same routine opening all the curtains, lights, even standing in front of windows where he could be seen to anyone who had no business hanging around. Within a week, Al felt safe to leave us alone and he was gone as quietly as he had come.

I was relieved that the immediate threat had been handled and I could get on my life without that hanging over my head. I had a son and he had been doing well in school until lately. I'd been so busy keeping us both safe at home that I hadn't thought about the schools.

Bringing politics into the classroom

As a single unwed mother, I tried to stay involved in my son's school activities and monitor his grades. He was a smart kid and always made straight A's before moving back to Agawam. Glad to find something to chat about during the surveilling, nonetheless, Al took me by surprise when he brought up the subject of the schools.

"Are you running into any problems with his school?" Al asked one night after our eleven year old son had gone to bed.

"I guess our son mentioned something to you about it or else how could you have known?"

"Just tell me what's going on."

Given what I'd already been through since returning to Agawam, problems at school were peanuts compared to the trouble I'd been fending off lately. I quickly updated Al on the school situation.

"Something's up. Our son never gets anything but A's. But not anymore."

"Did you talk to anyone at the school yet?"

"I prayed about it but with all that's been going on around here, I haven't had a chance to visit with his teachers yet."

Hanging around as my bodyguard, it gave Al and I a chance to have a heart to heart talk and consider how of all my politics might've been affecting our son. Was someone bringing politics into his classroom?

He was only nine years old when we returned to Massachusetts in 1978. But in less than two years, he'd accomplished quite a bit for a boy his age.

"Do you remember when that kid of yours started up his own business selling candy to the neighborhood kids?" I asked Al.

"I sure do. That kid's got a lot going for him," Al recalled.

As a single mother, I'd been proud of how our son always managed to pick up little jobs here and there to make extra spending money for himself. So, I wasn't surprised when he came up with the idea for a neighborhood candy store.

"Mom. I want to sell candy. Can I do it from our kitchen?" My son asked me, one day after he'd come home from school.

And that's how our neighborhood got its very own candy store. It seems neighborhood kids had been complaining how there was no corner store nearby for them to get snacks like candy bars after school. He didn't get rich, but he did learn a valuable lesson in self-reliance.

"Didn't he work in a bicycle store in town for a while?" Al asked.

"Yep." After he closed down his candy store," I explained.

Our son had decided he needed a better paying job so he could earn enough money to buy a unicycle. He liked the candy store but it wasn't turning over the kind of profits he had hoped for.

I remember waking up 5a.m. one morning to a noise downstairs. I was surprised to find my son rolling newspapers in our living room. I still remember that day as if it was yesterday.

"Whatcha doing?" I asked, relieved it wasn't a burglar or worse.

"I got a job with *The Morning Union* delivering newspapers," he proudly explained.

He said he didn't tell me only because he thought I wouldn't let him do it. "But I can do it Mom. I promise I'll get the papers out every morning on time," he assured me.

As it turned out, paper boys had to be twelve years old. He was only eleven, so he got a reference from our neighbor lady and the *Morning Union* newspaper decided to give him a chance. I figured it didn't hurt that his mother was on the council either. I was really proud of him.

"I still have that picture of him delivering papers on his unicycle," Al said ever so proudly.

"I know. I still can't believe how he could ride it with a full bag of newspapers on his shoulder" I said.

Before he even got the paper route, our son had made a deal with the owner of a local bike shop to work off the payment of a unicycle. He kept his word and after he had earned the unicycle he applied for a job as a paper boy.

As we talked about our son's accomplishments over the past two years, we both came to the same conclusion. Yes, our kid was doing well. So what was up with the bad grades?

"Taking on all those jobs was a good experience for the kid Elaine," Al reminded me. While asking, "Do you think that had anything to do with his grades dropping?"

"No. He had already quit the paper route long before the problem with his grades came up. And besides, I made sure he studied for his tests and did his homework every night," I assured Al.

"I guess he's doing okay despite everything you've been going through in this town," he said.

I guess that's when we both turned our attention back on me. Since moving to Agawam, threats, bribery, and even murder was all too common on my mind these days. I hadn't considered how kids, who come from conservative political families, might be harassed in public schools by their liberal teachers.

Now, looking back on my own son's experience in the Agawam public schools, it brings back old memories of my own pre-law school days in the mid 90's when I attended the University of Northern Iowa to get a B.A. so I could go on to law school.

Most of my professors didn't appreciate the fact that I was on the Waterloo School Board while attending UNI especially since I was known a committed Christian conservative. It made me an easy target for them and I was often harassed in the classroom because of my beliefs.

Producing and hosting a conservative television talk show didn't help any. Many of my liberal professors' classroom antics gave me ample material for my talk shows. Not surprisingly, liberal professors not only encouraged, but fostered a policy of bringing politics into the classroom and relished anything they could do to annoy me. I put up with it and held my own until one particular professor stepped over the line.

I knew she had a problem with me but I didn't think any professor would go so far as to tamper with my grades. Wrong! I got my first undeserved "B" in her class. I prayed unto God and I appealed it and even went public with the incident hoping to discourage other professors from using my grades to harass me. It worked. I only got that one "B" while at UNI.

235

Looking back, I wish I knew back then what I know now. I knew of other Christian students who were having problems with liberal professors, but it was a bit more different with me only because I was an elected member of a school board and I had been publicly opposing the indoctrination of our public school students by their liberal teachers.

Not able to see into the future while facing a similar problem with my own son's teachers in the Agawam schools, I prayed and took it to the Lord. I felt pretty sure I was the intended victim of any harassment, not my son. Al agreed.

"You're saying that whoever is behind all your troubles on the council, might have talked to someone at our son's school?" Al asked.

"Yes. Yes I do," I replied. "Maybe they thought I might pack up and move away from here to get him out of our school district."

Al didn't like the thought of that one bit. I knew he wanted to keep his son close by. "I'll ask around and see what's going on," he said, as he made his way out the door.

I really didn't want to have my own sit-down with the school administration. I should've felt guilty for making Al think that I'd move out of the area if nothing was done about the problem. But I didn't feel guilty one tiny bit.

Heck, if Al could makes things go away like my Dad could, then I figured he'd make this problem disappear too. I sat back while he worked his Mafia magic. Sure enough, in no time at all, the warning slips from school stopped and soon my son was getting straight A's again.

Given the problem I had faced with the school, it begs the question--do conservatives hesitate getting involved in politics because of how it might affect their families, especially their children?

"But I have a family!"

"Hi. Can I help you?' I asked as I opened the door to find a nice looking man in his mid-twenties on my doorstep.

"Do you have a minute to talk?" he asked. "My name is Michael Cascella. I live in Agawam and I voted for you."

"Glad to hear it. What's on your mind?" I asked while wondering whether he was for me or against me.

I sometimes had drop-in visitors wanting to talk politics, but Cascella told me he only dropped by to thank me for the work I'd been doing on the council. He was a welcome sight indeed. I hadn't even been on the council a month and I'd had a rough week fighting the good ole boys when he dropped by. We talked for a while and one thing led to another.

"I don't know how you do what you do," Cascella said, sounding more like an apology than a compliment.

"It's not easy," I reminded him. "I could use some help if you'd be willing to speak up at council meetings or write letters to the editor."

Shaking his head, Cascella said, "I can't get involved and fight them like you're doing."

"Why not?" I innocently asked him.

He somberly replied, "I have a family."

His answer was all too typical and I understood. But he, like everyone else in town, knew I was a single mom. Poor guy, I couldn't let this moment go by. Without saying another word, I stepped away from the door so he could see my own son who'd been sitting on the staircase listening to our conversation.

"And what is he a dog?" I asked, while pointing to my son.

Yes. I really did say that. Even now, after all these years the words still ring in my ears. I just spit it out probably because everyone in Agawam, and all of Western Massachusetts thanks to the media, knew what I'd been up against.

Everyone knew my story. They knew I was an unwed mother struggling to survive working a 9 to 5 job like most people. And here was this young man so worried about what the Agawam boys would do to him if he got in their face.

Sure, I knew he was seeing what was happening to me and didn't want any part of it. He most likely wanted to encourage me to keep on with the good fight. That's probably why he dropped by the way he did.

Most people didn't reach out to me like Cascella did. They were either too afraid that the monkey on my back would jump onto them, or their conscience would get the best of them and they'd have to get involved. Cascella seemed to be with the latter.

He found his voice

As for Cascella, I like to think he must have prayed about what he could do to help me after he left, because one day, while reading *The Agawam Advertiser* Letters to the Editor section, I was amazed to see his name in print for the all the world to see.

Published December '79, Cascella had written a splendid letter to the editor slamming Theroux, our council president. He came right out saying Theroux "has brought that august body from being laughable to being ludicrous."

He further wrote, "The voters wisely chose Elaine Bonavita, a champion of the people, to represent them, but Theroux, his 'like-minded' colleagues, and their master, Peter Caputo [Town Manager] chose to stifle Ms. Bonavita, thereby negating our voice. She tried to bring up real issues…"

Yes indeed. Cascella had found his "voice." I saved his published letter which I have kept all these years. In Chapter 12, Michael Cascella even volunteered to help me start up a conservative town newspaper, which I appropriately named *The Agawam Voice*!

In towns with a mob problem, like Agawam, its people oftentimes lose their voice fearing for the safety of their families. Unfortunately, whenever this happens, truth is suppressed in the liberal media.

Often well-meaning small town newspapers lose their voice fearing the loss of advertisers who fear retaliation if liberal bias is absent. A scripture comes to mind.

"For God hath not given us the spirit of fear; but of power, and of love, and of a sound mind."

- 2 Timothy 1:7

Sometimes fear can be a good thing, especially with public officials who may decide against accepting bribes for fear of getting caught. Sure, there are more who don't get caught, but when they do accept bribes, there is always the chance it is a set up like what happened to a certain California city councilman.

In November 2013, a scandal involving the city of Moreno Valley Councilman Marcelo Co made headlines when he was indicted and sentenced for accepting bribes involving land-use decisions.

During Marcelo's trial, the FBI claimed he had abdicated his promise to the people by brazenly taking a series of bribes in exchange for his influence on the City Council. His story was about selling influence and votes for favors. Nice to know it wasn't just Agawam's story. The only difference with the people of the city of Moreno Valley, is that the Feds got involved!

They didn't in Agawam. Not even when I contacted the FBI remember? As for what happened to the California councilman, getting nailed for taking bribes, it could've easily happened to me in Agawam. Heck, I never imagined my vote being worth very much. But it was!

How much am I bid for this vote?

Known as a conservative watchdog on the town council, I held the belief that the more you knew, the better you could cast an honest vote. I'm glad to say that I never supported anything that smelled bad. For most people that was a good thing. For others, my reputation for casting an honest informed vote often meant it would go down in flames if anything smelled suspicious once I was onto it.

Naturally, some of the other members on the council didn't want to be seen openly supporting something under those conditions. And that's how I discovered some votes were worth more than others. While no one around town ever openly claimed that money was paid for votes, everyone knows that old saying about voting, "it begs abuse and things can happen!"

Shortly after I was seated on the council, a land use vote came before us for a proposed condominium development. It was common knowledge how I was going to vote only because I had earlier discussed the pros and cons of the land use project on my radio call-in talk show with *WREB Holyoke Radio*.

As I always did before making a decision on the council, I met with interested members of the community who, one way or another, might've been impacted by the development. On this particular project, it was met with opposition by the locals and I didn't like what I heard, so I decided not to support it.

Before the vote even came before the council, I was approached by the developer. It just so happened he was a friend of my father's and he had donated $50.00 to my campaign. In 1979, $50.00 had the same buying power as $178.00 today in 2017.

Out of respect to Dad, I met with the developer before voting on his project. I figured what could be the harm? People didn't sell their soul for $50 did they? So, I really didn't believe he was going to call in a favor and expect me to honor it for a mere $50 donation.

As you can imagine, I was truly disappointed when the developer reminded me of his $50 donation. He actually had the audacity to come straight out and ask me to support his condominium project knowing full well I knew why the locals opposed it.

"If you vote for it," he said, "the council will approve it."

"Sorry, you know I can't do it."

When that approach failed, he made me an offer he thought I couldn't refuse.

"I know you would like to bring up your son in a better neighborhood," the developer suggested. "I can make that happen for you."

"I guess you didn't hear me." I reminded him. "I've already made my decision."

But the developer wasn't one to give up so easily. I knew he was used to getting his way and I was in his way for sure.

"Maybe you didn't catch my drift. You can have your own condo. All you have to do is vote for my development."

All I remember to this day is how I could have been the owner of a brand new condo with a clear deed in my name. It was a generous offer, if it wasn't a set up to entrap me. Either way, even if my father's friend was on the level, it was a bribe for my vote. And I couldn't do it.

In politics, like in Moreno Valley, bribes go on all the time behind closed doors. More important to the story, is the fact that bribes, once accepted, puts you in a position to be blackmailed for future votes. There are all sorts of reasons public officials may be approached to sell their influence on a council or board.

I have no doubt that had I accepted the developer's bribe, it would have been used against me eventually. Memories of my arrest record's footprints were still fresh on my mind. For all I knew, it was a set-up to get rid of me and hold onto the evidence like they'd done with my arrest record. Then if I didn't do what they wanted, they'd leak it!

Even though it was my first bribe, I decided against going public with it. I couldn't afford to take on one more battle with anymore of my father's so-called "friends." Other public officials, finding themselves in my shoes, might've taken advantage of such an opportunity for political gain.

In the news: Councilwoman Says Developer Offered 'Bribe'

Another city councilor made the news a few years later on May 12, 1990 when a *Los Angeles Times* Staff Writer named Kenneth R. Weiss leaked her own story of bribery:

> An Oxnard councilwoman on Friday accused an Orange County development company of trying to "bribe" her...Councilwoman Ann Johs said a representative of Warmington Homes made the offer April 2 in an informal meeting on a 77-acre development proposed for the northeast corner of Oxnard Boulevard and Gonzales Road. "They were offering something to gain a vote, and that to me would be a bribe," Johs said. "They wanted my vote on their project."

"I can make it a lot easier for you," our Agawam Town Manager was saying to me in the privacy of his office. "Whatever you want, that's in my power to do, it's yours."

Peter Caputo was brought in by the Agawam faction who held a wide majority on the town council. He had already been in place when I took my seat on the council in the fall of 1979. That was one manager that creeped me out every time I got up close to him, so sitting in a closed door meeting with Caputo creeped me out even more. He smelled dirty. And now I had proof!

241

I should've sent him a thank you card for coming right out and bribing me for my silence the way he did right after I had stumbled onto something that his boss, whoever that was, had wanted to keep quiet. Yep. This was one town manager that was as good as gone. It was an answer to prayer, or so I thought. I hadn't yet put it together that Caputo's boss might've had something to do with poor Floyd's death.

For a big shot like Caputo, he sure was stupid. He knew I wanted his resignation even before he called me into his office trying to bribe me. So why did he do it? I had no idea at the time. I was still a rookie trying to stay alive and not end up fish food like others I'd known who'd crossed the mob.

Before Caputo's bribe, I had decided not to go public with such things. After my talks with Floyd, I knew I had nothing to gain by going public, whereas my enemies had everything to gain. They could twist anything around and make it come back on me. So why did I do what I did? Why didn't I heed Floyd's warning to me? I guess because he died before he could tell me why.

Before you go judging me as bringing more trouble on my plate, you should know about the fake resume leaked by Agawam's former Town Councilor Valentine Moreno. He was a gutsy ole kind of a guy and he really gave the good ole boys a run for their money in those days.

I don't know how Moreno lived as long as he did in Agawam but I guess it was because he never uncovered anything about the mob while on the council that was worth getting himself killed over like poor Floyd obviously did. Moreno did report someone had blown up his car once and come to think of it, he did get kind of quiet after that.

As the story goes, Moreno had been quoted in the local news just a few months earlier on Caputo's fake resume and I still have a news clipping of *The Morning Union* February 8, 1980 with him in it that came out again after I got on the council.

Union staff Suzanne McLaughlin tied the story to my own arrest record situation when she reported on the town council and how it was "reminiscent of its failure last summer to investigate the controversy surrounding former Town Manager Peter Caputo's resume."

I can still see the ole guy calling out "Whitewash!" which the "former Councilor Valentine Moreno mumbled after the council last August voted to retain Caputo when it became publicized that the bachelor's degree listed on his Agawam resume was from an unaccredited college in Canada that sold the degrees for $25."

Incredibly, the council kept Caputo on as manager! Once I got on the council a few months later, I figured with all the publicity Moreno had gotten with Caputo's fake diploma, I could use his stupid bribery attempt to garner enough support on the council to call for and get his resignation. Which I did!

I figured there was nothing to gain by my remaining silent about Caputo's bribery attempt given the card I was holding with his fake diploma. There was, however, everything to lose which I was soon to discover.

An Agawam tradition

On February 20, 1980, *The Morning Union*, now *The Republican,* ran a story titled <u>Chief showed officers Bonavita's arrest records: Cop</u>.

That story came out right after I called for and got Caputo's resignation. Whereas Caputo had something to hide, the Agawam boys did nothing once it was leaked by Moreno. My secret past, on the other hand, didn't get such a pass from them. I recall Richard Theroux eager to hang me out to dry in his official role as President of our council.

The Morning Union alerted Agawam when it reported, "The day before Ms. Bonavita's mug shots were picked up from the West Springfield Police Department by an Agawam detective, Ms. Bonavita called for former Town Manager Peter Caputo's resignation at a council meeting, claiming he had tried to make a political deal with her."

Bribes must've been an Agawam tradition, or else I don't think I would've been in so much trouble with Caputo's boss like I found myself in. Naturally, I was a bit more cautious when I got bribed again after Caputo was gone.

Back in 1980, council approval was required for all licenses and permits. Unless otherwise provided by statute, it was unlawful for any person to transact and carry on any business, trade, profession, calling or occupation in the city without first having procured a license from the city.

I recall getting a visit from the applicant for an appliance store license. I had not yet made any public comments on his application, so I just presumed my reputation preceded me and he assumed I would vote it down.

"Thank you for meeting with me Miss Bonavita. Can I ask you how you plan to vote on my license application?"

"I haven't made up my mind yet. And I won't until I look into it more."

I'd heard that some town folks were planning to come out against his store opening up in their neighborhood--something about parking issues. Fearing I would speak out against his application, and kill his chances of council approval, the applicant came right out and offered me a washer and dryer in exchange for my vote. I had the idea that he fully expected me to go along with it too.

As broke as I was, I would've killed for a new set of appliances like that. Whoosh! "Get thee behind me Satan," I was thinking. As usual, I turned down the bribe and said nothing to anyone. I voted against his license of course and I reminded myself I had done the right thing.

The high price of information in Agawam

I remember how I always collected information from wherever I could get it. I usually met with supporters and opponents before any controversial votes came before our council. But I also had people come forward and volunteer information that I could've never gotten without them. They were informants of mine and most of the time it wasn't anything that could've gotten themselves killed over.

On the other hand, there were three who come to mind after all these years that had something worth dying for. Just as some votes were worth more than other ones when offering bribes, I soon found out that not all information had a price on the head of those who leaked it.

My first informant who paid with his life for turning over information to me was Floyd Landers. You would've thought I'd learned from what they did to him after he ignored their warning to stop talking to me.

What I did and why I did it, I can't explain. Like Floyd, the other two informants were both political insiders and they came to me. I did not seek them out. Heck, I didn't even know they had anything I could use until they contacted me. Unlike Floyd who had been a member of the town council, none of my other informants were.

Unmasked

Like Floyd Landers, two more informants of mine turned up dead the day after our last rendezvous. Heart attacks I was told. No bullet riddled bodies turning up in the river like Gary or my boss Victor. No. Now everyone around me was suddenly dying of heart attacks.

Shortly after the arrest record and phony assault charge incidents had settled down, another informant, whom I will call Sarge, contacted me. His background made him a valuable informant considering what I'd been going through with the Agawam police chief.

Hoping to stay under the radar, I never questioned how my informants, like Sarge, got the information as long as what they gave me checked out. I was good with it. But unlike Floyd, Sarge made sure I played by the rules to keep us both safe.

"No one can ever know that I'm talking to you."

"Sure. Not a problem Sarge. I never reveal my sources."

Sarge had some good stuff on the boys and even our police and I knew he must've witnessed it all before retiring as he had done. Still, I never knew why he was doing what he did. I never asked. The less I knew about him the better. It didn't last long.

"I was warned to stop talking to you."

Sarge sounded just like Floyd when he too had been warned with those exact words.

"Why are you doing this?" I asked him.

"Someone's got to do it. May as well be me," he said without any hesitation. He had blue blood in him alright.

"But why are you even talking to me, if you were warned to stay away?"

I was thinking of poor Floyd. Hadn't he done the same thing? That was the last time I saw Sarge alive. I convinced myself that it might have just been a coincidence him dying of a heart attack right after our last secret meeting. But I knew in my gut, they killed him just like someone had done to Floyd. I was absolutely convinced of it when it happened again with another informant of mine.

Someone must've been surveilling me again, for all I knew. Maybe I didn't notice because I figured Al had chased them off the time I was being surveilled when my arrest record mess was going on. But that's the only thing I can say in my defense when I agreed to meet with another informant after Sarge's suspected murder.

The informant whom I will call Shoppie approached me after Sarge had been dead for a while. I never talked about Floyd or Sarge to Shoppie because I never talked about them to anyone until now.

What Shoppie gave me wasn't something worth getting killed over, or so I thought. Heck, the information was usually on the Gold Dust Twins and it was always right on. Yep. Shoppie was the real thing alright!

Looking back, that's probably what brought on the surveillance around my house again. The Gold Dust Twins were always suspect with me whenever big money tickets came before our council. Since I hadn't noticed any surveilling around my home, I stayed in touch with Shoppie. I looked forward to his next contact. The telephone was ringing.

"I can't meet up with you tonight." I recognized the voice on the other end of the phone. It was Shoppie.

"Not a problem. Is everything okay Shoppie? You sound kind of nervous."

"I'm putting something in your mailbox later tonight. You'll know what to do with it."

"What's going on Shoppie?" I was almost afraid to ask.

"I was threatened to stop talking to you."

"Not again," I nearly blurted out over the phone. "Tell me what they said to you Shoppie. I gotta know."

"Leave us alone, is all the guy said and that was enough for me. I got the message Elena."

I was familiar with that message. Isn't that what the Mafia says whenever they have someone deliver a message for them? Yes. I'd heard it myself. *Leave us alone.* It's never "leave me alone" because it's not about the individual delivering the message. It's about their boss and their crime family. And that's why I had no reason not to believe Shoppie had been contacted by the Mafia. But I wanted a name from him.

"I think they're serious this time and might try to kill me if I keep talking to you," is all he would say. But it left me wondering if he'd been warned before and had stupidly ignored it like Floyd and Sarge had done.

"Who threatened you Shoppie?" I pleaded for him to tell me. "A name, dear God," I silently prayed while on the phone, "just let him give me a name before he hangs up." But he didn't.

"Best you don't know kid. Gotta go now. Take care." Click! The phone went dead.

"Shoppie?" I took a deep breath. I paused as I looked down at the phone.

"Sweet Jesus in heaven," I thought to myself. "It couldn't be happening again. Or could it?" I stared into the receiver of my telephone fully expecting Shoppie to suddenly appear or something. But he didn't appear then, and never again.

That was the last time I ever heard from him. I did get Shoppie's package after I'd gone to bed that night. I was awakened from my sleep when I heard a noise outside. I slept light those days.

I didn't think it was a prowler. I prayed it was Shoppie. I remembered him saying how he had something he wanted to give me. I cautiously opened the front door and looked around. It was dark out and Shoppie was nowhere to be seen.

If it was Shoppie dropping off a package as he said he would do, then he sure hightailed it out of there fast enough. "Good," I thought to myself while praying no one was following him or surveilling my house. But it was too late for praying.

At Shoppie's funeral it was rumored he died of a heart attack. I thought about Sarge. Their deaths couldn't be a coincidence. I began suspecting their deaths were no natural heart attacks either. I was no Sherlock Holmes back then, but anyone with half a brain couldn't go on thinking that all three of my informants had just up and died all the same way.

Hadn't both Sarge and Shoppie told me the same thing on the last night we spoke? Both warned, just like Floyd, and both turn up dead the next day? Growing up around the mob, like I did, I am not one to believe in coincidences, especially when people kept turning up dead around me.

Who was killing my informants in Agawam? And why were their deaths reported as heart attacks, if they were being bumped off as I suspected they were?

Why heart attacks instead bullets?

For years, that question has haunted me. A bullet in the head and you were fish food. Yep. That's how your everyday mobsters had done it in the old days back in 1972 when I hung out with them. So, how were they making it look like death by natural causes to those around me since I returned to Agawam?

But it wasn't 1972 anymore. It was 1980 and I was a public figure standing up to anyone who came after me, even the mob that I had once been so close to. And yet, I knew Floyd, Sarge and Shoppie's killers couldn't go around putting a bullet in their head like they did with my boss Victor DeCaro or my friend Gary Dube whose bullet riddled bodies were pulled out of the river in 1972.

In the dark world of organized crime, I could understand how Gary and Victor both invited retribution upon themselves by what they did. But dear God in heaven, what did my informants do that was worth dying for? Was it to scare me off or shut them up?

Unarguably, the organized crime syndicate sometimes uses symbols to indicate what others should learn from a particular killing while simultaneously serving as an implicit warning. Despite the lack of any identifying marks on my informants, I knew these had to be assassinations ordered by the Mafia. Little did I know that I wouldn't solve the mystery until I began writing my memoir nearly thirty-six years later.

I knew the Genovese family well enough to know they wouldn't knowingly bring attention to themselves in any town business, be it police or the town council. I was a wild card for sure. They knew I wasn't running off to Texas again like they'd gotten my father to persuade me to do after witnessing Victor's assassination.

No. The boss in Agawam did not want to send any message involving the killings of my informants. I think it was enough that they suspected I might've known about them threatening my informants who just happened to turn up dead after being warned. For me, that was proof enough. What puzzled me was the heart attack thing instead of bullets.

Back then, I had no way of proving the Mafia was going around assassinating people by induced heart attacks. Sure, I suspected it after Shoppie's heart attack, but I had no way of proving it. As with everything else I'd witnessed over the years, I kept my mouth shut.

I learned a long time ago, that keeping your mouth shut keeps you alive around the mob. It worked for me. Today, I don't have to keep quiet. Everyone who ever wanted me dead is dead themselves. Anyone can go online these days and find what I did when I decided to search *induced heart attacks*. I still needed closure after all these years. And bingo! Thank goodness for the internet.

Assassinations by induced heart attack and cancer
Source: *sott.net* [Signs of the Times] website
Press Core, Thursday, 16 Dec 2010

"In 1975, during the Church Committee hearings, the existence of a secret assassination weapon came to light. The CIA had developed a poison that caused the victim to have an immediate heart attack. This poison could be frozen into the shape of a dart and then fired at high speed from a pistol. The gun was capable of shooting the icy projectile with enough speed that the dart would go right through the clothes of the target and leave just a tiny red mark. Once in the body the poison would melt and be absorbed into the blood and cause a heart attack! The poison was developed to be undetectable by modern autopsy procedures."

For the sake of this whodunit, if induced heart attacks were confirmed as a secret assassination weapon in the year 1975, then isn't it reasonable to assume that Floyd, Sarge and Shoppie might've been victims themselves of a mob assassination by induced heart attacks?

Who's the Boss?

Probably the only reason I am alive today is because Floyd, Sarge, and Shoppie never gave up any names to me, even though I tried to get it out of them. In their memory, I am hoping this whodunit will be solved by a clever reader of mine.

As for any other wannabe heroes, I am sure no one needed a body to turn up whose mouth was stuffed with cash, or a bullet to the head, to get the message to stay away from me like those who got on the wrong side of Big Al Bruno and Skyball Scibelli who reportedly committed such crimes while I was in Agawam.

The word was out in Agawam. No one was talking to me anymore, not even my favorite news reporter.

Bias alert warning

As a retired investigative journalist and newspaper publisher, I respect journalists who make every attempt to report the news as it happens. None of that FAKE news stuff. Back in my Agawam days before I started up my own newspaper, I had taken a liking to a particular news reporter whom I will call Jennifer. She had my respect and had done her best to keep any bias out of her stories.

"What's going on? You seem upset about something?" I asked Jennifer when she walked over to me after another crazy council meeting had just been adjourned.

"I was warned by my editor to make some changes in how I've been covering you at these meetings," she cautiously explained.

"Whatever happened to the idea of take no sides?" I asked.

"Guess, my editor thinks I'm making the town look bad every time you look good," she explained.

"Not again," I thought to myself. "Now they're warning my favorite reporter? What next?"

Despite the accepted practice of editorial control over their journalists' stories in the *Union* and *Daily News*, the news coverage had been as good as I could expect given what I was dealing with at the time. Before I'd started publishing my own weekly town newspaper, I depended on Joy to present a fair and balanced story on our council meetings. As the story goes, those days were over after what happened to my favorite reporter.

> **Bias by spin**-Emphasizing aspects of a policy favorable to liberals without noting aspects favorable to conservatives.
>
> **Bias by story selection**- A pattern of highlighting news stories that coincide with the agenda of the Left while ignoring stories that coincide with the agenda of the Right.
>
> **Source:** *Media Research Center* website - America's Media Watchdog

As it turned out, Joy told me her editor had made a conscious choice not to present a balanced story to their readers. Joy never said, but I just assumed her editor must've been taking orders from someone with a controlling interest in the newspaper. Either that or he'd been warned himself.

According to Reuters, their motto is to take no side and tell all tales:

> "As Reuters journalists, we never identify with any side in an issue, a conflict or a dispute. Out text and visual stories need to reflect all sides, not just one. This leads to better journalism because it requires us to stop at each

stage of newsgathering and ask ourselves *What do I know?* and *What do I need to know?*"

Associates working for the Mafia could be anyone in our communities, not just police and politicians. Many have been known to be editors of newspapers. So why not any of the editors at the *Union* and *Daily News*? My mind was a blur of meaningless thoughts as I waited for my favorite reporter to tell me more.

"So whatcha gonna do?" I asked.

"I'm going to do what I always do. Report the story. I intend to present both points of view, including yours."

I was worried for her and prayed she'd be okay. I knew the mob didn't go around killing reporters unless they nosed around and got too close to something. For all I knew, she wasn't doing anything to get herself killed. Her stories covering me in public meetings weren't worth her life.

Reading the breaking news about Agawam politics in the paper the next day, it looked like her story had been chopped up by an editor. It wasn't anything like what my favorite reporter would have written.

I was worried about Joy. If she hadn't written the story then who did? Wasn't she warned not to write up a fair and balanced story on me again?

At our next council meeting, Joy wasn't there. I decided to call the newspaper to find out what happened to her. I suspected, but I had to hear it from her own lips.

"I've been assigned to obituaries," she somberly explained over the phone.

This principled journalist, good to her editor's threat, had been assigned to obituaries. At least she was still alive. Her job may have been killed off but at least she lived to see another day.

Joy's story deserved mentioning in this chapter. People need to know why there's so much FAKE NEWS out there. It's a problem today same as it was back then. President Donald Trump has his tweets and back then I had my own newspaper to deal with the fake news.

Joy's story is the reason I started up *The Agawam Voice* Newspaper while I served on the town council. It was an alternative to the fake news put out by *The Daily News* and *The Morning Union* that my favorite reporter was no longer reporting for. Bias alert follow-up--Those two newspapers have since merged and today they operate under the name of *The Republican.*

After what happened to Joy, I was naturally suspicious of any mobologists working for *The Republican* operating in real time like Stephanie Barry does for *masslive.com.* Of course, the local mobsters like Big Al Bruno and Skyball Scibelli that Barry writes about are all dead. You don't get threatening calls from the dead eh?

Actually, I appreciate Barry's organized crime online vignettes. If not for that, I would not have been able to pull off my own in-depth organized crime investigation, as I have done in this memoir. It's when she goes out of her way, as she has done, to prove that the Mafia is no longer active today that I take umbrage with her reports.

It troubles me and because it does, Barry's theory on the Genovese family today is another valuable clue for this whodunit. If you're wondering about the mob problem in Agawam today, you can read all about in Chapter 16. But be forewarned, it is not for the faint of heart!

A Catholic Priest's confession

Reporters were good listeners but I still needed someone to confess to and seek counsel during the darkest days of my life on the Agawam Town Council.

I was a faithful communicant of St. John Evangelist Catholic Church when I lived in Agawam on Walnut Street and I spent a lot of time at the Rectory with my parish priest Father Huller.

I recall the time I paid him a visit after I'd been struggling with all of what had been going on around me. I was inconsolable and prayers were no longer enough.

Priests hear confessions and they can't repeat what you confess to them. I figured it was about time for me and my parish priest to have a come-to-Jesus meeting in the privacy of his rectory.

Bribes, threats and murders understandably interfered with my spiritual life. Besides prayer and scripture study, I was attending Sunday mass regularly when I noticed a familiar face. I immediately recognized him as a member of the Springfield mob from another run-in I'd once had with his associates long before I came back to Agawam.

I watched in disbelief as he walked right up to the altar to receive communion. His hands folded together looking quite pious. I quickly repented of any wrongful feelings. Judge not lest ye be judged, I heard myself saying as I tried to think about the Holy Family and not the crime family.

Naturally, I mentioned this to Father Heller. Now, I was sure I'd made it very clear who this man was and what he did for a living in the mob. I will never forget my priest's exact words to me that day.

Father Huller gently laid his hand on mine, leaned into me and looking into my eyes calmly counseled me, "Now, now my child. We mustn't judge."

"What?" I tried to humbly spit out. To which Father Huller again, repeated his counsel to me.

"Elena. They do good things for the Church," Father Huller tried to convince me.

Even now, I keep asking myself, did this priest know that "they" were the Mafia? As I tried to keep calm, I blurted out the words before I even knew what I was saying.

"But Father, they're killing people." I stupidly reminded him.

Letting out a deep sigh and shaking his head, I can still see Father Huller patting me on the head like a child gone astray.

Without another word, he counseled me to "go home and pray." While assuring me, "in the morning you will feel better and forget all about this my child."

Here I am Lord, I'm listening

No, I thought to myself. I wasn't ever going to "forget all about this." And here I am, finding myself still talking about our conversation thirty-six years later. Being respectful of my parish priest, I obediently thanked him for seeing me and left.

Walking back to my house, I was rehashing our conversation while asking myself, "Who in their right mind, could be okay with what the mob does? What would the Pope have said?"

Fast forwarding to October 2015, in his morning Mass from the Vatican in Rome, Pope Francis reflected on the apparent worldly success of people who do evil, even mentioning "an elderly widow whose son had been murdered by the Mafia."

Pope Francis appealed to the people saying, "Indeed, in the book of God's memory, the wicked have no name: 'He is an evildoer. He is a con man. He is an exploiter.'" These are people, he said about the Mafia, who "do not have names; they just have adjectives."

I didn't have the Pope to confer with in Agawam, but I knew it was never okay to excuse any evil in our midst simply because the Mafia does "good things for the Church," as Father Huller had expected me to accept.

If my priest couldn't come to grips about the mobster in his parish, then he sure wouldn't want to hear about what happened to me at work either.

Using bullets to send a message

I remember it just like it was yesterday. It was in the winter of '79 right after I had called for the resignation of the Town Manager in Peter Caputo. Despite everything going on all around me in Agawam, I had managed to land a good job when I came back from Texas.

Everything was going good for me on my job until I got another warning message. I had just arrived for work one morning when I was met with what definitely looked like a spray of bullet holes in all the front windows of the building. It didn't take a genius to figure out who did it and why. For me, it was just more proof Agawam had a serious mob problem.

As I rushed into the building, looking around expecting to see bodies everywhere, I was relieved to learn that only the windows had been shot out. I figured it must've been done during the night after everyone had left for the day.

"What happened here?" I called out to my cousin Jerry whom I worked with in the Data Processing Division.

255

"Don't know," he said, shaking his head as if in disbelief. "Found it like that when I came into to work this morning."

"Any signs of a break-in?" I asked.

"I asked around when I came in," he replied. "Nothing was disturbed inside the building."

"So, all they damaged were the windows?" I asked one more time, wondering what he was thinking. My cousin was no dummy, he kept up with the news. He knew what I'd been up to on the council lately.

"Yep. Sure looks that way," he said while trying to look busy with some papers on his desk.

He went back into his office and I took a seat at my desk wondering what to expect next. I didn't have to wait long to find out.

Someone was peeking their head into my office and motioning to me. It was the office manager. She was a real bear when she wanted to be and I think she was enjoying her job right now.

Usually Mr. Johnson Sr., who owned the company, liked to drop by and visit us in Data Processing every morning in person. I knew it couldn't be good if he was sending the office manager to summon me.

I walked out onto the floor where Mr. Johnson Sr., a kind elderly man in his 80's, was sitting at his desk. He had retired years ago and turned the company over to his son, but he still had a say in everything. The old man motioned me to take a seat.

"I'd rather stand thank you."

I saw the pain in his eyes and knew this couldn't be easy for him. I waited until the old man was ready to speak.

"I guess you saw the windows?" he asked, as he pointed to the bullet holes in all of the windows alongside his desk.

"Yes. I saw that when I came in this morning sir," I managed to say.

"I'm sorry Elena."

The old man was struggling for words as he pretended to be looking for something that'd gone missing on his cluttered desk.

"I know sir," I replied softly as I waited for him to speak the words I couldn't think.

"We were warned, but we didn't think it would ever come to this," he tried explaining.

"And you never said anything?" I asked.

"No. We just thought it was idle threats and chose to ignore it."

As always, no names were mentioned about who was behind the message. So they'd been warned like all my other informants. Sure, everyone has choices to make. But keeping my job was definitely not worth anyone dying for like Floyd had done. I decided to make it easier on the old guy who was not taking it too good.

Mr. Johnson closed his eyes for a moment not knowing what to say. So I said it for him, "I'll pack up my desk and leave."

But I couldn't resign. If I did, we both knew I wouldn't be able to collect unemployment. I knew my enemies would get to other businesses if anyone dared to offer me a job after word of this ever got out. So we came up with a plan that worked for both of us.

Mr. Johnson Sr. refused my resignation and instead laid me off so I could collect unemployment. I thanked him and I was relieved knowing I'd have an income to fall back on temporarily.

I applied for unemployment and even now, I still get a good laugh from that day so long ago. I'll never forget the claims clerk who processed my unemployment application. The tired looking woman sitting behind the desk was busy scrawling some notes while asking me questions. All of sudden she just froze when I explained why I'd been laid off.

"My employer felt it was in their best interest not to have anyone on the payroll that might be unsafe to be around," I politely explained. "Someone shot out their windows and the bullets had my name on 'em."

Dropping her pen and pushing her chair away from her desk, she nervously asked, "You're that Bonavita woman?"

"Yep. That's me alright."

"Just sign here. Your unemployment checks will start coming in two weeks," she abruptly announced while motioning for me to leave without further instructions.

You didn't have to ask me twice. I got up and headed out of there before she had time to rethink why she'd just approved my application.

Good to her word, the checks arrived in the mail like clockwork. It was only half of what I'd been earning at Johnsons, but no one was hiring me and it wasn't because I didn't try.

So, I never expected to get another message so soon. The telephone was ringing.

CHAPTER ELEVEN:
MY NEW CHURCH FAMILY

"Hello? Is this Elaine Bonavita?" A sweet angelic voice, on the other end of the telephone, was asking.

"Yes. This is Miss Bonavita."

I answered the phone as I usually do with cold calls from strangers. I was a public official on the town council and I was used to getting lots of phone calls from townspeople wanting my assistance. I assumed this was such a call. But it wasn't.

"I am a missionary with the Church of Jesus Christ of Latter-day Saints." The young woman on the other end of the phone informed me.

"How can I help you?"

The caller didn't waste any time and got right to the point of her call. She asked if they could share a message with me about Jesus Christ. The word "message" got my attention.

I couldn't help but ask myself who these people were, who had another message for me? As I listened to the missionary on the other end of the phone, I couldn't help but think how every message I'd ever been given was either a warning or a threat usually followed by someone's death.   I was still shaken from the bullet riddled message that had just cost me my job at Johnsons. And here was someone calling me with another message.

Normally, I might've hung up on the caller. Sarge and Shoppie's mysterious deaths were still too fresh on my mind. Understandably, I would've been suspicious of meeting with any stranger, much less welcome them into my home as the caller was asking me to do. And yet, I recall never experiencing that dark feeling as I usually did when the mob was involved, just the opposite.

Instead of hanging up on the caller, I felt the Spirit remind me of how I'd been praying. No. It was more like I'd been crying unto God. For three days straight I'd been pleading for Heavenly Father to tell me which Church He wanted me to join.

My readers might recall in Chapter 5, how I had experienced a type of spiritual renewal while living in Texas after attending some Catholic Retreats. When I didn't find any answers I stayed with the Catholic Church, even though I had a hard time accepting my parish priest's attitude toward the Mafia. I knew the God I worshipped was not okay with this evil that was spreading in our community.

As I did once before in Texas, I gave up my search for the true church and vowed not to keep searching anymore. Believing there weren't any more churches for me to investigate, I cried all the more unto God after visiting with Father Heller one night. As I wept, I waited for an answer as I normally would get in similar situations when praying out loud for help. But this time nothing happened.

Never one to give up easily, I repeated my cry unto God for three nights in a row. Finally one night, in frustration, I felt impressed to do something out of the ordinary. I laid prostrate on the floor for what seemed like an eternity and then I just screamed it out to the heavens.

"If there isn't a Church that you want me to find, then just leave me alone!"

Yes. That's exactly what I screamed out to the Lord our God. I got up off the floor, wiped away my tears, and was relieved that my endless search was finally over once and for all. No more searching I thought. No more looking for an answer that I didn't even have a question for. It was over. I could stop and move on. Or so I thought.

The Message

Thinking back on those three intense days of praying with no answer in sight, I held onto the phone and resisted the temptation to hang up on the caller. It took me a few seconds to catch my breath and come to grips with the fact that Jesus had a message for me? "Well, wasn't that what I prayed for? Maybe this was it," I thought.

"A message from Jesus Christ, you say?" I asked the sister missionary in disbelief.

As we talked I learned that the LDS Church, nicknamed the Mormons, had a chapel in Springfield only minutes from where I lived. That got my attention real quick. Monikers had a way of turning things upside down in my life for good or bad.

"You're telling me there is a Mormon Church in Springfield?" I asked in total amazement. "I never heard of the Mormons before. I didn't even know you had a church around here."

"Yes. And we would like to schedule an appointment to come and tell you more about the Mormon Church." She explained.

"I was just praying about how there were no more churches for me to check out," I tried explaining. "And here you are calling me. Yes. I need to talk to you right away. When can you come?"

The two sister missionaries were in my home the very next evening and I agreed to take the ten lessons from them to learn more about their Church. In less than two weeks, I had taken all of the lessons.

After sitting in on the first discussion from the missionaries I learned we had a living prophet on the earth. I remember my excitement and my response. "I knew we had to have a prophet today-- just like in biblical times."

When the sisters left, I walked over to the rectory to bring the good news to my parish priest at St. John's. As Father Huller ushered me into the rectory waiting room, I sat down next to him.

"What's on your mind today, Elena?" Father Huller asked.

"Father," I said rather excitedly. "We have a prophet on the earth today! It's Spencer W. Kimball, and he is the President of the Mormon Church."

President Spencer, who died in 1985, was the LDS prophet at the time I was investigating the Church. I guess I was just so excited to find what I was searching for after all those years, that I got carried away and shared the good news with Father Huller. I even started reading from a pamphlet the sisters had given me.

"According to the Mormon Church," I began reading, "Latter-day Saints consider the church's president to be God's spokesman to the entire world and the highest priesthood authority on earth, with the exclusive right to receive revelations from God on behalf of the entire church or the entire world."

You could have heard a pin drop. Poor Father Huller. I watched as he took a deep breath and leaning towards me, looked deeply into my eyes. As patiently as he could, he kindly reminded me of who the head of the Catholic Church was.

"We have a Pope," he replied, as if trying to get me to give up the Mormon prophet idea.

I was disappointed in his reply. But not discouraged. I knew truth when I heard it. And I knew the message the sisters brought me had indeed come from God. I guess that's why I ignored Father Huller's advice and accepted their invitation to attend Church the following Sunday at their Springfield chapel.

Today there is still no chapel in Agawam-- only in Springfield. But due to the growth in the Church, the LDS Chapel in Springfield, a 600 member congregation located on 376 Maple Street, is now a part of the Massachusetts Stake instead of the Hartford Connecticut Stake.

Sitting towards the back of the chapel with Sister Connie R. Redford and her companion Sister Jo A. Harefeld, I watched as Bishop David Owen Sutton conducted the sacrament meeting. After the opening prayer, Bishop Sutton took the pulpit and made some announcements and then he did something that surprised me.

"We have a special visitor with us today."

Yes, he did welcome me right from the pulpit and even introduced me by name. He also mentioned how glad they were to have me visiting them while acknowledging my position on the Agawam Town Council.

Doing what he did, it kind of reminded me when the Pentecostal minister in Texas had stepped down from his pulpit to hand me his own personal bible. I liked it.

"Does your bishop always recognize visitors from the pulpit like he just did with me?"

"We always welcome visitors," the sister explained. "But not like that."

Those Mormons made me feel glad to be there. I wasn't an invisible face like I had always been in the Catholic Church. I loved everything about the worship service, and was surprised at how comfortable I felt around the Mormons. The spirit was strong and they were some of the friendliest people I had ever met at Church.

Feeling confident that this was where I was supposed to be, I continued to take the discussions from Sister Redford and Sister Harefeld. Everything went well until the subject of tithing came up. Back in those days, the Catholic priest just told you to "give what you can" and I usually put $5 in the collection plate every Sunday.

"Well Sisters, I always put a little something in the collection plate and plan to keep right on doing it." I assured them.

The sisters didn't judge me at all. Instead, they taught me the true principle of tithing wherein the Lord has commanded we give ten per cent of our gross income. They quoted scriptures and I believed them.

"Can you do that?" The sisters reverently challenged me at the end of our discussion on tithing.

Wow! Even now, I can recall my shock at hearing this principal of tithing for the first time in my life. I was quickly adding up what I would have left from my weekly unemployment check if I tithed ten per cent on it.

The sisters knew my financial situation as a single unwed mother. They didn't know much more about me because Mormon missionaries aren't allowed to watch television and hadn't kept up with the news. Understandably, I didn't want to burden them and fill them in on anything they didn't need to know.

Given what was going on all around me, I was just happy for the sisters staying focused on their message. For me, I could feel the light they were bringing into my life which seemed to be snuffing out the darkness in my world.

Although I questioned how I could pay tithing when I could hardly pay my bills, I sincerely wanted to accept the challenge to obey God's commandment to tithe.

"I will tithe," I promised them. "But only as long as it works. If I can't make it financially, then I won't do it okay?"

The sisters merely smiled and nodded as if they knew something I didn't. I am sure they must have heard this before because they assured me that it would work just fine and left me with a prayer as they always did after our discussions.

The next time we met, it was my last lesson with another challenge when I was invited to be baptized.

"I love going to church and I'll keep attending with you," I assured the sisters. "But I don't think I need to be baptized again." I innocently explained how I'd already been baptized as a baby in the Catholic Church. I figured I was good on that part of it and we left it at that.

There were no more lessons. In my eagerness to learn everything, I'd taken all missionary lessons in less than two weeks. The sisters left me with a prayer and invited me to read and pray about the Book of Mormon to know if it was true. I glanced over at the Book that had been laying on my coffee table for the past two weeks unread.

It was late and I wanted to turn on the TV to catch the evening news as I'd always done. But as I reached down to turn on the television, I was stopped by what felt like an invisible barrier between me and the television set.

In those days, we did not have remote controls. You had to physically turn the knob on the TV to turn it on. But try as I might, I could not touch the knob.

After several attempts to turn on the TV, I gave up and sat back down on the couch. I had no idea what was happening. Suddenly I felt the strongest prompting, like a radio voice in my head, instructing me to pick up the Book of Mormon and open it.

I no sooner picked up the Book of Mormon when it opened right up to Chapter 8 in the Book of Moroni, who was a prophet of God as were those in the Old and New Testament scriptures.

To my utter amazement, the chapter addressed the baptism of little children and it was an epistle written by Moroni's father, who was a prophet named Mormon. I couldn't believe my eyes. This was the very question I had just raised with the sister missionaries moments before they left. And here was the answer right in front of me. In the Book of Moroni, Chapter 8, it reads:

13 *Wherefore, if little children could not be saved without baptism, these must have gone to an endless hell.*

15 *For awful is the wickedness to suppose that God saveth one child because of baptism, and the other must perish because he hath no baptism.*

19 *Little children cannot repent; wherefore, it is awful wickedness to deny the pure mercies of God unto them, they are all alive in him because of his mercy.*

20 *And he that saith that little children need baptism denieth the mercies of Christ, and setteth at naught the atonement of him and the power of his redemption.*

I no sooner began reading when a light, brighter than natural sunlight, suddenly filled the room. It was ten o'clock at night and only one small reading lamp was lit in the room. The brightness of the light took my breath away.

I could not do anything except remain seated. I never doubted what I had experienced was a confirmation to me from God that I needed to be baptized into the Church of Jesus Christ of Latter-day Saints. I made the call.

"Hello?" I recognized one of the sister's voice on the other end of the telephone.

"Hello Sister Redford? I want to be baptized right away," I excitedly announced over the phone.

The sister missionaries informed the Bishop of my decision to be baptized and I was interviewed the next day in preparation for my baptism. I committed to keeping the Word of Wisdom which meant no more coffee for me or wine either. As a single woman, I also committed to keeping the law of chastity.

I had no addictive habits so I was good to go on that end. It was the thought of ending my affair with the love of my life Big Al that crushed my soul. I prayed mightily for the strength to walk toward the light that the Lord had blessed me to experience the night I opened that Book of Mormon.

My affair may have been over, but so were my years of searching for the true church. I had found it and I was determined to become more involved in a relationship with Jesus Christ who loved me enough to die for me.

I scheduled my baptism for Saturday December 13, 1980. But on the eve before my baptism, I became suddenly ill. The pain racing throughout my entire body was unbearable. I tried to convince myself it was a panic attack. What else could it be I thought? Maybe I was having remorse for leaving the Catholic Church. Hadn't I always been taught it was the only true church too?

A copy of the Book of Mormon was given to Sister Bonavita by the missionaries.

If I believed that about the Catholic Church, then what was with the six years of searching for another church like I'd been led to do by the Holy Spirit? The pain worsening in my body, I prayed and was immediately prompted to call the sister missionaries.

Under attack by Satan

"Hello Sister Redford?" I barely could speak, I was in such pain. But I got out the words, "I don't think I can be baptized tomorrow." I said while holding back the tears.

"Stay right where you are. We'll be right over." That was all she said. So I waited.

The sisters showed up in less than a half hour with two other missionaries. I recognized one of the two young elders from Church as Elder Jeffrey Lynn Weeks. I'd asked him to baptize me. So when Elder Weeks asked me if I wanted a Priesthood blessing from them, I eagerly accepted.

The elders laid their hands on my head, after anointing me with consecrated oil, and gave me a blessing as directed by the Spirit. I wasn't expecting what happened next.

While laying their hands on my head, I immediately felt a flush of warmness, as it began moving ever so slowly, from the top of my head down through my entire body. I could feel the pain leaving my body as it passed out through my feet.

The experience lasted only as long as the elders' hands remained on my head. I was reminded of the admonition of the apostle James who taught about the gift of healing as one of the gifts of the Spirit. In LDS practice, church members believe "a gift may be present in the one who administers and the one who receives."

"Is any sick among you? Let him call for the elders of the church; and let them pray over him, anointing him with oil in the name of the Lord. And the prayer of faith shall save the sick and the Lord shall raise him up; and if he have committed sins, they shall be forgiven him."

- James 5:14-15

I was immediately healed after receiving the priesthood blessing from the elders. I learned something that day about the forces of evil. I learned that Satan's attacks upon those who choose to follow Jesus Christ are very real.

I knew what had happened to me the night before my baptism was no anxiety attack. After the blessing, I never doubted I was under attack by Satan. Hadn't I been surrounded by evil battling the dark world of organized crime before the missionaries found me?

If it was to Satan's advantage to keep me away from the truth, then I did the right thing by letting the elders administer a blessing to me. I thank God I didn't listen to Satan's message and instead embraced the message of Jesus Christ sent me through the sister missionaries.

The ninth president of The Church of Jesus Christ of Latter-day Saints, David O. McKay, a prophet of God, once taught, "There is your story. ... Your weakest point will be the point at which the Devil tries to tempt you, will try to win you, and if you have made it weak before you have undertaken to serve the Lord, he will add to that weakness.

 Resist him and you will gain in strength. He will tempt you in another point. Resist him and he becomes weaker and you become stronger, until you can say, no matter what your surroundings may be, "Get thee behind me, Satan: for it is written, Thou shalt worship the Lord thy God, and him only shalt thou serve." (Luke 4:8)

My baptism went on as planned Saturday morning December 13, 1980. I was baptized into the Church of Jesus Christ of Latter-day Saints while I was still unemployed and yet, I never did have to stop tithing.

Tithing really works! I never stopped tithing 10% back then and not even in the thirty-seven years that I've been an active member of the Mormon Church.

My baptism is breaking news

I was used to getting phone calls from the local media whenever I did something outrageous on the town council like calling for someone's resignation or an investigation. I never expected the media to show any interest in my baptism. But they did!

It was kind of exciting to be able to talk about something more positive for a change. To my astonishment, I was flooded with phone calls wanting to interview me.

The Daily News and *The Morning Union* along with local television and radio stations were all very interested to know why I left the Catholic Church to join the Mormons. Thankful for the opportunity to share my conversion testimony, I was only too happy to take their calls.

I should've expected a dark turn in the story, but I wasn't worried. I gave my testimony and I prayed the Lord would use it to touch souls. As for my detractors, they were touched alright, but not as I'd hoped they'd be.

When my political foes inside the Agawam faction were asked to comment on my baptism, I remember one of them whose quote I have never forgotten.

My baptism story made breaking news much to my surprise. Leave it to the liberal media to take something so pure as a baptism and make it political. But it really was my testimony on the front page of *The Daily News* and that was a good thing despite some contrary comments from my political foes when one of them said something like, "We don't have to worry about her anymore. She's finished now that she's joined the Mormons."

Incredibly, the media pounced like a hungry coyote on the thought of what everyone perceived to be my political undoing. It seems they figured the Mormon problem trumped the Mob problem. As such, my detractors were now claiming I'd lose my support base which was made up largely of Catholics.

Everyone knew I was a faithful communicant of St. John Evangelist Catholic Church in Agawam. And now, thanks to the media, everyone knew I'd left the Catholic Church.

Did I change after my baptism? Absolutely! Did the people I continued to represent change their opinion of me? They did! But more importantly, so did my twelve year old son three months later.

Elisha multiplies the widow's oil in Agawam too!

On the *BibleHub* website under C.H. Irwin's narrative of 2 Kings 4:1-7, we read of the widow who was preparing her last meal for her and her son when she was visited by the Prophet Elisha. Her story reads kind of like my own experience shortly after my baptism into the Mormon Church.

I had been on unemployment, and I was struggling financially after I had lost my job at Johnsons, which meant I was living on half my usual income. Al hadn't been coming around regularly anymore since I ended our affair after I was baptized. And so I wasn't getting the extra cash that he'd usually leave on the table every time he dropped by.

Understandably, it took a leap of faith for me to tithe 10% of my unemployment checks as I was expected to do as a member of the Church. Understandably, prior to my baptism, there never was enough money for the bills, much less food. However, after I started tithing, food didn't seem to be as scarce anymore.

I still remember the day my son walked into the kitchen and opened the refrigerator and just stood there staring for what seemed the longest time.

"Close that refrigerator if you're not gonna get anything."

"Mom, where's all this food coming from?"

"The Lord is providing for us. Now close the fridge."

I had no other explanation. The blessings of tithing was still new to me. There was no more money coming into our household than before my baptism and even less now since I was tithing. Yet, we had more food in our fridge and cupboards than I ever remembered.

Another scripture comes to mind about the story of the Widow of Zarephath who shared her last morsel of food with the Prophet Elijah when asked to do it and as is recorded in 1 Kings 17:8-24.

Watching my son standing in front of the refrigerator staring at the food packed onto every shelf, I reminded him about the day we were expecting two sister missionaries for dinner but three showed up instead.

Sister Missionaries with Elena Bonavita Photo taken 1981 in Bonavita's kitchen in Agawam.

It was right after I'd been baptized and money was still tight. I had invited the two sister missionaries for dinner as is the custom in the Mormon Church.

"Do you remember that day?" I asked him.

"Do I ever!" he replied.

"Yes. When I opened the door, there were not two, but three missionaries standing there." I reminded him.

"And I remember how I pulled you aside and whispered how we didn't have enough food to feed three of them," he recalled.

"And what did I say to you?"

"You told me that the Lord will provide Mom."

We never said a word to the missionaries, but it was true we didn't have enough food for three of them. I had only planned a meal just for the four of us that day.

I left the food on the stove so the sisters wouldn't see how little food we had. I gave them the larger portions and sat down to eat. After the missionaries left, my son had another question for me which sounded all too familiar.

"Mom. Where did all that food come from?"

"I don't know. But it was a miracle for sure."

My son was referring to the second helpings that I gave out despite our not having enough for our unexpected guest. After the plates were empty, I walked back over to the stove to see if there was anything I could scrape together to offer the sisters who I knew did not have enough to eat.

To my amazement, there was more than enough food to fill everyone's plate with seconds. Even now, I am all amazed at how the Lord provides to those who feed his servants even when they have barely enough for themselves.

In the weeks following my baptism, my son attended church with me but did it reluctantly. Some of the neighbor kids had been making fun of him because I had joined the Mormon Church. At first, he didn't want to go inside the chapel so he sat in the car while I was in church.

That didn't last long. The next Sunday he started coming inside and sitting in the lobby where I knew he could hear the sacrament speakers. I never forced him to come in the chapel or attend classes. I just prayed he would do it on his own because he wanted to, not because I was forcing him.

One Sunday, I was sitting with the missionaries inside the chapel, during Sacrament meeting, when lo and behold my son comes walking in and sits down right beside me. After that, he continued attending church with me for the next three months. And then, to my delight, he surprised me with a message of his own for me.

"Mom. I want to…"

"You want to what?" I asked, as he sat at the kitchen table watching me prepare dinner after we'd just gotten home from church.

"I want to be baptized!"

"Why? I asked in sheer amazement. He had never talked about it to me and I never pressured him to be baptized. So, I was surprised indeed.

"Because I want what you have," he said smiling and winking at me as I turned around to look at him.

So, he had noticed after all. I never pushed my son into following me into the Church. "Teach by example," the sister missionaries had always said.

Yes. I had made some major changes in my life to commit to baptism and my son must've noticed. Children do watch what parents do, that's for sure. I know my son had felt the presence of the Spirit in our home after I cleaned up my act and gave my life to the Lord.

He noticed other little things too, like the tithing miracles that brought more than food into our home. True to his word about wanting to be baptized, my son followed through and in the spring of 1981 he was baptized into the Church of Jesus Christ of Latter-day Saints at the age of twelve less than three months after my own baptism. Today he holds and honors the priesthood and is a faithful member of the Church.

After the front page story, and my conversion testimony had gone public on television and radio too, I was a bit of a curiosity to the community. Instead of shunning me, like my detractors had predicted would happen, the good of people of Agawam rallied around me more than ever before.

A power greater than the Mafia

Before my baptism, it was just a mob problem I'd been dealing with. After my baptism, my eyes were opened and I could actually feel myself in the middle of a spiritual battle fighting a secret combination that held sway over our town.

Clearly, I was used to giving back as good as I got in our town council spats. But after making baptismal covenants, promising to do God's will and not mine, I soon discovered it was a whole new set of rules out there. Being LDS, I was expected to act more Christ-like.

In other words, I was expected to be more forgiving and kind while turning the other cheek. As I examined my life before the Church, I had to admit I hadn't always done that. Merciful heaven, I did what I had to do to stay alive hadn't I?

I may have been baptized, but I was still a risk taker on a crusade to save our town and I needed the townspeople to stand with me. I naively assumed the Christian community would rally to the cause even more after my baptism. I was on fire with the baptism of the Holy Ghost and it did not get past the media.

Prior to my baptism I had always been the subject of numerous editorials. I lost the news clipping but I can still smile when I was described by one local newspaper as hearing "voices from God" and determined to save Agawam as "Joan of Arc" had saved ancient France from its enemies.

I kind of liked it. Although I have to admit, the editorial kind of spooked me when it talked about my being "burned at the stake" by my enemies, like Joan had been. Maybe it spooked the nice people of Agawam too because they didn't jump into the battle like Joan's followers had done.

The more I found myself around the Christian community, the more I began to understand why nice people didn't want to take risks. For example, we know nice people want everyone to like them. Undeniably, Christians are nice people. I include Mormons in this group because we are **CHRISTIAN** despite those who might disagree.

To my dismay, as a fighter who'd been used to standing for truth and justice even before my baptism, I had to face the fact that most nice people won't stand up for their rights. Especially if it makes them come across as a troublemaker. Nice people, I'm told, want everyone to like them. Me, not so much!

I had to reconcile the fact that I could not hope to stay alive in Agawam and be a nice person too. I wished I knew back then what I understand today about the scripture that Jesus taught about being in the world but not of the world. As a politician in Agawam it was a challenge for sure!

I have to agree with leaders in the Christian community who teach us today that good people, on the other hand, "will have enemies." Good people, they argue, "will stand up to evil and corruption because they don't care what others think of them."

I can agree because I have seen for myself what oftentimes happens to good people who "care more about what God thinks of them than their fellow men." And yes, "good people are killed for their beliefs." But not always. I appreciate the encouraging words we often hear from the churched community who hold the belief that "when bad things happen to you, even though you've been a good person, God will use it to give you a platform to do more good."

Sadly, I had experienced the truth of this for myself as I stumbled blindly in the dark world of organized crime. Good people like Floyd, Sarge and Shoppie immediately come to mind.

Mario Facione and Elvis Presley are two other good people who made the news and earned a place in my memoir, but didn't care what others thought of them after they'd both been taught by the LDS missionaries and wanted to be baptized.

Mario, pictured with the two young missionaries from the Church of Jesus Christ of Latter-day Saints

Mario's story is told in his book, titled <u>Mafia to Mormon: My Conversion Story</u>. After his baptism, he spent his life sharing his conversion testimony at many LDS Fireside talks, college campuses, and in a film documentary. But Elvis died before he got the chance to tell his story.

Elvis almost a Mormon

Elvis Presley's personal story about the Book of Mormon, found by his bedside at the time of his death, intrigues me only because I knew him as a friend. His story was eventually told in the movie "Tears of a King" which was released in 2007 as a biography and drama feature film.

What are the odds that we were both contacted by the missionaries after he and I went our separate ways after our Palm Springs escapades in 1969?

Elvis, who died in 1977, reportedly had many close ties to LDS families. Some of whom claim he had actually set a baptism date but died before he could be baptized. I find it interesting, how unknown to either of us, we both had been given a copy of the Book of Mormon.

Looking back, I am deeply touched to know that, like me, both Mario and Elvis didn't care what people would say. They knew the Church of Jesus Christ of Latter-day Saints was true and wanted to be baptized. I guess that's because it's what good people do.

Sadly, Elvis died before he could be baptized. Naturally, I can't help but imagine what his life would have been like if he had lived the life of an LDS Saint, instead of dying a drug addict as he had. Didn't Mario Facione experience a marvelous change of heart after he walked away from a life of crime, money and power to follow Jesus Christ instead of the Mafia?

Seeing how it turned out so badly for Elvis, I am grateful to my Heavenly Father that my life was spared so many times. It allowed me to live long enough to receive a message from His missionaries in 1980 and be baptized.

Another Mafia to Mormon testimony

Have you ever wondered what Jesus meant when he warned the people, "Woe unto you, when all men shall speak well of you!" (Luke 6:26)

I wisely took to heart Luke's admonishment and accepted the fact that I was not a nice person. But I was a good person and that meant I could, as a "good" Mormon, continue to battle the evil I'd been confronting since returning to Agawam.

Before my baptism, I figured I would continue to live as long as I kept my mouth shut about the mob problem in Agawam. After my baptism, I knew I'd live only if I kept my baptismal covenants. How could I ever reconcile the two and still be the good person God expected me to be as an elected official?

I suddenly found myself a wanted Mormon alone in the dark world of organized crime. Unlike my former parish priest Father Huller, my LDS Bishop never counseled me to look away from the obvious mob problem in Agawam. I never doubted the local Mormon Church leaders knew who I'd been battling in Agawam. It was the same story for Mario Facione.

As he explains in his book, he'd only been a member of the Church about four months when his Bishop asked to speak with him after Sacrament meeting one day. Mario was under the mistaken belief he thought he could continue working, as an associate for the Detroit mob, after he'd been baptized.

"I don't know what you're doing or how you're doing it but you can't serve two masters," Bishop Duncan said to Mario, "Get rid of one. You must make the choice."

Good advice indeed. Although I had to get used to new ways in the LDS Church, I didn't have to choose between two masters as Mario did. Long before the Mormons found me, I had already accepted Jesus as my personal savior. I just didn't commit my life to Him until I was baptized.

Forced to choose between two masters in Agawam

Right up until my baptism, I relied on my most loyal supporters to get me through the worst of what my pal Chief Stanley Chmielewski had been doing to me. Dad was nowhere around but my beloved Big Al always seemed to show up every time the chief came after me. For all I knew, Big Al and Dad could've been a mob tag team working behind the scenes to keep me and my son safe.

And so it happened that when my father showed up unannounced at my doorstep in the summer of '81, I was surprised to see him. As it turned out, Dad had a message for me from our pal the Police Chief.

Opening the back door of the kitchen, I greeted him like a daughter seeing her long lost father for the first time. "Say Dad, what brings you here?" I asked ever so innocently.

But he wasn't smiling and given the serious look on his face I immediately quit my silly bantering. "Uh oh. This was no social visit," I thought to myself. "Was it gonna be another one of his sit-downs," I wondered?

The drama playing out at that moment reminded me of another time back in '72 when my father dropped by Gram's unannounced and the next thing I knew I was being shipped off to Texas in exchange for my silence and my life. Today, standing there in my kitchen, Dad had the same look about him.

"Do you want to come in and sit down?"

No. He didn't want to sit down. Instead, he stayed standing by the back door with the strangest look on his face. Finally he spoke.

"I got a visit from Chief Chmielewsky."

As if expecting to see squad cars surrounding the place, I ran to the front of the house leaving Dad standing by the back door.

"What's the matter with you? Will ya stop doing that? Dad demanded.

"You here alone, Dad?

Ignoring my theatrics, Dad spit out what he came to say.

"Just shut up and listen."

Dad then proceeded to tell me how the Police Chief, who was suddenly his best pal, had taken him for a ride in his squad car and asked him to give me a message for his boss.

You could have knocked my socks off, because I couldn't believe what I was hearing. My enemies who had tried everything to get rid of me, even resorting to blackmail, threats, murder, and setting me up on false assault charges, were now coming to my dad to make a deal with me? I guess I should've been expecting the unexpected since I'd just been baptized into the Church.

"Okay I'm listening." I said. I was all ears. I was going to commit this conversation to memory lest I ever forgot. And I never have!

I guess it was a compliment to me that the Chief's boss sent a message through my father instead of coming to me directly. The boss of the Agawam "group" would've had to have been an idiot to think I'd go along with any deal they could offer me. So they asked Dad.

"Are you listening or off daydreaming somewhere?" Dad suddenly interrupted my thoughts.

According to my father, the police chief made it real clear what the offer was his boss was putting on the table. My father carefully repeated to me what the Chief instructed him to say.

An offer I couldn't refuse

"You and your kid (that's me) can have anything you want in this town—all the money and power you could ever want." Just get her to stop fighting us," Chief Chmielewski pleaded with my father. Or so Dad told me that's how it went down.

There it was on the table--MONEY. Integrity and courage I had plenty of and the mob knew it. But money? Ahh! Now that was a different story. I was poor as a church mouse and everyone knew it.

The only thing I can say is that someone had already made me a better offer and beaten them to it. I had a better power than anything the mob could offer me. I'd just been baptized into the Church of Jesus Christ of Latter-day Saints a few months earlier hadn't I?

I'd been getting used to the power of God since being introduced to the constant companionship of the Holy Ghost following my baptism. I gotta say, I really loved it!

Still, Dad made the mob's offer sound so innocent, that I think he truly believed I had no reason to refuse it. So when I just stood there with my mouth open and nothing coming out, Dad tried again.

278

"Just do whatever they say," he argued. "What's so hard about that?" He was yelling now and I could see his face facing turning beet red as it always did whenever he got angry. "That's all you have to do!"

I listened as my dad encouraged me to accept what might have seemed an irresistible offer to any other politician in Agawam.

"You know I can't Dad and you know why," I said, as I reminded him of my baptism into the Mormon Church.

Sure, Dad saved my life and stopped a contract on me most likely ordered by "Skyball" himself a few years before I got back in Agawam. For all I knew Dad might've even saved my life again when he made a deal behind my back to put me on the town council. And now he probably thought he was saving my life again by trying to get me to take their offer.

Whoosh! All the money and power anyone could ever want. Yes. That's exactly what I would be turning down. "Get thee behind me Satan," I prayed.

Dad didn't say it, but I would find out soon enough what happens to those who turn down an offer they can't refuse. Looking at the expression on my father's face, I was worried for both of us. I was worried because the offer had been made to both of us, not just me.

"Dad," I said. "I know you won't understand, but I have a duty to more than the people of this town."

To which Dad angrily responded, "You don't owe anyone anything."

Poor Dad, I guess he didn't think I was talking about my duty to God. Realizing he wasn't going to change my mind, Dad did what most parents do in the heat of the moment, as he angrily shouted, "You're no daughter of mine!" And with that, he walked out of my life.

I can't imagine the humiliation he felt when he had to go back to Chief Chmielewsky and tell him he had failed. I wasn't thinking that Dad might've been worried because he knew they'd kill me for sure this time. At the time I honestly thought Dad was angry with me simply for walking away from such a sweet deal he could've had too.

Even now, I feel sorry I let my father down the way I did. Not sorry about not accepting a bribe. I was sorry I couldn't pray with him like most fathers and daughters would have done in a similar situation. As I watched Dad drive away, it pained me to think I might never see him again given what we'd both just been through.

That alone is one of my saddest regrets in our relationship. But I had another Father in my life who I had promised to obey the day I was baptized. Hadn't my Heavenly Father rescued me even more times than Dad had ever done? Two fathers and two choices. I knew what I had to do. One was a relationship I wasn't prepared to ruin for all eternity.

Another father in my life

I'd like to say that I felt safer in Agawam than I had before my baptism. But nothing much changed on that end of it. I may have changed after I stepped out of the waters of baptism, but my enemy hadn't.

The first change I noticed, I was directed to use my voice in a more godly way thanks to the influence and power of the Holy Ghost. I was headstrong and foolish in those days only because I really didn't know how engaging evil could be done any other way. Drawing closer to my Heavenly Father, I soon realized I didn't need to worry about losing my voice in order to keep the spirit at my council meetings either.

Determined to choose the right and fight the wrong, I did what I'd always done before my baptism. I prayed. I needed to hear the voice of the Lord and so I prayed to my Heavenly Father knowing He really does hear and answer prayer.

As a Latter-day Saint I quickly learned about fasting with prayer to know God's will and more importantly how to accept His will and do it. Soon, I learned how to communicate with my Father in Heaven that went beyond praying and crying out unto God as I'd been prone to do. I started fasting once a month with more faith in prayer.

And that's how it was that I found my voice again after I'd been prompted by the Spirit to start up my own conservative newspaper. It was appropriately named *The Agawam Voice*.

CHAPTER TWELVE:
A VOICE IN AGAWAM

"You really gonna start up a newspaper Mom?" my son was asking, as he looked over the paperwork scattered across my desk.

"It's better than the two-hour call-in radio talk show I get to do only twice a month," I replied.

It wasn't a paying job, but it did give me a voice ever since the local media decided to transfer my favorite political news reporter to the obituaries. I figured doing a call-in show twice a month was better than nothing. I remember like it was yesterday.

"Go ahead. You're on the air with Willard Womack and Agawam Town Councilor Elena Bonavita." Willard announced to his radio listeners.

I couldn't believe my luck when Womack invited me to co-host a talk radio call-in show with him. He had his own 3 to 5pm daily show with *WREB Radio* out of Holyoke, Massachusetts, but as luck would have it, Womack was one of my biggest fans. The radio station admired my "moxie," or so they told me

For me, *WREB*'s invitation was an answer to prayer. Willard Womack was a popular on-air personality ever since the radio station switched to a talk format in 1972. *WREB* left the air in 1991.

Our call-in talk radio show, airing twice a month, aimed to turn politically divisive communities like Agawam into a type of echo chamber more like what the Fox News Channel does today.

I'd been praying for a way to reach Agawam residents after getting shut out of fair and unbiased coverage of my council activities. I feared losing my support base which so much fake news tends to do. And besides, there was another reason that a talk radio show was a blessing for me.

There's an old adage someone once said, "If you only counsel yourself, you end up with your own thoughts." Using a call-in talk radio show was a great sounding board for anyone in my situation, not to mention the people who were listening in on my shows.

Giving a voice to the people of Agawam

Going on the air with *WREB Radio* was all about politics and it was an overnight hit. Of course, my detractors had their supporters call in to take me to task for making Agawam "look bad." But I relished those calls too. It gave me a chance to set the record straight.

I can still see the lights on the call-in board that lit up like a Christmas tree every time we went on the air.

"Hi. I have a question for Bonavita," the caller would say. To which I'd lean into the microphone saying, "You got her, what's your question?" Like some talk show hosts strive to do, I too wanted to be more like a sounding board than a megaphone.

Lots of callers were just plain frustrated with not being able to get a straight answer from their elected officials or couldn't get on the city or school agenda to address some serious issue.

"I'm in the phone book, if you need to talk," I'd often remind my callers. Agawam folks took me up on it and that's how I got a better feel of our town's problem. I enjoyed taking those kinds of calls at home and luckily, I didn't get too many harassing calls. The talk radio show was a blessing for me and the people.

To my surprise, my voice got even stronger after the mob got so bold as to send a bullet riddled message to my boss at Johnson's. What's that old saying? When one doors closes, another one opens? And it did!

The Agawam Voice makes its debut

Where do I begin? It all happened so fast. I was doing my talk radio show with *WREB Radio* in Holyoke and I loved it. But I knew it wasn't enough. I needed a stronger "voice" than what talk radio afforded me. Besides, it was only twice a month. So I prayed about what I could do.

I'd been collecting unemployment after losing my job at Johnsons and I was ready to take on more than the talk radio show while serving on the town council. The impression given me by the Holy Spirit was like a radio voice inside my head instructing me to start up my own town newspaper. I'd been a praying fool long enough to know to check it out.

Back then, Agawam already had a small town newspaper, *The Agawam Advertiser* which is still in operation today and its policy regarding media bias was no different from any other liberal mainstream newspaper.

In view of its corrupted political machine with a suspect mob problem in Agawam, I didn't see how I could compete with the *Advertiser*. As the story goes, I guess the Lord knew there were enough "good" people in Agawam who would welcome my Christian conservative newspaper. I hadn't forgotten how faith in the Lord is always the best plan when we can't see what He can.

Meanwhile, I knew enough not to ask any of the mainstream liberal media newspapers in the area for help setting up my own newspaper. They were part of the problem! I prayed some more not knowing what to do.

You can hear God's voice

I'd no sooner prayed about finding a publisher, to help me, than I was prompted to contact a small town family owned newspaper in West Springfield. It was right down the road from Agawam and nothing like the others, I'm glad to say.

In fact, its publisher and owner admired what I'd been doing in Agawam and didn't hesitate to help me when I contacted him. Indeed, if not for him, I'd have no story to tell in this chapter. Phillip Coburn passed away a few years ago and I am glad to report that his family continues to operate and publish the West Springfield Record as did their father.

"Hello may I speak with the editor please?"

"You got him. This is Phillip Coburn, what can I do for you?" A friendly mature voice answered on the other end.

I introduced myself and we got to talking about what I wanted to do with my own newspaper. I remember our conversation like it was yesterday.

"Can I drop by at your convenience to talk with you about it?" I asked without taking a breath, fearful he might hang up once he had a chance to think about getting involved with me.

By no surprise, he'd recognized my name right away and in spite of it, Mr. Coburn invited me to set down with him the next day. He knew who I was alright and he liked it! The West Springfield Record editor miraculously volunteered to train me in the dos and don'ts of the newspaper business. I was ecstatic. It was more than I'd ever hoped for when I acted on the spiritual prompting to contact him.

Mr. Coburn knew that I had only a high school diploma plus a one semester secretarial course taken back in 1966. It wasn't much for an aspiring newspaper publisher, much less an editor. But that was all I brought to the table! Thanks to Mr. Coburn, who adopted me as an apprentice, I soon found myself learning the newspaper business.

Mr. Coburn offered to print up my newspapers for me if I used the same format as him. The West Springfield Record had the compact newspaper which is a broadsheet-quality newspaper printed in a tabloid format. It worked fine for me and I went with their format. Mr. Coburn was good to his word and he trained me for the job as a publisher but he was only printing up my newspapers for me. That only left me to hunt down other equipment that I'd be needing before going into business for myself.

The hard part was scraping up the cash for a strip printer (to print headlines), office supplies, and finding a volunteer staff. One day while praying on my knees I inquired of the Lord how I would ever find a volunteer photographer. Suddenly the phone rang.

"Hello. Is this Bonavita the town councilor?"

"Yes. What can I do for you?"

"My name is Tom Ferrari and it's what I think I can do for you," he promptly replied. "I hear you're starting up a newspaper. Could you use a photographer?"

Talk about answered prayer and right while I was still on my knees. As it turned out, Tom was a photographer and had his own equipment and was ready to come on board. He even offered his services, which meant he was signing up as a volunteer on my staff.

I couldn't believe it. To this day, I don't know how Tom managed to call at the exact moment I was on my knees praying for a photographer. But one thing was for certain—Heavenly Father had heard my prayers and He made sure Tom did too!

I know, because the next time I was on my knees praying for help to staff my editorial team, the doorbell rang.

I got up from my knees and opened the door to find a handsome stranger on my doorstep. His name was Burt Prokop and he had dropped by to talk town council business with me. By the time we finished our chat, he had the answers that he had come for and to my surprise I learned he was a writer.

You can imagine my excitement. First a photographer rings me up on the phone when praying on my knees and now a volunteer reporter had walked right up to my front door while I was praying again. I told him what I was up to with my newspaper and one thing led to another, and before I knew it, he had signed up as a volunteer staff reporter.

Another local named Michael Cascella, a very vocal supporter of mine, who'd been writing letters to the editor in the *Agawam Advertiser,* gladly volunteered when he heard I was looking for an assistant editor. He was a pretty good letter writer, so he easily qualified for the job.

Now that I had a staff, it was time to name my newspaper. I already knew it would be a voice for the townspeople, so I named it *The Agawam Voice.* While I may have had a name for my paper and a volunteer staff, I had another problem. I didn't have any money to roll out my first edition.

Who starts up a business with nothing in their bank account? Remember, I was still collecting unemployment at the time and money was tight now that I wasn't working at Johnsons anymore. For all I'd been through lately, I never imagined the Lord would actually bankroll my newspaper. But that's exactly what He did. Since my baptism into the Mormon Church only a few months earlier, I'd been gaining a greater understanding of how faith precedes the miracle.

Having such a powerful partner like Heavenly Father for my newspaper, I was encouraged to push on. But I needed sponsors for a sight unseen first edition. If that didn't call for a miracle in Agawam, then I didn't know what would. I'd been spending a lot of time on my knees in the days following my baptism, but it was all worth it.

Prayer was power indeed, especially when praying in faith and asking for righteous things.

And so it was, that I soon learned the power of God was nothing compared to the power of the Mafia or anyone working for them either.

The good people of Agawam hear His voice

Why is it we often tend to think we did it ourselves when it was actually God's hand in it? Yep. Looking back, it wasn't anything I'd done so much as what Heavenly Father was doing for me. As it turned out, the good people of Agawam who supported me must've been listening to the voice of God too. I didn't know that a miracle was already on its way.

Every cold call I made that day was a success. In fact, every available advertising space, and then some, was sold out. To the surprise of my staff, I had just enough money to print our first edition in the spring of 1981. The scripture "Ask and ye shall receive," came to mind.

With my newspaper I figured I'd be reaching 3000 households with 8 pages of unbiased information they'd get nowhere else. Crazy as it sounded, I envisioned my newspaper as an even better sounding board than my call-in talk radio show could have done with *WREB*.

Back in 1981, that kind of circulation was really amazing when you consider the *Agawam Advertiser* only has a circulation of 6000 today and it's not free to its readers either. I'm proud to say my newspaper was free! No one got paid on my staff, not even me. Every penny from advertising went into putting out the paper. There may not have been any profits, but I had no debt and plenty of blessings that kept my newspaper going! My volunteer staff was incredible.

"How much do you plan to charge for each copy of your paper?" My staff questioned during our one and only organizational meeting.

"Nothing." I replied. "I'd like to keep it more like a service to the townspeople."

"It might work for a while, but who's going to want to deliver the papers for free?"

"Good question. I hadn't thought that far ahead yet."

More praying together as a staff and we soon found a volunteer with a pickup truck willing to deliver the 3000 papers to local stores who'd also volunteered to carry them. Counters by cash registers carried a sign encouraging shoppers to take one FREE.

The plan to balance the media bias and fake news was working thanks to the Lord and so many good people. Our papers soon found their way into households eager to hear the rest of the story not reported in other media sources.

I kept some copies for posterity sake, and looking back, I don't know how the merchants kept advertising with me. My editions looked so high school and unprofessional. I was using my old worn manual typewriter for the text as well as an outdated strip printer for the headlines.

The letters were often crooked and without anyone to edit the text, typos became a fashionable trademark of *The Agawam Voice*. Obviously, I couldn't afford to hire a printer, so I had settled for the outdated strip printer and turned my bedroom closet into a darkroom to develop the film.

Once I set up my office in the living room, I was open for business! I just needed to figure out how I was going to make up the ads for our sponsors.

"Ask and ye shall receive"

Advertising presented another challenge. I had no budget for professional artwork or setting up logos of my sponsors' trademarks. Unfortunately, some of the merchants who advertised in my newspaper didn't have an ad already prepared to give me.

I knew how to write up an ad. Yep. I prayed and it would just come to me. Seems, I had a knack for writing and never knew it until I prayed for it. After I prayed over my first edition and inquired of the Lord how I might make up advertisements by myself, I discovered another hidden talent.

Back in the '80's we didn't have design templates to make print ads like we do today. I had to make mine up from scratch. The amazing thing is that after I prayed, I put my hand to the paper and as if by some invisible force, I was able for the first time to sketch objects to near perfection!

I should mention that I fasted and prayed several times before starting up the first edition. The power of prayer and fasting is a wonderful principal and it is a common practice among the Mormons which I learned and embraced.

It not only helped with putting out the newspaper, but by fervent prayer with fasting, I was able to feel the spirit and peace in the midst of all the political chaos around me. Going into business with a newspaper, meant my staff and I had to decide how we'd present our views without compromising those godly values I had recently embraced.

It wasn't a church, but it worked like one

Normally, newspapers in cities run by Democrats like those in Massachusetts tend to be liberal, like the majority of the populace. After my baptism into the Church of Jesus Christ of Latter-day Saints, my political views changed dramatically. For one thing, I switched from the Democrat Party to the Republican Party.

In keeping with tradition, Italians are mostly Catholic and Democrat. This was true of my own Italian family and most of Agawam as well. Up until my baptism, I hadn't been involved in partisan politics. Like many city councils back then, Agawam was non-partisan.

Once I took a closer look at the Democrats' platform, I was perplexed to discover they were pro-abortion, or as they like to call themselves, pro-choice. I was perplexed because the Pope, the head of the Catholic Church, had always come out against abortion.

The right to kill anyone, much less the unborn child, was not what I wanted to be affiliated with and that was a wake-up call for me after my baptism. And that's why I switched parties while serving as a town councilor.

Thanks to my new Church family, I quickly identified as a fiscal social conservative. Once I registered as a Republican, I decided my newspaper should reflect the views of a Christian Conservative as well. I even dedicated one full page in the paper to CHURCH NEWS.

A lot of good things came from that section in *The Agawam Voice*. I recall a time that I'd been working in my office sorting through stories for our next edition when the doorbell rang.

"I wanted to meet you so I could thank you in person," the lovely stranger introduced herself.

"Please, won't you come in?"

As the story goes, she had read the Church News section in my newspaper and decided to call the missionaries whose contact information I always published for my Church.

"You made an appointment with the Mormon missionaries?"

"I sure did. And I even set a date for my baptism."

The woman was baptized and even met a wonderful man in our ward and they were married and later sealed for time and all eternity in the temple too! I was truly blessed to be able to give a voice to the Lord's work in my newspaper as I had done for the brief time I had it. But sometimes the adversary, who is Satan, just can't leave a good thing like a godly voice in Agawam alone.

An attempt to take my voice out of Agawam

Maybe someone didn't like my voice getting so much coverage like I'd been doing with my newspaper, or just wanted to get me out of town period. I'll never know what prompted the offer to send me to the Massachusetts State Legislature, but that's what happened shortly after I got my newspaper up and running.

The offer came out of nowhere, and unlike me, most local politicians would've killed to get such an offer as what I was made. You can imagine my surprise when I was invited to lunch by a powerful statesman in the Democrat party whose name escapes me after all these years.

By now, I had survived two scandals that had rocked our community thanks to our police chief's attempts to oust me from the council. Not to mention I had switched to the Republican

Party. But for some reason, that didn't seem to be an issue with him. That should've been a red flag!

"We can't beat you, so we'd like to join you." Yes. That's what he said alright.

The invitation to send me to the Mass. Senate was flattering and tempting to be sure and it left me speechless. I had to think this offer through very carefully. What was the catch? You know there was always a catch whenever an offer seemed too good to be true.

Sensing my hesitation, he tried another approach. "You'd make a great Senator and we would like to put our support behind you with no strings attached."

Gosh. It sounded like a good plan. "No strings attached" he said. Okay. But then, I got to thinking as soon as I got my ego in check. Who would be supporting me and who would be controlling me once I was elected? And there was the catch!

He didn't expect my answer I think. Heck, neither did I. But the words just spilled out of my mouth. "No. But thank you for asking!"

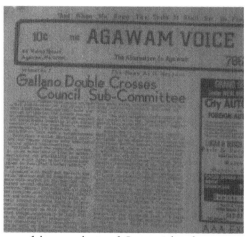

I never saw him again and I went back to my work on the town council and newspaper as if nothing had happened. As usual, I never spoke of it to anyone. I figured it came from the same "group" that had tried so many times to get rid of me before.

After turning down such an amazing offer, or bribe to get me out of town, I had time to think about his offer to put me in the State Senate. I figured the mobsters who'd been watching my every move and killing my informants, had to have been worried about something, or else why the offer for the Senate?

As I prayed for guidance to keep on track, I was reminded of the very reason why I'd included the scripture from John 8:32 on the nameplate of my newspaper which read, "And when we know the truth it shall set us free."

Stealing my voice

The phone was ringing and I was in the dark room printing up headlines for the next edition of the paper. There was that dark feeling again.

"You better come out here right away. They're stealing all your papers," the caller said, as I listened in disbelief.

It seemed not everyone was excited about a new "Voice" in town. I had only gotten out seven editions, when I started getting phone calls to report the theft of our May 14, 1981 edition. My first stop was a popular corner store in Agawam.

"You mean that someone just walked in your store and walked off with all my papers?" I asked in astonishment.

"Yes. These two guys come into my store and walk right up to the counter, looked me straight in the eye, and grabbed up all your papers and walked out with them."

It was the same story with every one of the stores who carried my papers. According to every store employee's description, I could only assume the thieves were henchmen or picciottos, a low-level soldier in the Mafia, who does the day-to-day threatening, beating, and intimidating of others.

The scene that played out that day in Agawam smacked of another racket favored by the Mafia. Hadn't we'd heard stories in the news, in the movies, about local merchants forced to pay for protection by racketeers working their neighborhood? As for Agawam, I could only imagine who those alleged picciottos were working for or taking orders from.

In the meantime, I got a phone call the next day from one of my supporters who wanted to report what he'd witnessed. It was a story alright but it was a day late!

"Are you sure it was my newspapers you saw the guys throwing in the dumpster?" I asked the local on the other end of the phone.

"I waited until they pulled off and took a look inside and sure enough, they were your papers alright."

After he described the two men which fit the same description as the storeowners I had already talked to the day before, I was satisfied we had our culprits nailed. I didn't bother asking why he waited a day before contacting me. He probably needed time to think about whether he wanted to get involved or not.

"Do you want to show me the dumpster where you saw them throwing my newspapers?"

"Sure. But I don't know if the newspapers are still in it. The trash might've been picked up. I guess I should've called you sooner."

"Let's go take a look," I said, while praying the sanitation department hadn't picked up the trash yet.

We drove to the dumpster hoping to find my newspapers still there, but it was empty. The trash had already been picked up and my papers were most likely sitting somewhere in the town dump.

I reprinted the stolen edition and thankfully some of the advertisers helped me out so I could do it without a loss. We were printing 3000 copies a week, so that was no small lump of change to write off especially since it was a free newspaper.

I didn't bother reporting the theft to the police. The Agawam police chief probably had organized it for all I knew. I took it to the Lord instead.

I already mentioned this part about the reason for stealing my newspapers back in Chapter 9. I had quoted my cousin Officer Norm Nardi who used the "M" word when speaking to the Liquor License Commissioners at a hearing for a controversial liquor license application. But I didn't go into detail in Chapter 9 explaining how that story lines up with my own story only because I promised to bring my readers up to speed in this chapter.

As the story goes, I wrote up an editorial in our May 21st edition, titled <u>Destroying Newspapers Does Not Destroy News</u>. I apologized to our readers and to our advertisers and this time it was me sending a message to the mob only I was careful not to mention the "M" word in my column.

Even now, I can see God's hand in all of it. The fact someone went to all the trouble to steal that one edition with the word "Mafia" in it, told a whole new story didn't it? Why weren't the store owners ever threatened or just warned to stop carrying my newspapers? Why only steal all the papers of that one edition? Just more questions for the whodunit eh?

Although I was able to reprint the entire stolen edition without it being stolen again, I couldn't keep replacing editions, so we needed a plan. I met with my staff and we prayed. We felt inspired to charge 10 cents for our newspaper from now on figuring that would deter any more thefts. The plan was never to collect any money for the paper, just keep giving it away free.

The plan was simple. We put the 10 cents on the nameplate while encouraging store clerks to place a complimentary copy in their customers' grocery bags. That way, if anyone tried to steal the 10 cent papers again, I could report the crime to the police as a theft and file charges since we had already identified the thieves once before.

The plan worked and we were in business again. After that no one ever walked off with bundles of my newspapers anymore. The interesting thing about someone in Agawam not liking my using the word *Mafia* in my own newspaper actually makes for another great clue to this whodunit. Take a look at what happened to someone else in Hollywood who tried to do something similar.

The Godfather movie producers had the same problem

Who hasn't seen *The Godfather* movie? Do you remember the time the Mafia protested the Godfather movie back in the '70's? I go into more detail in Chapter 16, but it's worth sharing in this chapter too.

In February 2014, Nolan Moore wrote up a fascinating review on the history of *The Godfather* movie production titled, <u>When The Real Mafia Tried To Stop Filming Of 'The Godfather'</u>.

Thanks to Moore, we get another clue for our whodunit. Nolan Moore identifies Joseph Colombo as the leader of the Colombo crime family, one of the infamous Five Families in New York, which by no coincidence includes my own family's Genovese crime family I believed was active in Agawam.

Moore details the action Colombo took to shut down production on the Godfather, and explains it was because "he didn't want all the unwanted attention the film would generate."

The Mafia tried everything, except killing anyone, to shut down the production. But nothing worked until the gangsters called for a sit-down.

According to Moore, the Godfather producers met with the gangsters and agreed to strike the word "Mafia" from the script. After that concession by the Godfather producers, the gangsters had no more issues with the movie.

Does that ring a bell with anyone? It should. If the word "Mafia" is what caused all the trouble for the Godfather producers then why couldn't it have been a problem for me too? It's not a stretch of the imagination to link Columbo's *Godfather* incident to the Genovese family's problem with my own newspaper printing the word "Mafia" in it as I had done.

As I see it, the Godfather producers and I definitely had something in common. Praise the Lord, we both lived to see another day and like their movie script, my newspaper was allowed to be published without further harassment.

The only difference in my true story is that I never conceded to the gangsters in Agawam because I never took the word "Mafia" out of the reprinted stolen edition. There's a moral to this story and it gets better.

Getting out of the business

Shortly after the stolen newspaper episode, I got it into my head that I could resign from the council and still serve my community through *The Agawam Voice*. I figured if I could turn it into a business then I could get out of the mob business once and for all.

So much had changed after I'd been baptized into Mormon Church. I had a whole new perspective on life but it contradicted the life I was leading in Agawam. For me staying in Agawam meant I had to keep living a lie about its mob problem and I was no longer spiritually comfortable with it. Maybe Father Heller could, but I couldn't.

Attending council meetings didn't help either. For all I knew, I could've been sitting next to those behind the killings of my informants, not to mention everything else done to me. I couldn't explain how I was still alive all this time in Agawam, but after my baptism I felt even more determined to keep my mouth shut.

It was no surprise that I began relating more to the Apostle Paul and that was frightening. Who can forget Paul's own story and what he went through after his own conversion to Christianity as he embraced the teachings of Jesus Christ? What happened to Paul is a story of itself that fits perfectly into my next chapter.

Hadn't Paul been fighting against the Church and killing Christians at the time Jesus appeared to him on the road to Damascus to give him a message?

"And he trembling and astonished said, Lord what wilt thou have me to do? ... Arise and go into the city and it shall be told thee."

- Acts 9:1-7

Just as Paul had been fighting the wrong people, I too must've needed to hear the word of the Lord to set me on the right path. Yes. God still sends his messengers to us as he did with Paul.

CHAPTER THIRTEEN:
GOD'S MESSENGERS IN AGAWAM

"You gotta take it back Elena," Anita said when I told her what I'd done.

"I know I've made a mess of it and I want to take it back, but how?"

My friend and mentor, former town councilor Anita Davilli, didn't feel good about my decision to turn in my resignation from the council and I was waffling too.

"Just tell them you changed your mind and let it go at that," she argued.

Poor Anita, how could I expect her to understand? I was not the same woman since I'd been baptized into the Church of Jesus Christ of Latter-day Saints less than six months ago. Good grief. I didn't even understand myself anymore. I felt trapped inside two worlds.

I knew the Church was true. Like the Apostle Paul who'd had a vision when the light blinded him on the road to Damascus, I understood his conversion story completely. I could never forget my own experience when a light so bright had filled my living room the night the sister missionaries had challenged me to be baptized into the Mormon Church.

Like Paul, I listened to the Lord and obeyed. It's been 36 years since my baptism and I've never regretted my decision. But I did regret my decision to tender my resignation. At first Anita had agreed it was the best thing to do. But so much had happened after I decided to do it, that we both had second thoughts. I was home the day Anita dropped by so we could figure out a plan.

We sat in my kitchen and I listened to my wise experienced friend as she tried to convince me to go public with my testimony. Hadn't the mainstream media done that already for me when I was baptized in December 1980? Yes. But that was different. So much had happened after that.

I took Anita's advice to go public with my letter of resignation dated June 30, 1981. Don't worry. The date is not a typo. I submitted my resignation so I could give a two month notice. I needed time to gage the pulse of the community. Who knows, I may have wanted to withdraw my resignation, which is exactly why the resignation story made headlines as it did. I had checked before tendering it and was satisfied that I could legally withdraw it anytime I wanted before its June 30th deadline.

I should've known the boys in the "group" wouldn't let me take it back so easily. Law or no law, they were good at making up their own rules in Agawam. As the story goes, it was a story all of itself for me to take it back.

The real story of my resignation

In the May 7th edition of *The Agawam Voice* Newspaper, I made breaking news on the front page. The headline told the story: <u>Councilor Requests Clerk Withdraw Her Resignation:</u> <u>Newspaper Seen As Alternative.</u>

The story explained what our town clerk Ed Caba was doing to make sure I couldn't take it back. "Mr. Caba when last contacted by *The Voice News* was still checking to see if her resignation could be withdrawn." I know. Unbelievable, right? And what about my not-so-friendly District Attorney who'd done everything to put me away?

District Attorney Matthew Ryan told *The Voice News* "this is a civil matter and should be decided by the Town Solicitor Lambert Ollari." Why wasn't I surprised? Wasn't Ollari the one who gave illegal advice to me and the town council when I called for an investigation into the Agawam police department over my arrest record incident?

But the D.A. surprised me when asked "whether or not she could withdraw her resignation, Ryan said "Off the cuff I think you could. Common sense would dictate that anyone could."

In the same *Voice* story and the *Morning Union* news, I cited spiritual reasons for my rash decision to resign. I never mentioned the real reason—the mob problem in Agawam that I couldn't reconcile with my life in the Church. Instead I reminded the people that I could still serve them "through *The Voice* Newspaper that the Lord has blessed me with."

Fearful of who might fill my seat, I was deluged with phone calls for two days and nights from people asking me not to resign which prompted me to withdraw my letter of resignation that I'd submitted a week earlier to the Town Clerk.

Here is what the *Morning Union* reported on May 12, 1984 about what I had done at a council meeting: "said [she] still intends to resign. 'I have withdrawn…only because it is my intent to re-submit a resignation,' Ms. Bonavita told the other 14 town councilors. She said if the council could have filled her post with 'someone of my flavor' she may not have rescinded her resignation."

As it turned out, little did I know what someone was planning to do to me if I tried to take it back. As you might suspect, those behind all my troubles in Agawam sure didn't want to give up my resignation that easily. Guess I ruined their celebration plans when I took it back.

Big mistake! I prayed before I did it and thought I had the right plan even though I made the mistake of not fasting and inquiring of the Lord *before* I withdrew my resignation. The only thing I can say in my defense is that I was new in the Church and didn't take that kind of a decision serious enough to do a fast. I wanted to resign and that seemed right to me.

As humans, don't we often tend to ignore God's will for us? I guess that's what I did. I thought I knew best and in retrospect I didn't. It got all mucked up and I was humbled by the experience.

After all was said and done, I opted to withdraw my resignation after Anita convinced me it was the right thing to do. I couldn't tell her why I wanted off the council because I didn't want her ending up like Floyd Landers. She loved me like a daughter and I knew Anita was finished fooling around. She'd heard the outcry of my supporters and she just wanted me to stay on the council. We both thought I made the right decision this time and I took it back.

When I said it got all mucked up because I didn't take my decision to resign to the Lord first, I really meant it. Here's where my story takes a surreal twist that prompted another visit from Anita after it hit the fan.

Resign or go to jail

"I guess you saw the paper before I called you? I can't believe I'm being charged for interference with our town manager's duties."

"Now see what you've gone and done by jumping the gun the way you did Elena," Anita was chastising me and rightly so. "Whatever were you thinking?"

"You think what I did may have brought on these charges against me?"

I guess I deserved that look she threw me. I didn't need an answer. We both knew what I'd done had most assuredly brought it all on.

I'd been so used to all the problems orchestrated by the police chief that I'd become numb to what I might have done to bring on my latest problem with mob. Never one to hold back, Anita ever so politely reminded me of how I might've given the idea to the "group" myself.

It seems the idea to bring me up on charges all started even before the Town Clerk had decided to officially accept my letter of withdrawal for my resignation. Thanks to me, we had a new town manager and he was no better than Caputo whose resignation I'd called for and gotten after he tried to bribe me. Only Bowen was better at what he did in following orders than Caputo had ever been. Bowen didn't attempt to bribe me to change my mind like Caputo had once done.

No sooner had I decided to withdraw my resignation, then it seemed someone was determined I was going to get off the council one way or another. It looked like a plan to replace me with one of their own associates on the council instead of waiting for the voters to choose.

I guess Agawam's boss thought our new town manager should give it a try, given how our Police Chief Chmielewski had already failed so many times in getting rid of me. Luckily for me, Manager Bowen was no mobster's handler and he fared even worse with me than our clumsy police chief. Nonetheless, as our town manager, Bowen did have my pal the town solicitor Ollari to give him free advice on how to get rid of me.

Sure enough, only five days after my plan to withdraw my resignation appeared in my own newspaper May 7th, Ollari apparently found a loophole. Although it wasn't illicit advice he gave Bowen, the loophole nonetheless opened the door to a commonly known practice employed by the mob that I was only too familiar with.

The story was headlined <u>Bowen Grasping At Straws</u> in *The Agawam Voice* May 21, 1981 edition, which reads in part:

> "In a letter addressed to the Agawam Town Councilors on Monday May 12th, Town Manager Richard Bowen charged Councilor Elaine T. Bonavita with interference in his duties and requested a council investigation into the matter. In an effort to remove the thorn from his side, Manager Bowen is calling for an investigation into the actions of a Town Councilor who has herself called for and failed to get three times investigations into the Police Department and bidding system."

We explained to our readers in the *Voice* story, "Bonavita is charged with violating Chapter 43, Section 92 of the State General Laws for allegedly discussing negotiations with a union representative of the town's firefighters. Maximum penalty upon conviction of these charges is $600 fine or six months in jail. Also at stake is Councilor Bonavita's eligibility to hold any town office."

I still hadn't forgotten what *The Republican* newspaper editor had done to my favorite reporter Joy. Working as a news reporter myself and covering Agawam politics, I was my own editor. I wasn't worried anyone would demote me to obituaries, like they'd done to her. But Bowen's boss was trying to fire me from the council permanently!

Looking back, it seemed like a page out the same play book used by the Agawam police chief against me. For example, how was Bowen's unexpected call for an investigation of a fake ethics charge any different than when the police chief had set me up on that fake assault charge when I faced a ten year prison sentence?

Well, at least this time, it was only six months' jail time if convicted. Anita was worried though and I tried to make light of it for her sake. She still didn't know the full story on the mob.

"You gotta give these guys credit Anita. They sure don't believe in giving up, do they?"

Shaking her head, as if in disbelief, Anita managed to say something like "I didn't think Bowen had it in him to do something like this to you. I really didn't."

"Well, one thing we know is that he takes his orders from the council and that points to Fred Nardi doesn't it?"

I baited her to see what she would say, but as usual, she wasn't taking the bait. Actually, it's kind of ironic that the "group" Officer Brown had warned me about chose to charge me with a Code of Ethics violation. After what I'd been through, I knew the mob could get anyone to say anything even under oath. Who can forget my own story in Chapter 9 when I was up on fake charges?

Despite bringing in two out-of-state witnesses to testify against me in court hoping to send me to the big house for ten years, I beat the charges brought against me. Like some miracle, I still can't believe it.

Of course, I was not guilty of the ethics charge either, nonetheless, it looked serious on paper as those types of things always did. There was never any question in my mind that they must've expected their felonious charge to hold up or they would not have wasted their time with it. But since when had that ever stopped them before?

I often wondered what they had on their witness, who they claimed was a union representative, which made him the perfect fall guy willing to bear false witness against me. From my own experience, I knew the Mafia were real good at bribes, threats and if all else failed--murder. The poor *patsy* they found, willing to do such a thing, was doomed for sure.

Adding to the suspense of Agawam politics, I couldn't help but think that my detractors might've wanted everyone to think that I had only tendered my resignation because I had known what was coming which would've made me look even more guilty.

Violation of state ethics and public corruption laws are intended to protect the innocent and punish the violators of public trust. It wasn't so much the six months' jail time that seemed to have brought on these fake charges against me, as it was that someone had hopes that I'd be ineligible to serve in any future office if found guilty.

While doing research on this chapter, I came across Chapter 43 of City Charters of the Massachusetts State General Laws. It makes for some pretty interesting reading, especially Section 92 about the penalty of both imprisonment and to "never again be eligible for any office or position, elective or otherwise, in the service of the city."

Wow. Reading Section 92, it left little doubt that my enemies were going to make certain I never held office in Agawam again eh? As it turned out, I prayed and I felt prompted to do nothing and just wait to see what came of it because it was, after all, up to the council to decide whether or not to investigate the charges Bowen had brought against me. That didn't seem very likely, given how any investigations I had ever called for with the police department never made it to the council floor.

To this day, I never knew what came of the fake ethics charge against me. All I know is that I have no memory of any battle with Bowen and the "group" after I made my next move that must've surprised the heck out of everyone, including me!

This is where my story gets difficult to talk about. It is more personal and I never went public with it until now. I can only say that two things interrupted my life that I had absolutely no control of at that time.

As the story goes, I continued putting out my newspaper after I withdrew my resignation despite the mysterious lingering illness that was rapidly worsening. I felt like I was dying again and didn't know what to do. To make matters worse I felt no peace in my decision to stay on the council and yet, I was resigned to the idea that if I did I'd still be wanted by the mob.

Maybe I was too absorbed with the ethics charge, or too sick, to think about what was bringing on that dark feeling I always got whenever I was in danger. Whatever it was, I sure wasn't thinking about what the mob was going to do to me after I turned away my own father like I did. Sure, I had walked away from the mob's offer of "all the power and money" I could ever want, but why did I forget what they wanted from me in return?

Hadn't the police chief told Dad that I could have it all if I just stopped fighting them? Dad never said, and I never thought to ask, what would happen to someone who refused that kind of an offer by the mob? Even to this day, I always wondered why they just didn't flat out kill me like I suspected they had done to Floyd, Sarge and Shoppie after I had turned them down too.

As always when I was in danger, that eerie dark feeling persisted even though I thought I had put all my problems to rest. Naturally, I decided to take my questions to the Lord this time with fasting and prayer. Should I re-submit my resignation? Or should I even seek re-election? More importantly, what was I to do with my newspaper? And what about the mob, what was their plan for me?

Having the gift of faith as I did, I prayed fervently for instruction and believed I would get it. The scripture, "Ask and it shall be given you" took on a whole new meaning for me while I'd been fasting to hear the word of the Lord. What happened next would change my life forever.

God's messengers were waiting with another message

The doorbell rang and when I answered the door I found two missionaries that I'd never seen before, standing on my doorstep. I knew they were elders, a term used for young Mormons on their mission, because of the recognizable Mormon missionary name tag they all wore. It is a symbol of the Church they've been called to represent and of the Savior Jesus Christ whose messengers they are.

Like the apostle Paul who'd been given instruction by the Lord in His appearance to him on the road to Damascus, I found myself wondering why God's messengers chose to appear to me out of nowhere too!

"What brings you here today elders?" I asked, surprised to see them.

"Sister Bonavita, may we come in?" the elders asked.

Normally, church members make appointments to have the missionaries in their home for dinner or to administer a blessing in the absence of a priesthood holder in the home. I had no priesthood in my home and I'd been fasting for an answer to prayer and I was glad to see them even though I hadn't called to make an appointment.

They introduced themselves as the zone leaders assigned with the Mormon Church for our area in Agawam. I let the elders in and we all just kind of stood around in the living room as I waited for them to tell me the purpose of their visit. I vividly recall what one of the elders said to me that day.

"The Lord sent us here Sister Bonavita and we don't know why."

I immediately felt the presence of the Holy Spirit and I knew something was up for sure. I just didn't know what it was. I told them that I had been fasting and praying about something and I didn't know what to do. I never did mob talk with church members and yet, I didn't have to say anything more to them. Amazingly, as if prompted by the Spirit, those young elders just seemed to know what to do after that.

I listened as the elders explained to me how persons desiring guidance in an important decision can receive a priesthood blessing. Unlike the time when I was taken ill the night before my baptism and I called the sister missionaries who brought the elders to give me a healing blessing, I didn't call anyone this time. And yet, here were God's messengers at my door unsolicited. Or were they?

Standing in my living room, for what seemed like an eternity, I got to thinking what really might've brought the elders around. But those young boys didn't know anything about the mob problem in Agawam or how I was wanted by the mob. Gosh. I never even confided in my own Bishop only because I feared it might bring him into danger too.

Nope. No one in my Church family even knew I'd been walking around with a big target on my back for years. But I did need a miracle didn't I? Wasn't I fasting for help to know what to do? I didn't know how, but I knew those young elders had been sent to me by God Himself and I listened to the Spirit telling me what to do.

"Can you give me a comfort blessing Elders?"

"Yes Sister Bonavita. I believe that's why the Lord sent us here today."

As I prepared for the blessing, I set up a chair in the living room and took a seat. We had a prayer and then the two elders placed their hands on my head and spoke the words the Lord gave to them. I waited to hear the words encouraging me to stay on the council, but what I heard was not what I expected. I have never forgotten one single word of the blessing they spoke to me that day.

"Sister Bonavita, it is not the Lord's will that you should lose your life at this time. You are to leave this place immediately for the Lord has another work for you to do," the elder pronounced quite clearly.

Sitting alone in my living room, watching the elders drive off, I couldn't help but think that if I didn't take their warning seriously, I'd most likely end up the same way as my informants—dead by assassination of an induced heart attack.

Why not? Hadn't I been sick lately and growing weaker from the Lyme disease? And couldn't anyone have known about my weekly visits to Doctor Proulx given how I'd been on their watch list and surveilled since moving back to Agawam?

Add to that, the recent charges leveled against me by the town manager and I was probably another prime candidate to be set me up by the mob for an assassination by an induced heart attack for sure. It would have been amazingly stupid indeed if I had forgotten about the warnings to my three informants the last night I saw each of them alive.

Of course my informants had each gotten a phone call warning them to "leave us alone." Yes. They all did, but what about me? I think the only warning the mob had in mind for me of late was when the Agawam police chief outed himself by sending my father to me with a message from Chmielewski's boss.

Is that why another father in my life, Heavenly Father, had sent two of His own messengers to warn me with a message of His own?

And there came two angels

Since I was a veteran at running from the Mafia by then, I figured anyone in my situation might have been suspicious of the two young men dressed as missionaries. Could the Genovese family have sent two young hoods disguised as Mormon missionaries? Anything is possible in this mob whodunit given how the Mafia operates.

Hadn't its own hit men in the Mafia oftentimes disguised themselves as priests when ordered to kill someone? Or was that just in the movies?

To be honest, the thought hadn't crossed my mind at the time. Looking back, I can see how my readers might be wondering how I could have been so sure which "family" sent the missionaries to my door. Was it my Mormon church family or my father's own crime family, the Genovese? Or was it just another scheme of Dad's to exile me to Texas hoping to save my life again?

For the purpose of our whodunit, I decided to look up my former Bishop who presided over the Springfield Ward where I was baptized into the Church.

I contacted the church in Salt Lake City, Utah and they located my former Bishop who was still alive. I called him on the telephone and we spoke briefly. He was getting on in years and his memory wasn't so good anymore. I even had to remind him who I was. Gosh. Who could forget me?

"I'm sorry Sister Bonavita. I don't know remember anything. I wish I could help you," my former Bishop insisted after I explained the purpose of my call to him.

I wasn't surprised when my bishop claimed to have no inkling of why the Zone Leaders had paid me a visit that day. Mormon missionaries only serve under Mission Presidents not local bishops. But there are other messengers sent forth by the Lord.

As for those two elders who were sent by the Lord with a message for me, I know they were God's messengers because I felt the witness of the Holy Ghost in their presence. There was no dark feeling warning me of danger that I'd normally get if it was. Being in the habit of likening my own life story to stories from the bible, it made me think about the story of Sodom and Gomorrah.

What was it the two angels who came to Sodom were sent to tell the Prophet Lot? "And when the morning arose, then the angels hastened Lot, saying, Arise, take thy wife, and thy two daughters, which are here; lest thou be consumed in the iniquity of the city" (Genesis 19:15).

I'm sure a prophet like Lot didn't ask the angels for an ID or press them for proof of who sent them to him. He was a righteous man and he knew they were God's messengers, just like I knew when the missionaries were sent to me.

In fact, since leaving Agawam I am reminded of other instances when God's messengers would just show up unsolicited on my door step while I was either fasting or praying fervently seeking guidance for important decisions. I remember such a time when I'd been living in Texas and it was 1985.

I'd been fasting for two days with my boyfriend Scott. He was not a member of the Church like I was, but he'd been visiting Church with me right after we started dating. He had even been taking the lessons from the missionaries to learn more about the Church.

Scott and I had only been dating two months but we were madly in love and needed guidance about our future plans together. He agreed to fast and pray with me about whether or not we should marry. If not, then we'd break it off and go our separate ways.

And so it was that we got down on our knees and together we opened our fast with a prayer. I still remember what he said to Heavenly Father before he closed our prayer.

"And I won't break my fast until I get an answer."

Okay. I gotta admit I was worried. Here he was an inactive Catholic who had loved to party but had never been praying, much less fasting about anything before meeting me. So, I was worried how it would go for him.

As the story goes, I had gotten my answer after my 24-hour fast, as I normally did when fasting, but I couldn't tell him. I knew the Lord wanted us to marry. But I had to wait until he got an answer for himself. That's how fasting works.

Well, he didn't get an answer by the end of our 24 hour fast and so, true to his promise to God, he wanted to continue our fast until he did. We were now in the second day of our fast.

I was understandably concerned and we prayed together that evening that he would know how to get an answer to his fast. He knew I had my answer, so he was anxious to get an answer too. After we prayed again, he hung around my apartment so we could talk about what to do. It didn't take long to get an answer. But it wasn't what we expected.

The doorbell rang and when I opened the door I was surprised to see two missionaries standing on my doorstep. I immediately recognized the elders as the zone leaders assigned to our area in the Mormon Church.

"Elders! What brings you by this time of night?" It was nearly dark out and I hadn't called them or made an appointment with them either.

"Sister Bonavita. We don't know why we are here."

I listened as they repeated the words, that until that moment, I had only heard once before in my life and that was in Agawam when the zone leaders there had also appeared out of nowhere with a warning for me to flee the city. And that's how I ended up in Texas and met Scott.

Tears welling up in my eyes, I motioned for the elders to come in. No one knew we were fasting about marriage. It was just between the two of us. At least I thought it was. I'd forgotten someone else knew.

Heavenly Father hears and answers our prayers in different ways and I suddenly realized He had sent his messengers to me again for such a purpose.

"I think I know why you're here Elders."

I told them about our problem and Scott not being able to get an answer to his prayer while we were fasting. The elders looked at each other and nodded as if in agreement about why the Spirit had led them to my door.

"We know why we're here now Sister Bonavita," the elder replied. "We're here to help Scott get an answer to his prayer."

That was my cue to ask if Scott would accept a comfort blessing from the elders. He did and he got a beautiful blessing instructing him to take me to the Dallas Temple. In the blessing Scott was also promised that he would get his answer "on the temple grounds."

We went to the temple as instructed but we were too late. The temple had just closed for the day. Scott looking around said to me, "Isn't this the temple grounds we are standing on right now?"

Indeed it was! The gates had been closed but the temple ground extended a bit past the fencing. Ignoring the cars passing by on the busy street facing the temple, we knelt in prayer and waited for Scott to get his answer. Nearly ten minutes had passed and I was feeling ill from fasting 48 hours.

September in Dallas was blistering hot and the heat was beginning to take its toll on me.

Scott knew I had serious health issues when he met me, but it didn't matter to him. As of that time in my life, I still hadn't yet been diagnosed with Lyme disease. Feeling faint, I said nothing to Scott. I prayed he would get an answer but I needed to get back to the car.

Praying while holding onto the rail of the temple fence, I looked up to the heavens while thinking I needed Scott to pick me up and carry me to the car. Suddenly, without speaking a word to me, Scott stands up and swoops me up into his arms and carries me to the car where he asks me to marry him. He had heard the voice of the Lord and we were married a few weeks later.

Yes, today I can bear witness that the missionaries who were sent to me both times in Agawam and Texas were true servants of the Lord, much like God's messengers who are angels as those recorded in scriptures.

Escape for thy life, look not behind thee

Meanwhile back in Agawam in 1981, I did not ignore the message from the Lord warning me and my son to flee the city just as He had once sent two angels to Sodom with a similar message for Lot.

In what I can only describe as a complete act of faith on my part, I didn't hesitate to leave my past behind and move on with my life, and like Lot, never looking back. Three days after the elders had appeared on my doorstep, my son and I were on the road heading back to Texas in my pickup truck.

I never saw what the local newspapers reported on my resignation after I left town. I left all that behind me and never looked back until the Lord called me to write this memoir 35 years later. Out of curiosity, I decided to see what was out there and looked up the *Morning Union* Archives.

Reading about what I did for the first time since leaving Agawam, I was surprised to find my own father and grandmother had been interviewed and made the news in the July 1, 1981 *Union* newspaper after I left town. The story by *Union* Staff Reporter Helayne Lightstone titled <u>Council seat hinges on residency</u> quoted my grandmother saying, "She sold all her furniture…and moved. She left Tuesday (June 23rd) at 7 a.m. and got there [Texas] at 4 p.m. Thursday (June 25)." *The Union* reported that my mail was being forwarded to the North Street home of former Town Councilor Anita Davilli.

I found it interesting that my former council president, Paul Fieldstad, said "the determination of where Ms. Bonavita lives will be made by Town Clerk Edward A. Caba."

Dad and Gram were both dead now but it didn't feel like it as I read their story. As for the good people of Agawam, I wish I knew what they were told. I can only imagine the rumors swirling around my sudden disappearance. Like Lot, I didn't have any news on Agawam once I arrived in Texas. I only had what I had brought with me, and nothing more.

Thanks to a telegram tendering my resignation and a few other files that I held onto all these years, I can report what I actually did to secure my council seat after I arrived in Texas.

310

Not as much as I'd like to have, but enough to finish this part of my story. Now it was my turn to send Agawam a MESSAGE!

I didn't know at the time I was in Texas that the *Morning Union* had already contacted Dad and Gram and went with the story that ran on July 1st. Owing to some instinct I have been blessed with, I amazingly sent a message of my own to the Town Clerk by a *Western Union* mailgram dated July 2nd:

Here is what I wrote about what I would do: "Will not return from my vacation. Decided to stay July 1. Resignation effective June 30, 1981. Will return all my council books and material. Will write formal letter following this telegram."

Guess I was on "vacation" and decided to make it permanent so my resignation would be valid and my seat couldn't be filled until the next election. Although I was in Texas, I was smart enough to keep my legal Agawam address on my rental property until June 30th too. It was all legal and I did my best to ensure it would be the voters who'd replace me in the upcoming fall election and not the mobsters like Chief Chmielewski's boss who I'd left behind.

I figured it was safer to leave my seat empty rather than let the mob put in someone who would undo everything I had risked my life, along with others, to accomplish. I felt I owed that much to the memory of former Town Councilor Floyd Landers, Sarge and Shoppie.

I found the formal letter I'd written for the council dated July 4th that I mentioned in the telegram, and it reads more like a will. It was odd in a way because I'd left something of my own experiences for each of my fellow members on the town council.

One more thing I came across in the *Morning Union* archives was an article dated July 6th that mentioned what actions the council would consider at its meeting that night. Fill a vacancy on the Town Council was at the top of the agenda. The *Union* reported, "The controversy over filling the post appears to hinge on whether Ms. Bonavita was technically a resident of Agawam on that date. The town attorney (Ollari) has been asked to render an opinion tonight."

I leave my story there. What was it Lot was told after the two angels had taken him and his family out of Sodom before it was destroyed? "Escape for thy life; look not behind thee, neither stay thou in all the plain; escape to the mountain, lest thou be consumed" (Genesis 19:17).

But his wife looked back

I never understood why, but I didn't look back after the Lord warned me to flee the city. Like Lot who fled Sodom and escaped to the mountain, I too escaped with my life and obeyed the Lord when I moved to Texas. Never realizing I was doing the same thing as Lot had done, I left my story in Agawam and never looked back.

Until the writing of my memoir, I was never even curious about what happened after I left. And it's not like I didn't try to find out after all these years, because I did. But I should've remembered the rest of Lot's story after his family fled Sodom and were told by the angels not to look back. "But his wife looked back from behind him, and she became a pillar of salt" (Genesis 19:26)

What can I say about my own experience when I looked back, even though I waited more than 35 years to do it? You can read all about it in Chapter 16 if you want to know what happened when I attempted to contact Agawam authorities while writing this memoir. Spoiler alert! It's not a story for the faint of heart. But it is the reason why I leave off with my story about my resignation.

Meanwhile back in 1981, I needed to do one more thing to make it all official after I'd arrived in Texas.

My bishop claims he's an FBI agent

As soon as I got to Texas, I checked in with my new bishop as is the practice of our Church whenever its members change their address or move as I had just done. As I found my way to his office after our Sunday services, I was welcomed to the ward by one of the brethren who introduced himself as the bishop's secretary.

"We sure are glad to have you in our ward Sister Bonavita."

"If you're busy I can check in with you next Sunday."

"Not a chance of making you wait that long Sister Bonavita."

He invited me to take a seat in the lobby while I waited on the bishop. As I chatted with some of the other church members hanging around the foyer, I got a chance to ask them about my new bishop.

"Well, I'll tell you." replied one old timer, who'd been reading the posted messages on the nearby hall bulletin board. "Bishop Allred's not your average everyday white collar worker, that's for sure."

I couldn't quite make out what he said so I asked a woman standing next to me, "Did he just say that our bishop is an FBI agent?"

"Yes. Bishop Allred is an FBI agent," she said whispering ever so reverently into my ear.

I couldn't help but think what if the Church had been monitoring my situation back east and wanted to ensure my safety out here by calling an FBI agent as my bishop? I was new in the Church and it made sense to me given all the miraculous rescues going on all around me since I was baptized.

No way, I finally convinced myself. I may have entertained such a thought at first, but only because I didn't understand how bishops are called by inspiration and not for the convenience of any Church member.

Did I really have an FBI agent for a bishop? Even now, I stand all amazed at God's love for me that somehow, someway, my loving and ever protective Heavenly Father had indeed called an FBI agent as my bishop in Texas. I came to know it was by no coincidence that Bishop Allred had been called by the Lord to serve as bishop in my new ward just before I'd gotten a visit in Agawam by the Lord's own missionaries warning me to flee the city. Only the almighty God Himself could've pulled that off.

Looking back, I wonder what the mob was thinking about that when they surveilled me in Texas? I pray those mobsters from my past had a witness of the power of God and, like Mario Facione had once done, contacted the Mormon missionaries to learn more about His plan for us in the restored gospel of Jesus Christ.

As it is, I never officially knew the story behind my FBI bishop in Texas. I never asked him and I never spoke about my past, or the mob problem in Agawam, to anyone once I moved to Texas. All I knew was that I felt safer after I left church that Sunday. My bishop was an FBI agent!

As I settled down into my new life, I couldn't help but think how it all seemed too familiar being back in Texas and still finding myself running from the mob again.

The first time I was exiled to Texas it was my earthly father Pete Bonavita who made a deal with the Genovese family to save my life. The next time I found myself in Texas it was my Heavenly Father who had arranged for His own Church family to rescue me from that very same crime family.

I guess that's why I wasn't expecting to hear from any crime family all the way out in Texas. For me, Texas was starting to feel more like a sanctuary, a safe place. Before exiling me to Texas I remember my Dad telling me that I wouldn't be troubled by anyone in the Mafia out in the Dallas-Fort Worth area where Mom lived. Yes. I am sure that's exactly what Dad had told me when he exiled me to Texas in 1972.

But this was 1981, nearly ten years later, so why was there another message waiting for me from the Genovese crime family as soon as I arrived in Texas--if there was no mob problem in Agawam?

CHAPTER FOURTEEN:
WATCHED BY ANOTHER CRIME FAMILY

"Hey Bonavita. The manager wants to see you in his office right away," someone was calling out to me. I looked up to see the cute workout instructor. He wasn't smiling.

I had only been back in Texas a couple of weeks, when I was called into the manager's office of a Bally owned Health Club where I was working out. It was the popular Presidents and First Lady Health Club in Hurst, Texas and no longer in operation today.

"They know you're here"

It was July of 1981, and I found myself sitting in the manager's office feeling more like a nervous kid called into the principal's office. "Uh oh," I thought to myself. "There was that dark feeling again."

I didn't think the manager was going to offer me a job and I was paid up on my gym dues. So, I just sat there and waited as he looked me over from across his cluttered desk.

Never taking his eyes off me, he calmly says, "I have a message for you."

"Oh no, not again," I muttered under my breath. "Not another message." And from the look on his face I could tell he heard me.

Squinting his eyes the way he'd been doing, whether it was suspicion or disbelief, made me even more uncomfortable. Finally, he leaned into his desk indicating he was ready to speak. It was a chilling message which I have never forgotten to this day.

"They know you're here and as long as you're a good girl, they will leave you alone," he explained.

"Sure," I wholeheartedly tried to assure him. Fumbling for the right words, I muttered something like, "I just want to get on with my life."

"You do that."

And that's all he said and with a gesture of his hand, I was dismissed. No more talk. I had gotten the message. He did what he was ordered to do and nothing more needed to be said. I could've said more but I didn't. I could've reminded him, "I'll leave them alone, if they'll leave me alone," but I didn't.

As I stood up to leave, I couldn't help but think of Sarge and Shoppie who'd repeated nearly the same words to me after they'd been warned to stop talking to me. Didn't the caller have the same message for them--"leave us alone?"

Glad to have gotten away with just a warning, I walked out of his office wondering what he did for the Mafia that he could feel so safe using such straightforward communication with me. It reminded me of all the other messages whenever I inadvertently stumbled into the Mafia's dark world of organized crime activity.

Mobologist Thom L. Jones has an interesting blog on organized crime operating in Sicily, Italy. Here is what Jones wrote about a mafiosa, whose risk lies in his choice of words:

> "Messages act as accomplices of Mafia activity, revealing the transactions of organized crime." More importantly, Jones pointed out it's the reason why messages are "fundamental to the existence of the Mafia."

Watching my back as I left the manager's office, I had to remind myself I was in Texas. "How could this be happening to me again?," I asked myself. "Didn't Dad tell me I'd be safe when he exiled me out here in '72? But if it was so safe in Texas, then why was I still being surveilled by the mob?"

At this point in our whodunit, there really is no mystery as to how anyone in the mob back east knew where to start looking for me. I had done something pretty stupid in my rush to get out of town. I gave them my address where I'd been living once I got to Texas.

What are the odds that a mob owned joint like Bally's health club was only ten minutes from where'd I'd been staying after I fled Agawam? As to how the mob found me so quick, I just figured I had been surveilled once I stupidly gave their associates in Agawam's town hall my home address on the telegram I sent the town clerk tendering my resignation. I guess that answers any question about how the Mafia found me again in Texas eh?

As for my home address, I planned to change that real quick, along with my gym. I wasted no time in cutting my ties with

Bally's. I took a quick shower, got dressed, packed up my gym bag and cancelled my membership. I didn't bother to say goodbye to the manager.

Bally's mob friends in Agawam

Back then, I didn't care to find out about Bally's association with the Mafia or their ties to the Genovese family back in Agawam. It was enough for me to know the mob owned the place. I decided to go online to find out more about that Bally's group only after I started on this memoir. I got lucky! The internet was burning up with sites linking Bally's to organized crime. Hello Dallas!

> **HOME_UPI ARCHIVES**
> **Bally's contracts with Belgians linked to organized crime figure okayed**
> June 24, 1981 Headlines in a UPI OC story By Louis Toscano

I realized what I'd dug up online had to be the same Bally group that branched off into the health club business in the 1980's. Sure enough, my research confirmed it was.

Interestingly, Bally's was the same outfit that had been linked to organized crime following ongoing investigations of the Federal Bureau of Investigation (FBI). The Feds conveniently named some of Bally's own associates that included the Genovese crime family.

What's worth remembering for this whodunit is the fact that some of those associated with Bally's, were none other than two of our favorite mobsters "Skyball" Scibelli of Springfield and "Big Al" Bruno of Agawam. And weren't those the mobsters I suspected who I'd been running from since 1972?

So for the sake of this whodunit, let's suppose it was Skyball who had put out a contract on me. I figured it had to be him, only after going online and finding an update on my boss Victor's cold case. Thanks to an informant, inside the Genovese family, who fingered Skyball as the one behind Victor's assassination, the Feds were able to solve his cold case a few years after I left Agawam.

If Skyball and my father were up to their old tricks again, I was definitely on someone's watch list in Texas. Looking back, it's no small wonder my mother and her husband Boots were so nervous being around me when Dad exiled me to Texas in 1972? After my close run-in with the mob at Bally's, I had no choice but to turn to my mother for more answers. It didn't go so good.

"Why don't you want me staying with you Mom?"

"No. And don't ask me again. You want to come here because you'll feel safer than at your apartment?"

"Well, they know where I live now Mom and I need to get out of there until I can get up the money to find another place."

"Let me talk to Boots and see what we can do to help you with some money."

"Thanks Mom."

Sure, I knew my mother didn't want me and my son in her home. I hadn't forgotten her chilly reception when Dad forced me on her like he did back in 1972. But I didn't want to stay in that apartment of mine anymore, only because everyone in Agawam had my address now.

Mom was good to her word and Boots gave me the money to move into another apartment which I listed under another family member's name until the dust settled down around me. But my old address wasn't the only thing I wanted to break from. Since leaving Agawam, I had some habits I couldn't get rid of so easily.

Old mafiosa habits are hard to break

While living in Agawam and being around all the corruption I had dug up, I found that some habits had followed me to Texas. I couldn't explain why, but I seemed to have the habit of stumbling onto activities that the Mafia wanted kept secret. And now, living in Texas, I naturally wanted to find out who was behind all my troubles and had even taken the trouble, themselves, to follow me all the way to Texas again.

What disturbed me the most about it was that I now knew those mobsters from Agawam were still surveilling me, thanks to Bally's manager. Unlike the last time I was exiled to Texas, I hadn't a clue I was being surveilled by the mob. Now I knew and

I couldn't help but want to find out more. I paid my mother another visit after I moved into my new apartment.

"It's all your father's fault. Why do you keep asking me such questions?"

"Because Dad never talks about it to me and I need to know."

"Why didn't you ask your grandmother before you came back here? She didn't have a problem telling you all those crazy lies about me. Why not ask her about your father?"

"I don't know. I guess I was just in such a rush to get out Agawam that I didn't think about it."

"Well, you should have. Now leave me alone and don't bring it up anymore."

"Sure," I thought to myself. "I was good at leaving people alone. Hadn't I been doing that all my life while on the run from the mob?" But I didn't say that to her, because we never spoke of such things out loud.

I had no more communication with my father since leaving Agawam. It was for the best I convinced myself. In the meantime, I had another problem. Where could I run? Texas had always been safe for me and I had to admit, no harm had ever come to me or my son when we lived out here back in 1972.

Once more, I turned to the Lord for answers. I fasted and prayed to know where I should go, or if I should just stay put. The answer was quick in coming and the calming spirit that I felt assured me I would be safe in Texas, only as long as I kept my mouth shut about what I knew in Agawam. Not a problem. I was good at that. I was still alive, wasn't I?

Yes. I was still alive and I planned to stay that way. Stress was something else! The good news was that I had managed to beat off some of the stress while working out at Bally's gym. I figured it was time to find another place to work out. I soon found a Gold's gym and signed up. I prayed the mob didn't own them too!

"You're new here aren't you?"

"Yes. I just joined up and I asked about a weight training program," I informed the cute employee at my new gym.

"You're in luck. I can set you up with a program, and even work with you myself, as a personal trainer."

319

"Great. When can we get started?"

"As soon as we figure out what goals you have in mind. Is your focus on strength, fitness or wellness?"

"All of the above."

I was still beleaguered by the undiagnosed Lyme disease and my symptoms seemed to lighten up a bit after I started working out at Bally's. Encouraged by the results, I wanted to take it one step further and try my hand at lifting weights. To my surprise, the more I worked out with my personal trainer, the more my symptoms seemed to ease up. I was hooked! And that's how I became a bodybuilder in a very short time.

Thanks to my trainer showing me the best way to build more muscle, I felt like I could take on the world and even the mob if anyone tried messing with me again. Oh that testosterone! I soon discovered I hadn't lacked any of it and that might've been why I was so aggressive in standing up to the mob all my life.

According to my trainer at Gold's, women with low testosterone find it hard to build muscle or burn fat easily. I didn't. Low testosterone, it seems, wasn't one of my problems. I was muscled up in no time, stronger than ever and feeling than better ever! I soon discovered that personal training at Gold's gym was the best way for me to get more than just health and fitness.

I wasn't as uncomfortable going home alone after work every night like I was before I started working out. I missed having my son's father Big Al drop by and keep an eye on us like he used to do in Agawam. I guess that's why I started dating guys from the gym who reminded me of him.

One of those guys was a famous wrestler named Kelly Kiniski who had recently signed for the Dallas, Texas based World Class Championship Wrestling. We dated for a while and I sure did feel safe around him. Between the muscle men I dated and my own confidence as a bodybuilder, I never gave the mobsters in Agawam another thought.

Besides building muscle, I was still busy building my new life in Texas. For me, that meant living the gospel and holding to the path the Lord had set me on when the missionaries found me in Agawam and baptized me into the Mormon Church. After that,

I had all the protection I could ever need, thanks to the constant companionship of the Holy Ghost, as long as I kept the commandments of God.

Looking back on my new life in Texas, I was indeed blessed. I not only enjoyed the support and love of my new Church family, but I had an FBI agent for a bishop.

Gratitude for my many blessings in sparing my life from the Mafia so many times, I am grateful to my Heavenly Father for helping me and providing all the things I needed to start over again as I did. I may have been alone raising a child without his father, but leaving Bally's gym was the best thing that could have ever happened to me. I found Gold's gym and a healthier life. More importantly, thanks to a better exercise program, I wasn't fearful of living alone as I was after leaving Bally's gym.

Bally's back on my mind

Back in 1981, there was no internet for me to check out Bally's so I went on with my life as if nothing had changed. Isn't that what I had promised Bally's manager? And besides, I had a bishop who was an FBI agent right? I figured if anything got too intense I could always confide in him and he'd know what to do. Until then, I decided not to get him involved.

Life was good and that's why I never thought about Bally's again until writing this memoir. Despite the good life since leaving Agawam behind, I'm happy to report that I still have an inquiring mind today. Which is why I wanted to pursue the clue to this whodunit involving Bally's health clubs.

What an eye opener my experience with that Bally's manager, was for me! Obviously when people think of the Mafia, they naturally think of racketeering, gambling, running drugs, prostitution and other underworld type business dealings with politicians etc.

Who could know the mob was involved with something so legitimate as health clubs? Much less doing it right in my own back yard in Texas? Even today, when I am asked if there is any Mafia in Texas, friends are so surprised when I tell them about Bally's.

So why am I bringing this up in my story right now? Let's not forget the main purpose of this whodunit. Isn't it to figure out if there really was a mob problem in Agawam?

What better way to do it then to take a closer look at Bally's own Mafia associates in Texas? I always thought it was kind of stupid for the Genovese family to be making direct contact with me like they did at my health club. Which begs the question, to what purpose?

For me, I was relieved just to know I had finally won and the enemy had surrendered. In other words, yes, someone in the Genovese family had stupidly put to rest the myth that there was no mob problem in Agawam. What happened to me at Bally's proved that. But that's just half the story isn't it?

On the downside, I was still wanted by the mob. If not, then why would the Genovese crime family based in Massachusetts go to such lengths to hunt me down in Texas? Why call on their Bally Las Vegas Associates who had ties to the Dallas Crime family as they most certainly had to do to send me a message like they did?

The Dallas Crime Family

Carlo Piranio, a native of Sicily, began the Dallas faction of the American Mafia in 1921. That got my attention because it was the same year as the assassination of my grandfather Tony Bonavita. According to *Wikipedia*, the Dallas crime family was an American Mafia crime family based in Dallas, Texas.

After my run-in with the Dallas crime family it was only natural I started thinking about my own protection. Looking back, wasn't it really about the mob's own protection that prompted the Genovese family to risk outing themselves to me again by doing what they did when I arrived in Texas?

In Chapter 9, I wrote about what Agawam Police Officer Norman Nardi did when he used the "M" word in public at the Liquor License hearing: "To listen to everybody you'd think we have a Mafia in the town."

One thing led to another after I ran that story in my newspaper and every one of my newspapers ended up in the town dump after they'd been stolen from all the stores carrying *The Agawam Voice*.

Looking back on that incident, it leaves little doubt that the Mafia had wanted their activities in Agawam kept secret. Else, why steal my newspapers? It's all about protection isn't it? Keep it all secret, use coded messages like what I'd always gotten and if all else failed kill anyone who leaked information threatening to expose the Mafia.

Wrapping up this part of the whodunit, we should be able to figure out if there really was no Mafia in Agawam, as the godfather's nephew Officer Norman Nardi had once publicly claimed. But if that were true, then who in Agawam had enough influence with organized crime to contact the Dallas crime family in Texas and call in a favor to threaten me and warn me to leave them alone?

If anyone is still in doubt at this point, here is what mobologist Barry Meier wrote about linking Bally Gaming to the Genovese crime family in a 1995 investigative report titled, Is Organized Crime Back at the Table?

> "Federal investigators, who stumbled onto Worldwide Gaming as a result of a run-of-the-mill bookmaking inquiry, later maintained that [its vice president] Christopher J. Tanfield, was an associate of both the *Genovese* and Gambino families.
>
> In early 1992, *The Village Voice* published an article that linked Mr. Tanfield with Eugene (Noogie) Gilpin, a reputed associate of the *Genovese crime family*.
>
> An. 1995: Bally is denied a permit by the president of a state regulatory board, Willmore Whitmore, to sell equipment to planned Harrah's casino in New Orleans on the ground that Bally allowed itself to be "infiltrated" by organized crime."

There's plenty more linking the two crime families to Bally. Following up on another organized crime lead, set up by Geoff Dougherty of the *Chicago Tribune* staff, I came across his April

3, 2005 online report, titled <u>Bally's no stranger to questions,</u> <u>controversy: The 1960's was a Bally world.</u>

Interestingly, Dougherty, like Barry Meier, also wrote about Bally linked to organized crime in his *Chicago Tribune* online report: "Four decades later, law enforcement agencies are once again interested in Bally, more specifically Bally Total Fitness Holding Corp."

Whoosh! That was my gym in Hurst, Texas alright. What were the odds that I'd pick the very gym owned by the mob and who just happened to be an associate of the Genovese family too!

Yes. It appears to be sufficient proof that Agawam did indeed have a serious mob problem after all. But does the mob ever really go "inactive" as imputed in recent updated organized crime vignettes published on *masslive.com* by *The Republican* journalist Stephanie Barry?

I don't need to delve into this controversy anymore. I think I have proved my point fairly well by now. As for my readers today, get ready to solve the mystery of this mob whodunit in real time from here on in. For some readers growing up in Agawam, this might be a frightening revelation of what's going on in your hometown today. For others, it will be quite an eye opener and a great twist to a mob whodunit for sure!

Fast forward to 2016

The only question that remains to be answered, from this point on, is whether or not Agawam is still under the influence of the Mafia in real time. Where are they today?

In other words, is the Genovese crime family active today at the time I began my research into Agawam? Or, should we take the word of mobologist Stephanie Barry who says they are inactive?

Before you jump to any conclusions, I'd like to re-introduce you to one of the more colorful characters whom I had the displeasure of knowing while we both sat on the Agawam town council.

You might recall my mention of the Gold Dust Twins back in Chapter 8. This former councilor, later appointed as Agawam's town clerk, easily got my attention again when he made breaking news in real time. He did it by regaining a seat on the Agawam City Council in the 2015 election after an absence of nearly thirty years.

I had to find out for myself why one of the Gold Dust Twins, known for covering up corruption in Agawam as I wrote about in my own newspaper, would suddenly want to get back into politics again? My habit of an inquiring mind paid off.

This whodunit is now part of an investigation, into the return of a Gold Dust Twin, in which you the reader will bring different pieces of my story together to solve the mystery in Agawam.

CHAPTER FIFTEEN:
RETURN OF THE GOLD DUST TWIN

"I am ashamed that the town has had to go through this," the Gold Dust Twin argued during a regular town council meeting.

And that's just the way it usually was when I was on the Agawam Town Council from 1979 to 1981. If you're wondering why I am devoting an entire chapter to one of the Gold Dust Twins nearly 35 years later, I invite you to take a walk down memory lane with us.

Besides his weekly lamentations made popular by his ongoing objections to each and every resignation or investigation I ever called for, Richard Theroux relished the reputation he had with insiders. Why? For the same reason he was known as one of the Gold Dust Twins.

My Auntie JuJu who had worked in the Town Clerk's office when I was on the council always had nothing but praise for Theroux. "He's such a nice boy Elena, if you'd only give him a chance," she would say to me every time I was around her.

Yes. My Auntie always saw the good in people and Theroux was always on his best behavior around her whenever he was in the Town Clerk's office. But he wasn't such a nice kid in our council chambers! Oh, the stories I could tell. Well, I can in this chapter I guess.

Town Council Happenings under the table

As Myles Munroe once said, "Your legacy must be in people...because success without a successor is failure."

I think the Mafia had the same idea as Munroe. I found that in Agawam politics it was more about securing the mob's chain of legacy within its organization of associates like those characters I write about in this whodunit. They are the politicians, officials, lawyers, and police chiefs all too easily compromised by the mob in any city all over the country, not just Agawam.

Normally, whenever associates are caught red handed and don't talk, the mob rewards them for their silence. If they talk, they're dead. Just ask my informants Sarge or Shoppie may they rest in peace!

The interesting part about a whodunit's legacy discussion is when the clues come full circle like with Richard Theroux. He is back on the City Council and in so doing he brings his past legacy with him. And this is his story through my eyes.

I knew Theroux as the reputed protégé of the godfather Fred Nardi when we all sat on the Agawam Town Council together in 1979. Back then, there were fifteen members with three at-large. Today Agawam is a city, not a town, and its City Council consists of eleven members who are all elected citywide.

There have been a few other changes like how Agawam is now a city even though it is still referred to as the *Town of Agawam* as proudly displayed on their website. And instead of a Manager, Agawam has a mayoral form of government today. I got a kick out of the message I found on the *Town of Agawam*'s website.

A Message from Mayor Richard A. Cohen reads in part, "Thank you for visiting the City of Agawam's website. Agawam.ma.us provides a wide variety of information about city government, city services, city events, and more..."

I got a good chuckle out of Mayor Cohen's message only because of what happened to me when I contacted the City of Agawam to get some information on their City Council and Police Chief. But you can read all about it in Chapter 16.

All of the members of the City Council are listed on the website as well, even the remaining Gold Dust Twin. Up until recently, former Town Councilor Richard Theroux was himself listed on the website as the Town Clerk which he had been appointed to right after he got off the Town Council in 1983. Today he is a City Councilor elected citywide instead of by precinct.

The legacy and the mob

There was a story to Theroux's jump from the Town Council to the Town Clerk's office, but I wasn't around in 1983 to find out what it was. All I know is that when I turned in my resignation and took off for Texas in the summer of '81, Theroux traded places on the Council for a Town Clerk position in '83, and the rest is history.

For some reason, I can't stop thinking about the offer I turned down when my father came to me with a message from our very own Police Chief Stanley Chmielewski. I only know that I walked away and protected my legacy of honoring my oath to the people I was elected to serve. Sure, I paid a high price but I never regretted my decision, even though I had to leave Agawam behind if I wanted to stay alive again.

But wasn't I on the same Town Council as Theroux? Yes. And wasn't I offered "all the power and money" I could want if I just "stopped fighting *them?*" Yes. That's what the Chief told my father to tell me. And who was *them?* Well, at the time I was in Agawam, I was still trying to figure out who our Agawam Police Chief was taking orders from. Now, at the close of this whodunit, we have a pretty good idea, I would imagine.

Maybe, it would be easier to answer such a question if we call Theroux by his mafiosa namesake--the Gold Dust Twin. Let's not forget why the original mobsters were even nicknamed the Gold Dust Twins in the first place. Weren't they best known for skimming union dues in organized crime? But I didn't know about their story at the time.

I did know about Theroux's story and he was the Town Council president when I was elected to take Floyd Landers' place. It didn't last very long for Theroux, I am happy to report. Not wanting to contribute to Theroux's dark legacy which I'd witnessed firsthand, I joined a voting block to help unseat him when the new council was seated two months after I was.

I backed a precinct councilor by the name of Paul Fieldstad for council president. I didn't trust him anymore than I could Theroux, but I wanted to see what happened when we overthrew the Gold Dust Twin.

Interrupting the mob's legacy chain inside its political stronghold was always kind of exciting and scary all at the same time. Heck, I lived for the moment those days, and so I celebrated our coup with my friend and mentor, former Town Councilor, Anita Davilli.

"He's not gonna forget what you did, Elena," Anita predicted, following the coup that upset Theroux's re-election bid as council president.

"Oh come on, Anita, can't you just enjoy this with me? Have you forgotten how he treated you when you were on the council?" I reminded her. Not another word out of her after that.

Fast forward to real time in Agawam politics

Today Theroux is 63 years old but he was only 19 when first elected to the Town Council. That would have made him about 27when I served on the council with him and I was 30 years old. By the time he was appointed Town Clerk in 1983, Theroux had served six consecutive terms on the council.

In August 2016, I began doing research for this memoir. I recall a piece of outdated breaking news by Suzanne McLaughlin in *The Republican* newspaper which caught my attention. The November 3, 2015 headline screamed out at me: <u>Longtime Agawam clerk Richard Theroux regains seat on city council.</u>

> "Theroux is leaving his City Clerk job as of January 1, 2016 after serving for 32 years. He will be returning to the city council where he was first elected at the age of 19, serving several terms as president."

My own message for the Gold Dust Twin

I know Theroux will be reading my memoir. I know because everyone including the Agawam police have already been alerted to what I am doing right now. But I get ahead of myself. What happens to me in real time while writing this memoir must wait until Chapter 16.

This chapter is all about legacy in organized crime and so in the pursuit of solving this whodunit, it is solely devoted to my old nemesis Theroux and no one else. As a fan of Fox News, I too hold the view, "we report you decide."

What better way to send Theroux a message of my own after all these years, than to do it through my own memoir – a mob whodunit? Given the mob problem I have already identified as having existed in Agawam while both Theroux and I were on the council, it is safe to assume some members had to be associates protecting the crime family that I suspected had been operating in the area.

By its very definition, according to who you ask, associates are people who work for or do business with a crime family. But it's said that they are not full-fledged members, just associates. It's also common knowledge that the Mafia can't exist without politicians in its pocket.

I can almost see the aghast looks on the faces of some of my readers who like my Auntie JuJu still think Theroux's "a nice kid." Listen. We've already had this discussion about nice people versus good people in a previous chapter. While no one would argue with the fact that voters need to be better informed to make better choices, I can't help but wonder why legacy is often overlooked by voters in elections, especially in communities like Agawam.

A fake legacy wins elections

Anytime we see a rising political star like Theroux go from the Council to the Town Clerk's office, it begs the question of how it could contribute to the mob problem in Agawam, if there was one.

Certainly a town clerk's position reportedly wields power in any community especially if the union contracts pass through the town clerk's office. Hiring a Gold Dust Twin as its town clerk, Agawam's town fathers had to have known about the original Gold Dust Twins Lepke and Shapiro, who started out skimming union dues and then graduated to killing anyone who got in their way after they partnered with mobsters like Lucky Luciano.

In Agawam, I stumbled into a similar situation that deserves mention in this chapter.

The whistleblower

I remember a time when I got tipped off by a whistleblower and I decided to call for an investigation into the town's bidding system. What a story that was!

I was a rookie member of the council and I might've never stumbled onto the situation if not for that whistleblower. Thanks to him, I quickly learned what happens when an administration fails to use sound procurement practices thus discouraging a competitive bidding system for its vendors. In other words, the whistleblower leaked a problem that pointed to someone intentionally controlling the bidding process.

"Why don't you go to Theroux or Nardi?," I asked the whistleblower.

"You know why I can't. You're the only one that can do something," he explained.

Sure, and maybe it was someone's plan to get me killed, too. When I didn't get a dark feeling talking with him, I figured if he knew what I did in this town, then he also figured I would live to tell about it, given my past track record with the mob.

When I did act on his tip, it did not go over very well with Theroux, but since I figured he wasn't the one going around killing my informants, I wasn't too worried. In fact, if I hadn't kept copies of my newspaper *The Agawam Voice* reminding me of that investigation, I might have forgotten about a scandal that rocked our community, involving its bidding process and the infamous Agawam Gold Dust Twins.

My call for an investigation as a councilmember warranted a few editorials of my own in *The Agawam Voice*. In it, we denounced Theroux's shameless defense of a corrupted bidding system, quoting his own disparaging comment on how he was "ashamed that the town has had to go through this."

The fox guarding the chicken house

Acting on the whistleblower's information, I did some snooping of my own into the administration's practice of preferred clients. What I found wasn't good. I wasn't comfortable bringing my suspicions to our own town's public works department, but I figured I had to trust someone.

I'd been baptized into the Mormon Church only a few months earlier when this problem came before the council. I prayed, of course, and when I did I felt prompted by the Spirit not to approach anyone in Agawam. Instead, I arranged for my newspaper, *The Voice,* to do an interview with the City of Springfield Superintendent of Public Works, Jean Laino.

To my amazement, Laino actually convinced me to call for an investigation based on the number of complaints I had been getting from contractors. He knew what was going on in Agawam alright!

As quoted in *The Agawam Voice*, Laino said, "Having preferred clients draw up specs is common. It's typical of small town politics. Fingers are already in the cash register and the specs are already sold...and it tends to make these [other bids] non-competitive."

Thanks to Laino's encouragement, I put the item on the next council agenda. That particular council meeting was attended by over one hundred townspeople--plenty of witnesses to council action that night, I thought. But in Agawam, that didn't always guarantee anything.

Despite sufficient evidence supporting an investigation, it was defeated 13-1. Guess who was the only councilor voting for an investigation?

A baseball bat and Theroux

In Chapter 14, I wrote about the Dallas crime family I ran into who gave me a message when I arrived in Texas after vacating my seat on the council. Acting on orders for someone in the Genovese crime family out of Agawam, I not only got their message loud and clear from their associate at Bally's, but it also confirmed my suspicion that it had been the mob behind all my troubles on the Town Council too.

In previous chapters, I also wrote about handlers in the Mafia who keep people like me in line, when we become a threat to their organization. As memory serves me, it was Theroux who was assigned as my handler only for our council meetings. Outside of the council chambers, it was Chief Chmielewski who, like Theroux, earned himself an entire chapter in my memoir.

Guess you could say they were a tag team and real good at it. Just ask poor Officer Brown who testified on my behalf about the Chief and Theroux's past history of schemes for the grand jury that was called to investigate the illegal dissemination of my arrest record.

My dumb luck, Theroux took the seat right next to me after I helped oust him as president. I couldn't do anything about it, of course. So, suffice it to say, whenever I opened my mouth, he made it a habit to jump all over me, almost literally!

As a councilmember, I didn't have to sit next to the Police Chief for hours on end, like I did with Theroux. So it was inevitable that I would take it to prayer when the Gold Dust Twin started getting out of control in his attempts to silence me.

His insults and snarky innuendos were creeping me out, not to mention it was embarrassing at our public meetings. I figured it was only a matter of time before one of us did something we might regret. So, I took it to the Lord and prayed about it. The next council meeting was spectacular!

"What's that baseball bat for?" Theroux asked as I laid it down on the floor between our seats at the council table.

"If you try to mess with me tonight, I'm gonna *whack* ya with it."

Oh, that I had a camera to take a picture of the look on his face. It was priceless! Well, I never did get a chance to use the bat. And I never did quite figure out why Theroux had that strange look of recognition on his face either. Did I remind him of something or someone perhaps? It wasn't until I began doing research for this chapter that I came across the story behind the baseball bat and the mob.

Who says God doesn't hear and answer prayers? I know the baseball bat was inspired of God or else how could I have known about the story of "Joe Batters" at the time?

I sure do wish I could've been a fly on the wall in the boys' clubroom that night after our council meeting. I wonder if they were asking how I could've known about the reputed mobster Tony Accardo aka "Joe Batters?"

The reputed mobster Accardo died in 1992, but he was still very much alive during my council days in the 1980's. While doing research for this memoir, I found this story online about him and I couldn't resist introducing "Joe Batters" to our whodunit.

According to *Wikipedia*, it was during prohibition that Accardo received the "Joe Batters" nickname from Capone himself due to his skill at hitting a trio of Outfit traitors with a baseball bat, at a dinner Capone held just to kill the three men.

Capone was allegedly quoted as saying, "Boy, this kid's a real Joe Batters."

Unknown to me, the night I unwittingly threatened Theroux with a baseball bat, I had no idea about a Chicago Boss named Tony Accardo. But judging from Theroux's reaction to my baseball bat and my comment about "whacking" him if he got out of line with me, he definitely knew about the reputation of "Joe Batters."

As I recall, the "Gold Dust Twin" didn't bother me that night or anymore as long as I had my bat handy. Had I known, I would've sent Accardo a thank you card. Instead, I went home and got on my knees to thank my Heavenly Father for giving me the idea about the baseball bat.

The story behind mob monikers

A fascinating mark of the Springfield Mob was how they had special nicknames for one another, like Springfield Boss Francesco "Skyball" Scibelli, Paul "the Penman" Cardaropoli, Salvatore L. "Big Nose" Cufari and lest we forget our very own Agawam mobster, Adolfo "Big Al" Bruno, who had lived right down the road from me.

Curious as to why the unusual nicknames, I found this explanation online: "Ever since Prohibition, mobsters have been giving each other monikers like Al "Scarface" Capone, Charles "Lucky" Luciano, and "Bugs" Moran. It's part of the persona, the Mafioso mystique."

It's kind of funny actually, given how I was totally ignorant of the story behind Mafia monikers when I served on the council. For example, when I started writing this memoir, I had completely forgotten about Theroux's own moniker until I came across an editorial in *The Agawam Voice* May 28, 1981 edition.

Taken from a page out of my own newspaper column under <u>News Analysis</u>, it reads:

> "Well it must be election year again…notice all the headlines a certain few councilors have been grabbing lately? …. Let's take a closer look at Councilors Andrew Gallano and Richard Theroux, better known as the Gold Dust Twins among the councilors."

Despite that subtle heads-up to the voters, Theroux was re-elected in my absence. Since that was the only issue of *The Agawam Voice* where I had mentioned Theroux's moniker, I sure am glad I kept it after all these years. Maybe the voters in Agawam won't overlook it this time if he ever runs again for any public office. And the same applies for anyone else in Agawam who has a moniker.

Monikers tell us so much about a person, whether they are full-fledged members of the Mafia or working for them as associates. According to online mobologists, the original Gold Dust Twins moniker was given to the "Gorilla Boys" by the name of Jacob Shapiro and Luis Buckalter. As the story goes, their client was the National Crime Syndicate, which just happened to be a confederation of crime families.

As reported in *Wikipedia*, "Shapiro and Buchalter took over [the] labor racketeering operation. The two partners soon began massive extortions of both labor unions and businesses as they created a massive criminal monopoly in the Garment District."

Now, I ask you, why would any elected official want to be named after such criminals like Shapiro and Buchalter, even in fun? The amazing thing about a whodunit, is how it can bring the past to the present telling the rest of the story.

The Gold Dust Twin today and the money trail

In 2016, I came across a story in *The Reminder* newspaper about an Agawam City Councilor who was running as a Democrat hoping to unseat State Representative Republican incumbent Nichols Boldyga in the 3rd Hampden District.

Red flags went up all over the place when I realized it was none other than my old pal Richard Theroux. Bragging on himself the way he likes to do, Theroux got the attention real quick of a Boston based Republican talk show host named Howie Carr. To his credit, Carr was successful in derailing Councilor Theroux's bid for a House seat in Massachusetts.

As a former radio talk show host with WREB while I was on the Town Council, I too enjoyed holding our elected officials accountable to the people like Howie Carr does today. Naturally, I've always respected Howie Carr and decided to look him up to see why he'd taken such a keen interest in Theroux's campaign for a House Seat. Everything is online these days, so it is available should anyone want to do more reading on Theroux's doomed campaign.

One of the breaking online news headlines by Laura Newberry caught my attention: <u>Agawam City Councilor Richard Theroux to challenge state Rep. Nicholas Boldyga for 3rd Hampden district seat.</u> The article details Agawam's longtime clerk, a seven-term city councilor, was enjoying support from Democrats like U.S. Rep. Richard E. Neal, Sheriff Michael J. Ashe Jr., and District Attorney Anthony D. Gulluni. He also served as a member and chairman of the Hampden County Retirement Board, where he invested a portfolio of over $300 million.

Did you catch that part about the retirement board portfolio? First of all, who in their right mind would trust someone with a portfolio worth $300 million who has a moniker like Gold Dust Twin, much less let him do it for 16 years?

I am not judging, but I'm guessing someone must've known Theroux alias the Gold Dust Twin was the right man for the job alright! Otherwise how do you explain it?

Knowing what Howie Carr must've suspected about Theroux's legacy of fakery, I can't help but think how pleased he must've been when another headline made breaking news: <u>Theroux ends bid for House seat.</u>

Theroux blamed his reason for dropping out of the race on "Republican attacks about his income." The article goes on to say,

> He said his family of four took a vote whether he would remain in the race. "I'm not going to get dirty," he explained. "I never have and I'm just not going to do that. That's why I'm out."

In the article, Howie Carr inducted Theroux into his "Massachusetts Hack Hall of Fame", because of his three public pensions amounting to $113,000. Carr's column called him a "triple-dipper," and even said he could become a "quadruple-dipper" if he were elected to the House of Representatives.

There's something else in the story written up by Chris Goudreau in *The Reminder* that brought up the past for me. For example, Theroux was quoted as saying, "Do I continue on a campaign that's going to go into the gutter?"

Listen. Theroux got called out by the conservative Republican columnist Howie Carr and he knew he was busted. But I get a kick out of the reason Theroux claimed he was really ending his bid for a House seat: "I'm not going to get dirty," he explained. "I never have and I'm just not going to do that. That's why I'm out."

Listen. If the Gold Dust Twin really didn't want "to get dirty," as he claimed, then why would I have had to bring a *baseball bat* to our council meetings when we sat next to each other?

And let us not forget all of the bribes I was offered as a councilmember, the same council Theroux was on, that filled up Chapter 10 of this memoir. I just can't imagine myself being the only councilmember ever offered bribes to switch my votes. If they thought they could get away with it with me, then it must've been an accepted practice in someone's circle.

And just one more thought on Theroux's story posted in *The Republican* by Conor Berry. It's always a good idea to consider the names of those who support a candidate. Who are they? What do they represent? And how did they get where they are? I noticed the D.A. Anthony D. Gullini threw his support behind Theroux's state run. In fairness to Gullini, he may have skipped a generation of mob associates, but based on my own experience with the Hampden County District Attorney's office, specifically former D.A. Matty Ryan's association with the mob, I'd be suspicious of anyone being endorsed by the D.A.'s office, today.

All in all, I feel the good people in the 3rd Hampden District owe a debt of gratitude to Howie for rescuing them from sending a politician, who is suspect in my whodunit, to the State House.

Now, I know what my critics may be thinking right now. Well, maybe Theroux turned over a new leaf and he's really a nice honest politician now. Sure, and I've got some ocean front property in West Texas I want to sell you, too. Howie Carr made a case against Theroux and that speaks for itself today.

As for the Theroux from my past, he had his chance to clean house and rid Agawam of its mob problem if he really wanted to do the right thing back then. But he didn't. Wasn't he in a better position than I was to do it? Of course he was! Who can forget how tight he was with the *godfather* of Agawam, who sat on the town council with us?

Instead of helping me fight corruption, Theroux appeared to do everything in his power to stop me. If he wasn't willing to go public to clean house, or even wanted to, then why didn't he ever come to me quietly like Councilor Floyd Landers had done? Or better yet, why didn't the Gold Dust Twin ever talk to me, like Sarge or Shoppie did, who risked their lives to leak information to help me? But that's all in the past, right? Or is it?

The front boss

Do you remember who delivered a message to me in Texas at Bally's health club on behalf of the Genovese family after I resigned my council seat in 1981? Given how this is a real time mob whodunit thanks to Chapter 16, we must now ask the obvious question—Who's giving those orders today in Agawam?

Based on my personal experience with the mob problem in Agawam, we should consider another question for our whodunit—Who was the "front boss" for the Genovese family when I was on the council, and more importantly, is there still one around today?

According to *Mafia Wiki*, the Genovese bosses had always used an effective technique so they could be as secretive as possible, using people they called "front bosses." It has been described as "a crafty method, in which the boss assigns a high ranking member of his crime family to conduct and portray himself as being the boss."

That "crafty method" was my thought behind this mob whodunit, probably because of my own quest to identify those behind the mob problem I repeatedly stumbled into around Agawam. If the Gold Dust Twin can return, why not the "front boss"?

Get ready for the past to meet the present as we uncover the final clues in solving this mob whodunit. Turn the page if you dare to know the rest of the story!

CHAPTER SIXTEEN:
A MOB PROBLEM IN AGAWAM TODAY

"I got a phone call from your friend Sara in Utah," Evan said over the phone.

"Why would Sara be calling you Evan?" I asked. "I only gave her your phone number in the event something happened to me and she couldn't reach me. What's the emergency?"

"She doesn't want you to call her anymore and she wants me to tell you she can't talk to you anymore either."

"But why not Evan? Tell me what happened because this doesn't sound like Sara at all."

When I got off the phone with Evan, I realized I had done something either really stupid, or really brilliant. Whichever, it didn't matter if it had cost me my best friend.

My friend whom I will call Sara was excited and happy for me when I decided to write my memoir in the fall of 2016. She's more like a sister to me and her husband was a bishop in our Church. They were both retired and lived in Utah where I had been living since I'd returned from serving in the Kingdom of Tonga as a member missionary for the Mormon Church.

It's a story of itself how I ever ended up in Tonga. Suffice to say, I wasn't sponsored by the Church, I just went on my own and served as a volunteer in the hospital and prison for six years. Sara just happened to be one of those special Latter-day Saints that I met when I relocated to Utah from Tonga.

Lucky for me, Sara had a bookstore before retiring and I figured she could give me a few tips on getting started with my own book. And that's how she ended up reading my first three chapters. One thing for certain, she was no editor. She just enjoyed reading and she liked what I was writing and it worked for me. I didn't need her as my editor. I could find one later.

In the meantime, I had some researching to do before I could get into Chapter 4 and start writing about being wanted by the mob. I ran some ideas by Sara and we felt it was a good plan for me to make some inquiring phone calls back East. My first call was to the cute lil mobologist reporting for *The Republican* on *masslive.com.*

Sara's voice is mistaken for mine!

First thing on my bucket list of research was *The Republican* newspaper. I was suspicious when I came across some updated organized crime vignettes published by one of *The Republican's* reporters named Stephanie Barry.

"Why are you doing this?" I asked Stephanie after I got a call back from her shortly after I had left her an email message.

In one of her latest organized crime vignettes on the Genovese crime family operating out of the Springfield, Massachusetts area, I was curious as to why Stephanie came across more like a spokesperson for the mob than a reporter. Watching her in action during a local television interview I pulled up online, convinced me even more.

I couldn't believe my ears. Was Stephanie really suggesting that the Mafia in Massachusetts no longer existed? Yes. To the trained eye of someone like myself who had been hunted down and threatened so many times by the Genovese family, there was no mistaking her message from them.

It sure sounded like code for "leave us alone." She had a message alright and it got my attention. Been there, done that, and I know a message being delivered when I see it. Only, this was the first time I'd seen a message from the mob on public television. Naturally, I was anxious to ask the mobologist about it when she finally contacted me. Who knows, maybe I was seeing something that really wasn't there. But so far, my gift for instincts had always been right on.

The day Stephanie returned my call I was standing outside in the foyer of a public library where I'd been doing research for my memoir. As such, I didn't have a chance to take notes over the phone, but if my memory serves me right, our conversation went something like this…

"Have you ever been threatened by the Mafia for writing about them the way you have?" I asked.

"No. No one has ever bothered me," Stephanie politely replied.

341

"Really?" I asked in feigned disbelief.

While we talked, I felt prompted to tell her about my latest project with my memoir and even invited her to work on it as my co-author. I figured it was worth a shot seeing as how her own organized crime vignette's timeline had tracked smack dab into my own family line.

To be honest, I had another motive behind the co-author idea. As a former newspaper publisher myself, I knew reporters might have to run it by their editors or publisher before committing to anything.

In *The New York Times* Employee Handbook titled Ethical Journalism, they come right to the point concerning their staff guidelines. It reads, "Simply asking oneself whether a course of action might damage the paper's reputation is often enough to gauge whether the action is appropriate."

Confirming what I already knew, Stephanie politely replied, "I'd be interested in doing that with you, but I'll have to ask my editor and get back to you."

I figured that was the last time I'd hear from her and I was right. Some things never change in Agawam.

Agawam goes on high alert

Stephanie Barry never got back to me but I got more than what I was looking for when we got off the phone that day. What happened next, sadly, is what cost me my best friend Sara.

If you've been following this whodunit and making notes along the way, can you guess what happened right after I talked with my cute little reporter at *The Republican*?

Like any good detective on the trail of the bad guys, I decided to do a little experiment. After all, the purpose of this chapter is to figure out whether or not there is a mob problem in Agawam today, right?

After my chat with the mobologist, I really wanted to see what would happen if I made direct contact with the Agawam Town Clerk's office. I figured I'd give it a day, before making the call, just to give them enough time.

I called the office of the Agawam Town Clerk Vincent F. Gioscia but he was unavailable. I decided to speak with the

Principal Clerk Beth Ceccarini instead. I came right to the point of my call and asked her if she could help me obtain the Town Council election records for 1977 through 1982. I did not give my real name.

Normally, public record requests like this must be made by GRAMA so I was surprised at Ceccarini's response. She said I could just do it over the phone and she'd see to it that I got the information. It made sense to me especially when she said, "I will do my best, but I'll have to go down in the basement to find the records for those years." She asked me for my email address before we got off the phone and I gave her Sara's, not mine.

Surveilled, unmasked and leaked again

I wasn't sure if the gang at town hall were onto me, but just in case, I'd already planned with Sara to give them her email address if they asked. We had talked about a plan to keep my identity secret just to be on the safe side when making calls to Agawam authorities. I wasn't really worried. But I guess she was.

"Are you sure you want to be doing this?"

"Sure. Why not Sara? Why would anyone want to take up with me like they'd done before? It's been 35 years."

"Well, just stick to the plan and get information on the elections and don't say anything else. Go ahead and use my business email address and I'll let you know if they send anything."

After we got off the phone, I wondered if *The Republican* had already leaked my telephone conversation with Stephanie to someone in Agawam. I didn't have long to wait for an answer.

I soon discovered that nothing much in Agawam had changed since I left. I eventually got a call back from Gioscia, the Town Clerk himself, whom I had left a voicemail for earlier in the week.

Still protecting my identity, Mr. Gioscia was most congenial when we talked on the phone. He even said, "Glad to help you in any way I can." That of itself, should've made me even more suspicious.

Not one to disappoint, I got the email Gioscia sent Sara after she forwarded it to me. A quick glance and I was puzzled because the documents I requested were missing. No sooner was I trying to figure out their game, when the phone rang.

"You got another email from Agawam lil sister," Sara informed me. "It's from Ceccarini."

Sara liked to call me her little sister. We were pretty close and we were like real sisters. So I feel really awful about what happened next.

It seems that Sara had opened up her email, but hadn't looked at the attachments before forwarding it to me. As I opened each of the three attachments to Ceccarini's email, I was perplexed as to why a Town Clerk's office would send me a link titled *Aloha* with the picture of a beach in Hawaii and nothing more than that on the attachment. Just a stupid picture!

Like the email I got from the Town Clerk Gioscia, the other two attachments sent with Ceccarini's email were just as useless to me. One had only a partial document with a few lines of print from a 1977 council election and the other I couldn't get open.

Between the two of them, I got nothing from Gioscia or Ceccarini, but I did have a lot of questions. I got to looking at the email Ceccarini sent Sara believing they were sending it to me. And keep in mind that this is being sent out from a town clerk's office.

What do you make of the word "*Aloha*" linked in Ceccarini's email? I didn't know what to make of it either. So I stupidly opened the link showing a picture of a beach with palm trees. What do you think happened when I clicked on it?

Totally unexpectedly, my computer suddenly started going crazy. It started acting like it had a ghost inside it. I couldn't get any response from commands and I ended up having to make a call to my IT guy for a diagnosis.

Something else was strange about Ceccarini's email. For some reason, I couldn't get the word *Aloha* to print out when copying the email to use in this chapter. According to *Wikipedia*, "Aloha" in the Hawaiian language, has come to be used as an English greeting to say goodbye and hello.

What town clerk sends an email like what I got from Agawam? First of all, we are not in Hawaii. And given her good ole Italian last name of Ceccarini, I don't think she's of Hawaiian heritage either. It's a sure bet Agawam wasn't saying hello to me in Hawaiian. Ahh. Nice to know some things never change. Do you think they intended to send me a message again, as in goodbye perhaps? Because I know they sure weren't saying hello.

For me, that meant I had a heads up on what to expect while doing research for my Agawam memoir. Good news for me-- bad news for the boys. Bad news, only because I would be inside Agawam's head for as long as it would take me to get out this memoir.

Meanwhile, back in Utah, Sara was having some technical difficulties of her own. Like mine, her own computer went crazy immediately after opening Ceccarini's *Aloha* email. I guess by now you know where I am going with this right? It was a mess for sure. My computer was going off the radar acting all kinds of crazy and so was Sara's!

Help, my computer is infected

Poor Sara. I felt so bad for her. Being unfamiliar with malware technology, she didn't have any reason to suspect anything or to suggest that she shouldn't have opened the "Aloha" attachment before forwarding it onto me. And neither did I!

If you go online, *Tech Culture* by Elinor Mills has a website, Help my PC is infected with malware! He explains the "warning signs of an infection that may cause the computer to stop responding, or just crash. Applications may not work properly, and disk drives may be inaccessible. There may be unusual error messages and distorted menus and dialog boxes."

Once Sara and I compared notes we realized we'd been infected with a virus. Both of us were experiencing every one of the warning signs mentioned by Elinor Mills. Wow! What a mess!

Even before she had opened the *Aloha* attachment on her end, Sara sent me a note with her forwarded email from Ceccarini. Sara's language shocked me when she asked, "How did you survive being around such scumbags?" And this from a woman who hadn't even yet discovered the malware gift they'd sent her!

I turned to my friend Tommy the IT guy for advice. He was the best in the business when it came to computers.

"So what do you think Tommy? Did someone do something to my computer? I can't even access my programs with my usual password."

"I can't believe what I'm seeing!"

Tommy was hesitant to come right out and say it, but I insisted he tell me what he thought had happened to my system.

"Have you been opening up attachments from strangers?"

"I think so. I got this strange email with an *Aloha* attachment this morning."

"Either you've been hacked into or the *Aloha* attachment is suspect," he finally admitted.

What seemed like an eternity, Tommy worked on my computer to sort out the problem. I was relieved when he was ultimately able to restore everything including saving all my files and my system from any further damage. First thing he did though, was to change my password. Next, he did some things to keep my book safe after I hinted someone might be interested in it.

And that's how my story, or my memoir, continued to live another day on my computer. It was disturbing, but not surprising to discover the mob still had control in Agawam. If not, then why the *Aloha* message?

If I wanted to know for sure, there was just one more phone call to Agawam that I had to make. I wanted to see what would happen if I made a cold call from my own personal cell phone to the Agawam Police Chief. Yep. Call me crazy, but who if not me to do it?

Up until now I figured they had just mistaken Sara for me when they had sent her the infected email. After all, it was my fault and I felt bad, so I needed to follow through. Not anticipating their next move, I couldn't wait to see what kind of a reception I'd get from Agawam's newest Police Chief.

The ghost of Agawam past lives

You might recall what I wrote about the effect of Agawam's in-house appointments on the legacy of police chiefs in Chapter 9. That's good, because it is relevant to solving this whodunit once and for all. In a December 2013 story, *The Republican* reporter George Graham wrote about Lt. Eric P. Gillis who was "tapped as Agawam's new police chief."

I may not have gotten the name of the person who filled my vacant seat on the Town Council for all my troubles, but I did get the names of those who filled the seat of my old pal Chief Chmielewski.

Normally city leaders will conduct a national search for a Police Chief's permanent replacement, as I encouraged Agawam to do for its Town Manager after I called for and got Manager Peter Caputo's resignation in 1979. Albeit no guarantee with that process either but it's better than in-house appointments.

What was the latest in-house appointment in the Chief's seat up to these days, I wondered? Only one way to find out. I made the call and waited to see what they'd do.

"Agawam Police. Can I help you?"

"Yes. Who could give me the names of Agawam's Police Chiefs since 1972?"

I didn't tell the clerk on the other end of the phone it was the year "Skyball" assassinated my boss Victor and that the Agawam police chief hadn't bothered with an investigation. If he had done his job, I might never have ended up running from the mob for the rest of my life.

I wasn't on hold very long, just long enough for a few flashbacks to 1972. Finally, my call went through and I was definitely not expecting to be sent over to the Police Chief's desk. But that's exactly where my call was routed. That was fine with me.

A woman took my call and identified herself as Chief Gillis' Administrative Assistant named Patricia Brennan.

347

"Hello. I was told you could give me the names of Agawam's Police Chiefs that have been sworn into office since 1972?"

The anxious voice on the other end excitedly demanded, "And who's this?" Click! The phone went dead.

What was that all about? I was going to call back and try again but I was unable to use my cell phone for several minutes after that. I waited it out seeing as how my phone had been fully charged prior to calling Agawam. Much as I tried to bring it back up after Ms. Brennan's incredibly rude hang-up, my phone would not respond to even a redial.

"So much for your friendly local police," I thought to myself as I wondered what to make of it. When I woke up the next morning I found another surprise on my phone.

"What happened now?" I asked out loud as I stared dumbfounded at my cell phone. I lived alone. I didn't expect anyone to answer me. I just stared stupidly at the 1% signal on my phone.

The battery was down to 1% at 5 in the morning. When I went to bed it was 70% just like I always keep it in case of an emergency. I knew I hadn't used the phone and so I didn't quite know what to make of it.

There was an emergency that night, but it wasn't on my end. Someone else had wanted my phone too. I made another call to my favorite IT guy. I explained the problem to him.

"Did you talk on the phone a lot before you went to bed?"

"No. I never even used my phone and my battery was nearly full like it always is before I go to bed."

"Well, that doesn't sound good. Did this have anything to do with your computer problem?"

"Maybe. All I know is that the problem's not with my cell phone because it's fairly new and the battery was fine right up until I went to bed last night. So what do you think someone did to my phone?"

We talked about who could do such things and he assured me that if the police wanted to tap my phone system they could. Sure enough, when I googled the subject after I got off the phone with Tommy, it confirmed my worst fears.

One website claimed "a cell phone being tapped, tracked, monitored or spied on could cause for fast battery draining."

Since it never happened again after that night following my call to Chief Gillis' office, I figured it was because I dumped my phone. It was too risky to use anymore. I wasn't taking any chances. I got a new phone under a new name and even got me a separate "burner phone," like those pay as you go devices, hoping to make it harder to track me while working on my Agawam project.

Another police chief is suspect

Actually, the whole squirrely issue with the Agawam Police Chief was kind of stupid when you think about it. If Agawam didn't want me to suspect foul play in their town after all these years, then why play around with my computer and cell phone the way they all did? Surely, they didn't think I wouldn't suspect anything.

As it stood now, I had no choice but to assume something was still rotten in Agawam. I wasn't sure how the ghosts from my past knew or if *The Republican* leaked the news about my memoir, but I suspected as much. They were all ready for me when I called, weren't they?

Flashbacks of my earlier days being handled by Agawam's Police Chief unnerved me to say the least. It helped knowing I had Sara I could confide in over the phone and pray with just as we had always done for so many years. I guess I'd been so busy writing and emailing Sara that I didn't notice we weren't doing that lately.

I should've suspected something was amiss when Sara didn't call me for a few days. That wasn't like her. Sometimes we'd talk on the phone twice a day. The phone was ringing. There was that dark feeling again.

"Leave us alone"

"Hello? What's up?" I asked, surprised to get such an early morning call from him. Evan lived nearby and like me and Sara he was a member of the Mormon Church.

"I got a phone call just now from your friend Sara in Utah," Evan explained.

"Is she okay? I haven't heard from her for a couple of days and that's not like her."

"She's okay and so is her husband. It's you she's worried about after getting a phone call warning her to stop helping you."

"Well, one phone call is nothing to worry about. Maybe it was just some idiot in Agawam trying to scare me off so I wouldn't finish my memoir."

"No. They seem to be taking it pretty serious," he explained. "Sara said they ignored the first threatening phone call and didn't want to worry you so they didn't say anything."

"What are you saying Evan? I was almost afraid to ask, but I had to know. "Are you telling me that she got more than one phone call threatening them?"

"I don't know what's going on in your world but she sure sounded scared," he said. "She ignored the first call, but when the same man called them a few days later she decided to call me since she doesn't trust using email or phone calls anymore."

I didn't say anything to Evan. I didn't want to scare him anymore than I had to. We prayed over the phone and after we hung up I had time to think about it more. It seems that the caller must've thought they could get to me by threatening Sara. But that never worked on me before, so I figured this next generation in Agawam hadn't figured that out yet. Or was it the next generation?

Hadn't my troubles started in the Town Clerk's office right before I called the Agawam Police Chief? And who from my past was still alive and might fear being exposed in this memoir that had been a Town Clerk just before Gioscia took his place? Bingo! The Gold Dust Twin returns and becomes suspect for our whodunit in real time. Wouldn't that explain why Sara got a call from Agawam?

When I couldn't get any more information out of Evan, I made some calls to Utah hoping one of my trusted friends out there could talk Sara into finding a safe way to make contact with me. I just had to know what was going on.

Who was the leak?

It couldn't have been a coincidence that all of the spying and threatening phone calls had suddenly found its way back into my life again right after contacting my cute little mobologist Stephanie Barry.

Poor Sara. I knew she wanted to talk with me, but that was no longer possible. I had to find a safe way to reach Sara. I had to let her know that no one was going to hurt her or her family. I needed her to know someone just wanted me to back off and were most likely trying to use Sara to get to me. So I sent a message to her through a mutual friend of ours.

It was no use. He couldn't get anything out of Sara either. I prayed he could persuade her to at least talk with him. As for me, I just couldn't wrap my head around the idea that she had really been contacted by ghosts from my past. Heck, they were all dead. So who had taken their place in Agawam?

As with my informants from the past, I never did get any names from Sara because the caller used a burner phone of course. But I was concerned because Sara's husband had been a Bishop. Who in Agawam would be threatening a Mormon Bishop and in Utah of all places? Questions like that were best left for my friends with the FBI in Utah.

I wasn't ready to give up on Sara yet. I decided to ask another close friend of mine in Utah to visit her. My burner phone was coming in real handy.

"Did you talk to Sara yet? Please tell me you did."

"Yep. I dropped by Bishop's home just as you asked me to do and I can tell you they confirmed Sara got two calls alright."

"Did Bishop tell you what the caller said?"

There was silence on the other end of the phone and then he spoke the words I thought I'd never hear again in my life. I can still hear the chilling words like a ghost from the past.

"Yes. He told me they said, "Leave us alone. Don't help Elena.""

"Okay. Thanks for going out to see them for me. I can handle it on my end from now on," I replied, trying to avoid worrying anymore people about me. But he wasn't ready to hang up.

"Why'd you think they were ever gone away? If they're watching you like this, don't go doing anything to stir the pot out there, you hear me?"

"Don't worry. They've been trying to kill me for years and it's only by the grace of God they haven't."

He prayed with me before we said our goodbyes and I can still remember his parting words. "Be careful and send me a text once in a while so that I know you're still alive okay?"

"Still alive?" I asked myself, as I got off the phone. I was sorry I had ever used Sara's email address, but if I hadn't done it, would I have had a witness to all of this today?

While being cut off from Sara was really hard on me, I don't know which hurt me more, walking away from Agawam in 1981 or losing touch with Sara until after my book would be published.

And yet, I couldn't help but think what the angels had said to the Prophet Lot after they brought him a message from the Lord to flee Sodom: "Escape for thy life; look not behind thee." Like Lot's wife who was tempted to look back and was turned into a pillar of salt, I too had been tempted to look back by contacting the Agawam authorities after all these years.

Like the Prophet Lot who lost his wife after she turned into a pillar of salt, I too lost my best friend Sara when she looked back wanting to see what had come of Agawam after I fled the city. Feeling like Lot must've when he had to accept his wife's fate and move on without her, I did the same thing and made plans to complete my journey without Sara, at least for the time being.

The Godfather movie had the same problem

I knew the mob was behind Sara's threatening phone calls. It was what they said to her: "*Leave us alone*." Normally, whenever a made member of the Mafia is threatening someone, they will use the term "*us*" and never "I" or "me." Their wise guys, or soldiers, acting under orders normally speak for their crime family and not themselves.

More to the point, messengers for the mob make sure you understand they are threatening you on behalf of their boss. The problem is they never name their boss eh? The only reason I was convinced Sara was in no real danger was because she was never any threat to them. It was me they wanted to scare off and nothing more.

Like a whodunit mob movie which I am hoping will come of my memoir, maybe my readers can figure out who is the "*us*" in Agawam that made threats to Sara hoping to scare me off so I wouldn't publish my memoir. Speaking of a good mob movie, who hasn't seen *The Godfather* movie?

Not too many people know about the time the Mafia protested *The Godfather* production back in the '70's. In February 2014, Nolan Moore published a detailed analysis, titled <u>When The Real Mafia Tried To Stop Filming Of '*The Godfather*'</u>.

Moore's analysis is the true mob story of another organized crime family named Colombo. Interestingly, the Colombo family reacted to *The Godfather* production much like someone in Agawam appears to be reacting to my own production of my mob memoir. But as Moore reminded his readers, no one was killed over it. And that's why I am not as worried about Sara either.

Nolan Moore identifies Joseph Colombo as the leader of the Colombo crime family, one of the infamous Five Families in New York. For those following my whodunit, it is important to note that the Genovese crime family, believed to be active in Agawam, is also based out of New York.

But the real interesting part of Moore's report is when "Paramount executive Robert Evans received a menacing phone call telling him to get out of town, or someone would break his face and hurt his kid." It's a story in and of itself how *The Godfather* ever ended up being produced into a movie and winning an Academy Award for Best Picture and everything else it could pick up.

According to Moore, "*The Godfather* producers met with the gangsters and agreed to strike the word "Mafia" from the script."

Hmmm. As I seem to recall, didn't gangsters in Agawam try a similar tactic on me when they stole an entire edition of my *Agawam Voice* newspaper simply because it too had the word "Mafia" in the stolen edition that I ended up reprinting? As I seem to recall, no one was ever killed over it either.

In its March 4, 2012 online publication of <u>The time the Mafia protested The Godfather</u>, journalist Devin Faraci wrote: "The

Italian-American Unification Council of Greater Kansas City spent their own money buying every ticket to the premiere showing....and played to an empty theater that first night."

The thought hasn't escaped me that any mob associates still active in Agawam might very well attempt to do the same thing like what was done in Kansas City. Will they buy out the first edition of my memoir like Kansas did with *The Godfather*'s own premier showing? Thank goodness for the online source of E-Books!

As for me, I can't take the word "Mafia" out of my script. Heck, that's the theme of my entire life story. Without the word "Mafia", I have no story to tell. And if I had no story to tell, I wouldn't have the hope of a book-to-film contract like *The Godfather*'s author Mario Puzo did with his own famous Mafia crime novel.

This production, my memoir, is in the hands of the Almighty God Himself. I have a testimony of how I was directed to bring it forth at such a time as this. It would be foolish indeed to let anyone scare me into stopping this work. Even more foolish, for me not to trust in God to protect me and those around me as He has always done throughout my life's journey as the Gospel took me out of the dark world of organized crime and into the light of Christ.

As I come to the end of my memoir, we all know by now that someone in Agawam does not want this book published. It is obvious given the reaction Sara and I got from the Agawam Town Clerk and the Police Chief when I innocently made contact with Agawam again after all these years.

I ever pray that whoever is behind all of this will find peace with our Lord and Savior Jesus Christ, as did Brother Mario Facione and Sister Elaine Bonavita when we received God's messengers into our homes and accepted the missionaries' invitation to be baptized into the Church of Jesus Christ of Latter-day Saints.

As for me, I will call upon God; and the Lord shall save me, evening, and morning,
and at noon, will I pray, and cry aloud: and He shall hear my voice.

He hath delivered my soul in peace from the battle that was against me: for there were many with me.
- **Psalm 55**

SOLVING THE WHODUNIT MYSTERY

This has been a mob whodunit offered to my readers in the hope that someone will be able to solve the mystery of who was behind all of the murders and mayhem in the town of Agawam during the period of 1970 thru 1981 as told in my memoir.

The whodunit also walks my readers through real time while I was doing research for this memoir in the fall of 2016. It is my hope that someone might also solve the mystery behind the surreal reaction to my inquiries in the Agawam Town Clerk's office and the office of the Agawam Police Chief.

Besides offering a thrilling mob whodunit to my readers, it is my sincere prayer that others in similar situations to my own might find the strength and the hope to overcome it as I did with the help of my Heavenly Father and His angels. I pray that my own experience, with a mob problem in Agawam, might also encourage other communities to get more involved who might not be aware of these problems with their own politicians and law enforcement agencies.

A MOB WHODUNIT QUESTION: Why would anyone associated with the mob fear the past if they are no longer active in Agawam today?

ARE YOU READY TO FIGURE OUT WHODUNIT?

Here are the questions from the clues I gave my readers in each chapter of this memoir…

WHO DO YOU THINK?

- Assassinated my boss Victor DeCaro in Agawam in 1972 and ordered a contract on me that my father cancelled by exiling me to Texas?
- Leaked my plan to write a memoir to the Agawam authorities after I contacted *The Republican* newspaper's mobologist?

- Made contact in 1981 with the Texas Bally's Health Club Manager who was ordered to give me a message from Agawam after I had resigned the Town Council?
- Was behind the leaking of my arrest record and unmasking my informants Sarge and Shoppie which resulted in their alleged assassinations by induced heart attacks?
- Warned Agawam Councilor-at-large Floyd Landers to stop talking to me and when he didn't, he ended up dead the following day?
- Warned Sarge and Shoppie to stop talking to me and when they ignored the threatening phone calls, they both died mysteriously of heart attacks the day after their last warning?
- Ordered the home invasion by the knife wielding street youth who wanted to kill me?
- Stole my *Agawam Voice* newspapers with the word "Mafia" in one of its stories?
- Ordered Chief Chmielewski to take my father for a ride, and asked him to deliver a message for them, offering me all the "power and money" we both could ever want if I would stop fighting them?
- Hacked into my computer and Sara's and our telephones right after I contacted the Agawam Town Clerk and Police Chief Gillis in the fall of 2016?
- Was behind the blackmail of my friend the Waterloo Iowa Mayor?

WHY DO YOU THINK?

- My father Peter Bonavita held such influence with the Genovese family and could broker so many deals with them to save my life as he did?
- The Agawam Police Chief Stanley Chemliewski felt he could send me a message through my father in 1981 offering me "all the power and money" I could want?
- My informants were dying of heart attacks each time they were warned to stop talking to me?

- The Agawam Town Clerk's Assistant emailed me the *Aloha* virus instead of the docs I requested of them?
- Councilor Richard Theroux wanted back on the Agawam Council in 2016?
- An Agawam Police Chief like Stanley Chmielewski was ordered to handle me if that job is normally delegated to an enforcer for the Mafia?
- Town Councilor Richard Theroux was given the moniker of a "Gold Dust Twin?"
- My bishop was an FBI agent when I arrived in Texas after fleeing Agawam in 1981?
- Someone infected and hacked into my computer and cell phone the same day that I contacted the Agawam Town Clerk and its Police Chief in the fall of 2016?

A NOTE FROM THE AUTHOR

Thanks for joining me in this whodunit mystery. This wraps up my true story in the dark world of organized crime prompting my own editor to declare, "You are the walking dead!"

I want to thank my Heavenly Father and my Savior Jesus Christ for giving me this opportunity to return to Agawam in the spirit of this memoir.

Indeed, my Agawam memoir is an unusual mob story, but it is also one of the most amazing God stories ever to be experienced by a convert to the Church of Jesus Christ of Latter-day Saints!

ABOUT THE AUTHOR

After nearly four years of a restful sanctuary in Texas, the Lord called Elaine Bonavita Jaquith to another work, just as He had promised in a blessing administered to her by the missionaries from the Church of Jesus Christ of Latter-day Saints at her Agawam home in 1981.

She married and moved with her husband to Waterloo, Iowa, where she became actively involved in the pro-life movement and was soon elected to the Waterloo School Board in 1991.

Despite a mysterious lingering illness, which later turned out to be Lyme disease, she continued to make local and national news for her strong stand as a Christian Conservative School Board Director fighting to restore God's values in our public schools.

After completing one term on the school board, she earned a B.A. Degree in English from University of Northern Iowa in 1998. After graduation, she returned to Texas and was accepted into law school at Texas Wesleyan.

In 2001, she served a six-year member-mission in the Kingdom of Tonga ministering to its people in both the hospital and prison in VaVa'u. She returned to America and relocated to Utah in 2007 where she served in the Manti Temple after a successful county-wide campaign, placing another Citizen Initiative Petition on the ballot that restored the people's right to vote on any proposed future coal power plant.

She was eventually diagnosed with Lyme disease in November 2013, nearly 45 years after a Lyme infected tick bite in Texas. A Western Blot Blood Test confirmed the diagnosis and allowed her to seek successful natural treatment which put the Lyme disease into remission after she'd been experiencing more than 60 of the 70 known medical conditions associated with the disease. She had been on oxygen therapy nearly 30 years before going into remission.

Her legacy of the Citizen Initiative Petition's tax reform under Proposition 2½ in Massachusetts remains in effect to this day. In recognition of her lifetime contributions to society, the author has been listed in *Who's Who of American Women* and *Who's Who in America.*

Today, the author resides in Texas and is working on her next action-packed memoir about another community where she lived and served and fought the good fight!

Made in the USA
Middletown, DE
09 June 2017